THE 69TH GENERATION

A Biblical Commentary on Daniel 9 and the Generation of Christ's Return

STEVEN MEDLEY

BALBOA.
PRESS
A DIVISION OF HAY HOUSE

Balboa Press books may be ordered through booksellers or by contacting:

Balboa Press
A Division of Hay House
1663 Liberty Drive
Bloomington, IN 47403
www.balboapress.com
1 (877) 407-4847

Because of the dynamic nature of the Internet, any web addresses or links contained in this book may have changed since publication and may no longer be valid. The views expressed in this work are solely those of the author and do not necessarily reflect the views of the publisher, and the publisher hereby disclaims any responsibility for them.

The author of this book does not dispense medical advice or prescribe the use of any technique as a form of treatment for physical, emotional, or medical problems without the advice of a physician, either directly or indirectly. The intent of the author is only to offer information of a general nature to help you in your quest for emotional and spiritual well-being. In the event you use any of the information in this book for yourself, which is your constitutional right, the author and the publisher assume no responsibility for your actions.

Any people depicted in stock imagery provided by Thinkstock are models, and such images are being used for illustrative purposes only. Certain stock imagery © Thinkstock.

Print information available on the last page.

ISBN: 978-1-5043-3402-0 (sc)
ISBN: 978-1-5043-3404-4 (hc)
ISBN: 978-1-5043-3403-7 (e)

Library of Congress Control Number: 2015908868

Balboa Press rev. date: 06/17/2015

ACKNOWLEDGMENTS

This book is dedicated to all those that have assisted and supported me throughout the process of the construction of this project.

My daughter Jennifer and her husband Dwight thank you for all of your love and kindness. And my grandchildren Nadine, Darrius, and baby Rebekah, I love you all.

For Donny, thank you for all of your financial support, friendship, and self-sacrifice. May God continue His good work, which he has begun in you.

For my mother Margarita, thank you for all of your love, and for never giving up on me. I also want to thank you for the Bible you bought for me that resulted in this book.

To Theresa the love of my life and soon to be wife, and to our precious daughter Angel, the two of you have thoroughly blessed my life greatly.

And at last I am most thankful to my God, who has loved and cared for me until this moment and beyond. All blessing, glory, honor and thanksgiving are wholly yours. This book is for you.

CONTENTS

INTRODUCTION

To all of my new found brother's and sister's in Christ Jesus, and to all those who may yet still be seeking and searching, by our shared and merciful God it is my extreme privilege to share these precious moments with you. According to His divine plans and purposes, be certain when I tell you that my thoughts and intentions are wholly devoted to your blessing and overall benefit as the God of all of Israel will see fit to perform it within us all.

To start, I would be less than truthful if I did not mention right off that I am neither a scholar nor a theologian as the world would like to classify me. I have neither seminary degrees nor any practical training in any institutions of biblical higher learning. I posses absolutely no credentials whatsoever that would recommend me for this most delicate and greatly important endeavor. I am also under no illusions, I am quite convinced that there may be many who will disagree with my findings and conclusions, and this too is of God and I am much at peace with it.

With that being said let me also say that I am a living miracle. I am God's testimony as to how much He can do with so little. If I am supported by any commendation at all it would be of that which He spoke in **I Cor.1:26-29 "For you** see your calling, brethren, that not many wise according to the flesh; nor many mighty; nor many noble are called. But God has chosen the foolish things of the world to put to shame the wise; and God has chosen the weak things of the world to put to shame the things which are mighty; and the base things of the world and the things which are despised God has chosen, and the things which are not to bring to nothing the things that are, that no flesh should glory in His presence." This is truly the strength of my resume. I was, and still may be, in the eyes of this world that foolish thing, that weak and base thing, that thing that is not; however, all glory be to God the Father and His Blessed son Jesus who has chosen me.

As with anyone that might find themselves in my position it is my only hope that the reader would judge by the Spirit of God whether this knowledge is of Him or not, and leave little consequence to the one who is sharing it, for I have already noted he is of no consequence at all. At the onset let it be clearly known that I have no hidden agenda's for or against any groups, churches, organizations, political parties, etc. Additionally I have absolutely no personal or selfish desires to be seen as significant in the eyes of anyone besides my Lord. There is no flattery or praise in which I seek, no self promotion, nor sinful pride or arrogance that would chose for me to be singled out as someone of importance. I am merely the slightest of instruments in the abundant arsenal of an All Powerful God, and only that.

I however am fully aware of by whom I have been taught. As God Himself so eloquently stated it in I Cor.2:10-12 "But God has revealed them to us through His Spirit. For the

Spirit searches all things, yes, the deep things of God. For what man knows the things of a man except the spirit of the man which is in him? Even so no one knows the things of God except the Spirit of God. Now we have received, not the spirit of the world, but the Spirit who is from God, that we might know the things that have been freely given to us by God." It is for this reason that I cannot, nor must not remain silent. Even as God spoke to the prophet Habakkuk in Hab.2:2-3 "Then the LORD answered me and said: "Write the vision, and make it plain on tablets, that he may run who reads it. For the vision is yet for an appointed time; but at the end it will speak, and it will not lie. Though it tarries, wait for it; because it will surely come. It will not tarry."

For those that are already saved the hope is that this writing should serve as a great encouragement in helping to strengthen and further establish your faith. A confirmation of all that we have hoped for and have known to be true, but until now, in this age, lacking the clarity of God's own end time revelatory understanding. It may also serve as a clarion call that certain course corrections may be needed given the dire content of the message. In either case it is meant to inform and to prepare an otherwise dull of hearing church, as many have seemingly fallen prey.

For the unsaved it is strictly an alert of the highest importance, a trumpet call, and the most stringent of warnings preceding the greatest severity of things to shortly come to pass. It is an outcry to seek the God of all creation and that through faith in His Son you would be forgiven yours sins and ushered in to the family of God, and thus preserved until the time of the end. In any case, there is no time for mincing of words, time is short and getting shorter so let's get started.

As a starting point of reference it should be noted that for the purpose of this study we shall only be using either the New King James Version of the Bible or the actual King James Version itself.

CHAPTER ONE

NO MAN KNOWS THE DAY OR THE HOUR?

Our journey begins with what is perhaps the most significant of all questions that could ever be asked, in my humble opinion of course. That question that many of the saints of God have pondered both past and present: "When will Jesus return?" I would be hard pressed to think of any question that has ever been meditated upon more, debated more, taught and misconstrued more, or that might be more important for us (the church) to resolve especially given the times in which we live today.

Even many of those that have found themselves on the outside of the belief of His promised return, even they in the deepest recesses of their soul have at one time or another considered if this could be true; and if so, they might generally follow that unsettling consideration with the very typical response of "at least not in my lifetime." The unfortunate truth is that there are many Christians today that would share this same response. Nonetheless, His return will await for none of us. There is an appointed time that only the Father has set, and as such He is the only one that can answer this seemingly unanswerable question. Naturally it is for this very reason that we will seek the answer to this great enigma in the only plausible place in which it may be found, that is within the confines of the Holy Inspired Scriptures. In **II Tim.3:16** we read, **"All scripture is given by inspiration of God, and is profitable for doctrine, for reproof, for correction, for instruction and righteousness"**.

Now many of you who are reading this may already be saying: "We cannot know the time of His coming. Jesus said that plainly." Well, if that's true I would have to agree there would certainly be no point in our even attempting to search out the answer when there is none available. So perhaps we should begin our search asking a different question, that question being: "Does God tell us in Scripture whether or not we can even know when He will return?"

As I see it, this is a good launching pad for our study. If in fact there is ample evidence throughout the Bible instructing us clearly that we can know, and more than that, that we should know, this should surely propel us forward in our search to find out that much elusive answer. After all, that would most assuredly ramp up the urgency of our need to find out the truth.

Using this as our starting point it serves to reason that we should begin in Matt.24, it is in this passage where the disciples asked Jesus the exact same question that we are now attempting to ask ourselves: **Matt.24:3 "When will these things be?"**

Upon the disciples asking Jesus this question one might assume that Jesus' response should have pointedly made it clear that the answer to this question is unknowable except by the Father only, as many modern day Christians so aptly reply, but He doesn't do that. On the contrary, He begins to give a very descriptive word illustration that would act as a definitive and precise picture as the answer to their question; this is impossible to ignore. In fact, from **Matt.24:5-33** Jesus methodically gives us a play by play of the events that would immediately precede His coming, drawing us ever closer to the conclusion of that great and momentous event. Even using such phrases as **"summer is near"** and **"it is near, even at the doors"**.

It is clear to me that Jesus in His response to the disciple's question walked the disciple's right up to the door of His coming by His instruction. It is extremely important that we realize that by the carefully chosen words that our Master employed that He did not leave them on the front porch; He did not leave them in the front yard; He did not leave them in front of the house for that matter, or down the street, or around the corner. No, he walked them all the way as far as they could be brought, to the very front of the door. It is only, finally, some 30 verses later, in **(v36)** that He says **"But of that day and hour no one knows, not even the angels of heaven, but my Father only"**.

This is in fact a primary verse that Christians today use to rationalize that we are unable to know when Christ will return. It is based on an errant interpretation of what Jesus really said. What I believe He really meant by this statement is: he could walk us all the way to the season of His coming, even as near as to the door of His coming, but the very precise moment in time that the Father will open that door is only known by Him.

Now picture the analogy of being at someone's door. Your there, you've arrived, all that remains is to enter in. You ring the door bell, and it is at this point that the only delay in your entering in is how long it will take for the person inside to hear the bell, walk to the door, and open it. This is how close Jesus had brought the disciples through the use of His prophetical remarks in Matt.24.

Returning to our analogy for just a moment, if while standing at that door you look down at your watch, you're curious as to how long it had taken you to arrive at your destination. Your watch reads 7:20 and you know that you left your house at 6:00. You quickly surmise that it took you 1 hour and 20 minutes to complete your journey. You are completely aware of the exact amount of time that had passed to conclude your trip, no mystery there. What you don't know and can't know, is how long it will take before someone answers the door. That is completely in the hands of the one on the other side of that door.

This for me is the equivalent of what Christ meant when He stated that "no man knows the day or the hour". Is it any wonder that in these remarks He skillfully utilizes the smallest of incremental times (day and hour) to further amplify the nearness to His coming in which we cannot know its exact timing. Contrast that with the obvious statements of "summer is nigh" and "even at the door" and in this He is loudly proclaiming a certainty of timing that God has already placed in the hands of men.

It is apparent to me that we (the church) have strangled the truth out of this teaching of Christ by plucking out a singular verse from an entire chapter of the Bible and amplifying it to mean something that it was never intended to mean.

The second most commonly used bible passage the church so readily uses to support its claim that we cannot know the time of His coming is found in **I Thess.5:2 "For you yourselves know perfectly that the day of the Lord so comes as a thief in the night"**. This sounds very self-explanatory, right? Wrong! Once again this is the danger of taking one solitary verse out of its intended context and creating an entire premise around it that cannot stand on its own when weighed carefully within the full context of the passage in which it was given.

One only has to go to two verses further to **(v4) "But you, brethren, are not in darkness, so that this Day should overtake you as a thief"; (v5) "You are all the children of light, and the children of the day; we are not of the night, nor of darkness."** It is plain when read within its context that the thief comes in the night, and we the saints of God are not of the night. This warning was never meant for the church, and yet it is commonly used to defend the fraudulent position that we cannot know the time of His coming.

So I ask you this: how important is this knowledge? On one hand we have many Christians who have unknowingly resigned themselves to the fact that we cannot know the time of His return based largely in part to a misinterpretation of two solitary verses of the Bible. These misinterpretations allow us to settle into the slumber of thinking that since we can't know, why worry about it. On the other hand, we see our Savior going through great pains to teach us the opposite that we can know and should know.

We see the Apostle Paul doing the same in his writings, even warning us in **I Thess.5:6-7 "let us not sleep, as do others do, but let us watch and be sober. For they that sleep sleep in the night; and those that get drunk are drunk at night. But let us, who are of the day, be sober..."**

Paul, is unmistakably creating a divisional line between "those" that are of the "night" and "us" that are of the "day". This is concrete evidence that the warning of Christ's return as "coming as a thief in the night" was not intended to be perceived in this way by His true Church, and yet this is the commonly quoted verse that many Christians use today to prove that the Bible tells us that we cannot know the time of His coming.

Paul was only repeating what Jesus had said earlier to the church in **Matt.24:37-43** when He said, **"But as the days of Noah were, so shall also the coming of the Son of man be. For as in the days that were before the flood they were eating and drinking, marrying and giving in marriage, until the day that Noah entered into the ark."** This goes back to our former illustration of the man waiting at the door to enter while others are completely unaware.

Now, I ask you, did God give Noah a timeline to observe and to understand? The answer is yes! In **Gen.7:4-16; (v4) "For after seven days, and I will cause it to rain upon the earth"; (v10) "And it came to pass after seven days, that the waters of the flood were upon the earth"; (v13) "In the selfsame day entered Noah"; (v16) "and the LORD shut him in."** I promise you this, as that 7th day approached Noah did not stray far from the door of that ark. By the arrival of that 7th day he was at the door and waiting expectantly on the LORD to say "Enter." As the Church of Christ, we have much we can learn from Noah. And unless we forget, God too has Given us a 7 to watch for, it's called the 7 seals of Revelation.

Going back to **Matt.24:42-43** Jesus continues, **"Watch therefore: for you know not what hour your Lord is coming.**

But know this, that if the goodman of the house had known what hour the thief would come, he would have watched, and would not have suffered his house to be broken into." In this passage it would seem apparent that the **"thief"** is not the Lord at all, in truth it is the lack of perception of that coming "hour" that is likened unto a "thief." It is the failure to recognize the time of the impending "day of the Lord" that results in the consequences which are described as when a thief breaks into a house. These are not the words of complacency. They do not beckon unto us to relax and to rest easy, but rather they represent a stern warning to "watch" (in the Greek the word "watch" means "to keep awake, be vigilant"). Common sense dictates that if we are warned to "watch" than there must obviously be something to "watch" for. In this case we are told that we are to be watchful of "the thief"; drawing a parallel to the "coming of the thief" as a prelude or nearly simultaneous event to that of the "hour of the Lord's coming". This is an analogy of an event that if we are not careful to be on the alert and observant, it will occur like a thief breaking into our home under the cover of night.

There is obviously a wealth of Biblical treasures that we could uncover that would greatly substantiate the truth that we can and should know the time of His coming, so much information that multiple books could be written on this subject alone, and many have been.

One only has to continue on to Matt.24:45-51, where we find the parable that Jesus taught of *"The Faithful Servant and the Wicked Servant,"* and immediately following in Matt.25, we find another parable of *"The Wise and the Foolish Virgins"*. In both of these parables we discover a united theme: one is

7

ready, waiting, watching, and prepared, and the other is not. These two parables were given by Jesus as further illustrations in response to the question the disciples had asked back in Matt.24:3, it is all one and the same teaching. It would not be until many centuries later that this message would be partially divided by the installment of chapters.

The terrifying truth is that we can see these parables being acted out today in our 21st century church. There has fallen a spirit of slumber upon the church even as it did in the night of the garden of Gethsemane. Jesus is at the door of the cross in **Matt.26:40-41 "Then He came to the disciples and found them sleeping, and said to Peter, "What! Could you not watch with me one hour? Watch and pray, lest you enter into temptation."**

In still another sharp criticism by our Lord of His generation, we read in **Matt.16:1-4 "...When it is evening, you say, "It will be fair weather; for the sky is red. And in the morning, it will be foul weather today; for the sky is red and threatening, O you hypocrites, you can discern the face of the sky; but can you not discern the signs of the times?"** Repeatedly we find passages that clearly demonstrate that we are to know the time of His return, completely contradicting the doctrinal stance that our modern day church in many cases seems to employ today.

Again I will say to you... how important is this knowledge? To best answer that question let's quickly go to **Luke 19:41-44** where Jesus Himself answers that very question for us: **(v41-42) "And when He had come near, He beheld the city, and wept over it, saying, if you had known, even you, especially in this your day..."** Jesus here is approaching Jerusalem. His long awaited prophesied arrival has finally come to the capital city of all of Israel, but it is not a joyful jubilant day, not for Him; for Him it is a day to weep. And why is He weeping? Because a great judgment will soon be unleashed on the nation of God's people as **(v43-44)** precisely declares. But why the judgment you might ask? **(v44) "because you did not know the time of your visitation."**

This statement speaks volumes to me. How could a just God bring Judgment on the nation of His own people for not recognizing "the time of...visitation" unless He had given them a timeline earlier that they had previously ignored? We know from scripture that these events will once again play themselves out in the time of His second coming just as Jesus warned. Therefore let us see clearly the deep importance of discovering this timeline. Oh that we would wake up!

Moreover, the disciples were not alone in their quest to answer the "when" question. The prophet's down through the ages understood the urgency of knowing God's own timeline as witnessed to us by Peter in **I Pet.1:10-12 "Of this salvation the prophets have inquired and searched carefully, who prophesied of the grace that would come to you, searching what, or what manner of time, the Spirit of Christ who was in them was indicating when He testified beforehand, the sufferings of Christ and the glories that would follow. To them it was revealed that not to themselves, but to us they were ministering the things which now have been reported..."**

Once again we see God's own chosen prophets "inquiring, searching, what manner of time", concerning the coming of Christ, and "to them it was revealed". How can this not serve as an example to us today?

Now here's another question: "Are timelines a rarity with God, or is this His prescribed method of dealing with man?" If found to be an unusual occurrence we might conclude that there is no reliability in which to hang our hat's on; but on the other hand if found to be a succinct, orderly, and systematic methodology, it not only becomes reliable, but an absolute certainty that one exists. Bear with me now as I present my case:

In **Gen.15:13-16** we see God Speaking with Abraham… **"your seed shall be a stranger in a land that is not theirs (Egypt), and shall serve them; and they shall afflict them four hundred years… but in the fourth Generation they shall come here again"** This is a clear timeline given to Abraham concerning the coming of a future deliverer and a set time for God's holy visitation. 400 years later God speaks to Moses in **Ex.3:16-17 "I have surely visited you, and seen what is done to you in Egypt: and I have said, I will bring you up out of the affliction"**. This would appear to be a direct reference to the promised timeline in which God had given to Abraham, some four hundred years earlier.

In **Gen.21:1** we read **"the Lord visited Sarah as He had said… at the set time"**. Earlier in **Gen.17:21** we read **"but my covenant I will establish with Isaac, whom Sarah shall bear to you at this set time next year."** Now I ask you, are these definitive timelines or not? In 400 years a deliverer will come; and in one year Sarah will give birth to the son of promise. Both of these are precise types and illustrations of the coming of the Messiah, both substantiated by God with an exact timeline preceding the event.

In **Num.14:26-35** God has brought the children of Israel out of Egypt, they are at the door of the Promised Land, but they have rebelled against the voice of God. In His righteous anger God administers the following judgment: **(v34) "According to the number of the days in which you spied out the land, forty days, for each day you shall bear your guilt one year, namely forty years."** In this timeline God goes even as far as to share His reasoning behind the allotted period of time. One thing cannot be disputed: God has told the people exactly "when" they should expect to enter the Promised Land. This again is a perfect illustration of the end times, in which the children of God shall cross over into "the rest" of God. Again, an impeccably exact timeline.

And what about the book of Joshua 6:1-5, where God clearly tells Joshua that the Israelites are to march around the city of Jericho for six days, and on the seventh day the walls shall fall and the city shall be taken. Imagine the climatic build up on the part of the Israelites as each day passed, drawing ever closer to the prescribed 7th day. The entire camp's faith had to be centralized on that approaching 7th day. No one there in their right mind was anticipating a long, drawn out, prolonged war over Jericho; neither did anyone suspect that the victory would come sooner than the prescribed 7 days. No one was in the dark as to "when" the much expected victory would take place. Additionally, this too is a strict shadow-type of the end time coming of our Lord.

Look now at the book of **Jonah 3:1-4**, God sends His prophet to the people of ancient Nineveh with a simple message, **(v4) "Yet forty day's, and Nineveh shall be overthrown."** Another unmistakable timeline.

In Isa.7 the Northern Kingdom of the nation of Israel has fallen into gross idolatry. God has continuously warned them of impending judgment if they do not repent and turn back to Him. Many years and prophets later and they have still refused the clear instructions of God. At last that fateful moment has come where God can no longer bear with their unfaithfulness, culminating with this decree in **Isa7:8 "within 65 years Ephraim shall be broken, so that it will not be a people."** As Jewish history would record it, it would come to pass at the set time in 722B.C. This proclamation would result in the fall and captivity of the Northern Kingdom, and they would be thoroughly scattered throughout the world to the point of no longer being a separate and distinct people. Once more an exact and precise timeline preceding this momentous event.

In **Dan.9:2** the prophet writes, **"I Daniel understood by books the number of the years, whereof the word of the LORD came to Jeremiah the prophet, that he would accomplish seventy years in the desolation's of Jerusalem."** Here we see Daniel searching the writings of Jeremiah and discovering God's timeline for the captivity and restoration of the Southern Kingdom.

Here is another example in **Mark 8:31 "And He began to teach them, that the Son of man must suffer many things, and be rejected of the elders, and of the chief priests, and after three days rise again."** Here Christ is alerting the disciples to a brief period of time in which it may seem that He has left them and will not return again, however, He encourages them to know that He shall be right back, in the thoroughly exact time-frame of "three days". This too is an unmistakable timeline.

And still yet another example, the admonition of Christ to His disciples in **Acts 1:2-5 "but ye shall be baptized with the Holy Ghost not many days from now."** This passage comes at a time immediately following the death and resurrection of Jesus. He is near to the moment of His Ascension when He speaks these words to His disciples. As the word of God declares Jesus was crucified on the Passover, factor in the three days spent in the tomb following the Passover, added to the forty days of Acts 1:3 that He remained with the disciples, and we see that His ascension takes place somewhere in the vicinity of 7 days before Pentecost which is the exact day that the disciples are baptized with the Holy Spirit (Acts 2:1). So I ask you... does 7 days qualify as being accurate with Jesus' timeline of "not many days from now"? Now there may be some that would argue: "Wait a minute, that's not an exact timeline." My answer to you is you're right; but it was not intended to be exact. This is a further illustration of "no man knows the day or the hour."

These are all God given timelines and they are everywhere. They are so frequent and abundant in supply that they often go unnoticed as nothing unusual. Unfortunately time does not permit us to do a thorough examination of this indisputable fact. We have not even begun to scratch the surface of these timelines as they exist throughout the Word of God, but at least for the sake of this study we have begun to initially make our case.

Bearing all of this in mind consider this: Has God changed that He shall not do as He has always done? **Mal.3:6** emphatically states, **"I am the Lord, I change not"**; and in **Heb.13:8 "Jesus Christ the same yesterday, and today,**

and forever." It is beyond foolish to think that our loving and merciful God would act completely opposite of His word, studiously recording the timelines for every crucially critical biblical event in history past, only to ignore His own unchangeable ways and character, leading into the greatest and most prolific event to ever occur since the creation of the earth itself. If that sounds ludicrous that's because it is. Even the seven day creation has been interpreted by many scholars (which I agree) as a 7 thousand year timeline for the totality of God's redemptive plan. Similarly the Millennial Kingdom is clearly revealed to consist of a time-frame of 1,000 years, and on and on it goes.

Still not convinced that we can and should know the time of His coming? Time will not allow me to share the overwhelming abundance of proof that exists everywhere throughout scripture. For me it is clear…God is a God of timelines and this fact should be indisputable.

What I have shared here is the smallest of samplings to awaken your interest, to cause you to question for yourself whether or not you are on the right side of truth concerning His return. However, the greatest proof of all would be to actually find such a timeline. After all, if it truly does exist and we can find it, and understand it, that should slam the door shut on the argument that we can't know. Why would God provide a timeline for the coming of Christ if He didn't want us to know? Why would He warn us to remain awake, sober, and watch? We will go to that exact timeline in the next section that we will cover and hopefully begin to put all of this to rest; but first I will leave you with one final thought: **Amos 3:7-8**

"Surely the Lord GOD does nothing, unless He reveals His secret to His servants the prophets."

In another passage of scripture we read in **Gen.18:17 "And the LORD said, Shall I hide from Abraham what I am doing?"** Again, on the eve of destruction, this time for Sodom and Gomorrah, God forewarns His children first and then proceeds to accomplish it. Let us not forget that Jesus Himself said in **Luke 17:28-30 "Likewise also as it was in the days of Lot... Even thus shall it be in the day when the Son of man is revealed."**

For me, the conclusion of the matter is not just one of can we know or not, but rather, do we care to know? Perhaps the allure of believing that we can't know is actually a comforting sublime denial, carefully shrouding us from the responsibility that each believer shares to make ready and prepare for the coming of the King. Could it be that we say outwardly "Come Lord Jesus", and we even pray "Thy kingdom come", but what we really mean on the inside is "not in my lifetime"?

As we go forward in our quest, within the prophet's writings we shall find our answer of Christ's return. And having said that, I believe this is as good a place as any to take a pause and reflect. Ask yourself dear brothers and sisters in Christ have we become so enamored with this world, with our own precious lives, with our goals and our ambitions, that maybe subconsciously we have deemed ourselves more important than the plans and purposes of the God who has created us? Has the thought of Christ's return become an inconvenience to our own carefully crafted laid plans? Has it become a fearful and dreaded event, one to be silently spoken of, or wished away? Does this world offer us more, so much more in fact that we have become staunchly entrenched in our own desires to stay? My prayer for us all is: **Matt.11:15 "He that has ears to hear let him hear."**

THE TIMELINE

As you may have already figured out, my writing style does not exactly overflow with poetic technique. You will certainly not be mesmerized with my great acumen or my skillfully employed usage of the written language. You will not find yourself gushing over carefully contrived quips or profound quotes from the past. There will be no latent smattering of genius or historical withdraws from biblical scholars of yesteryears. No short experiential stories to cement the point. No ebb and flow of soothing verse leaving you richly entertained and longing for more. No, there will be none of that, and I would not lie to you by saying that any of this was intentional. I will however say this: It is my gift to be so extraordinarily ordinary in my delivery that the message itself cannot help but to assert its proper place of superiority over the messenger. If I am able to remain as a semi-invisible voice throughout this writing than I would have accomplished my purpose. It is in truth my highest reward if in fact you come away with little to impress you with me, but cannot help but to remember what you have read and learned.

Now, enough of this foolishness let's get down to business. The task at hand is where to look for the timeline that will tell us when will Jesus return? Without trying to sound egotistical it is a fact that I have studied through the entire Bible many times. I have made it my life's work to dissect it from Genesis to Revelation, always holding fast to the hope that by understanding it to the best of my God given ability I would one day be given the opportunity to share with others what I have learned. I say all of this to serve as a simple prelude to my following statement: In all of my study and research there is only one clearly defined passage of scripture that in my opinion details the precise timing of the coming of the Lord. For that matter, it is unquestionably the most definitive by far, that passage is found in Daniel 9. In all of God's Holy word it is unparalleled and has no equal as the masterpiece of all of God's timelines. And should we expect anything less of the timeline that would herald into the world the coming of the Son of God? Interestingly enough it is also the exact passage of scripture that Jesus Himself pointed the disciples to back in **Matt.24** when they too asked **"when will these things be?"** Going back to **Matt.24** let us now look at **(v15) "When you see the abomination of desolation, spoken of by Daniel the prophet..."** What we see Jesus doing here is He is subtly pointing us to God's own timeline concerning Himself and His coming. He is directing the disciples to search the writings of Daniel in response to their question.

More precisely in **Dan.9:27** we read **"and for the overspreading of abominations he shall make it desolate"**. This verse is the only verse in the writings of Daniel that uniquely qualifies and matches the statement given in Matt.24 by Jesus. Furthermore, it is the very last verse of that chapter, demanding that the reader goes back and reads the entire chapter as a whole in order to understand this singular statement.

In short, what we can deduce from all of this is that Jesus desires us to know. He even pronounces a blessing on those that would read this passage when He says in **Matt.24:15** **"whoever reads, let him understand"**. Once again He shows Himself to be the Supreme Teacher, ever so cleverly providing a definitive answer to their question while simultaneously protecting its contents from those whom God has not chosen to reveal it. At Jesus' own behest let us now go to Dan.9 and see what we shall find.

First, let us begin with a little background concerning where we find ourselves at the time that this chapter was written. The nation of Israel has fallen under great judgment as a result of its disobedience to God. The Northern Kingdom (consisting of 10 tribes) was many years earlier in 722B.C. conquered and taken into captivity by the Assyrian Empire. This should have served as a dire warning to the remaining Southern Kingdom of Judah (consisting of 2 tribes), who likewise was storing up the wrath of God due to its grave defiance and continuing iniquity. At last the judgment of God was poured out on them as well and they too were conquered and taken into captivity, this time by the Babylonian Empire in 586B.C. It is here that Daniel finds himself and his people in a far away land, enslaved and under complete subjection to the ruling power.

It is here in **Dan.9** where Daniel discovers that God has given a timeline for the captivity of his people. In **(v2)** we read, **"I Daniel understood by the books the number of the years, where the word of the LORD came to Jeremiah the prophet, that he would accomplish seventy years in the desolation's of Jerusalem."** Daniel has been made aware that the time of Judah's captivity was drawing near to its close. As the man of God that he was, he began to seek God through fasting and prayer on behalf of the nation of his people, knowing that he and his people were at the door of a great promised deliverance of God, as the result of his finding this timeline.

It is here that we find our way to **Dan.9:20-27**; Daniel is praying and then suddenly in **(v20) "And while I was speaking, and praying, and confessing my sin and the sin of my people Israel"; (v21) "Yes, while I was speaking in prayer, even the man Gabriel,... being caused to fly swiftly, touched me about the time of the evening sacrifice." (v22) "And he informed me, and talked with me, and said, O Daniel, I am now come forth to give you skill and understanding."** Exactly what Jesus had intended back in **Matt.24:15** when He had said **"whoever reads, let him understand."**

Going back to **Dan.9:23, "I have come to show you, for you are greatly beloved; therefore understand the matter..."** Isn't it interesting that Daniel seems to receive this amazing revelation from God at the exact same time that he appears to be thoroughly ensconced in a search for a scriptural timeline? Imagine what he may have missed had he taken the doctrinal position of "there is no way that we can know", and us along with him.

In a moment we will get smack dab in the middle of the timeline that God gave to Daniel the prophet concerning the coming of Christ, and not just His first coming, but as we shall soon see, His second coming as well. That's right, the timeline representing both coming's of our Lord Jesus. Furthermore, if that is not exciting enough, within that same timeline we will find the third and final coming of God the Father following the 1,000 year millennial reign of **Rev. 22:1-3**; and simultaneously tucked into the mix, the coming of the Holy Spirit on the day of Pentecost in Acts 2. I told you it was the masterpiece of all timelines.

First, a quick reading of **Dan.9:24-27, (v24) "Seventy weeks are determined upon your people and upon your holy city, to finish the transgression, and to make an end of sins, and to make reconciliation for iniquity, and to bring in everlasting righteousness, and to seal up the vision and prophecy, and to anoint the most Holy." (v25) "Know therefore and understand, that from the going forth of the commandment to restore and build Jerusalem unto the Messiah the Prince shall be seven weeks and sixty-two weeks; the street shall be built again, and the wall, even in troublesome times." (v26) And after the sixty-two weeks Messiah shall be cut off, but not for Himself; and the people of the prince that shall come shall destroy the city and the sanctuary; and the end of it shall be with a flood, and unto the end of the war desolation's are determined." (v27) "And he shall confirm the covenant with many for one week; and in the midst of the week he shall cause the sacrifice and the oblation to cease, and for the overspreading of abominations he shall make it desolate, even until the consummation, and that determined be poured upon the desolate."**

Now one must admit upon an initial reading of this text it seems a bit mind boggling to be able to sort out its meaning, so let's take it slow, step by step. The first thing I would like to draw to your attention is the three underlined sections of the passage. The first section clearly states "seventy weeks"; the second section clearly states "seven weeks and sixty-two weeks", or for the sake of simplification "sixty nine weeks"; and the third and final underlined section states "sixty two weeks". These are obviously three separate and distinct periods of time, one 70, one 69, and one 62, set in a very organized descending order. Three periods of time to represent three separate and distinct events, all coupled into one passage of scripture as I will soon show you. How fitting it is when we consider that our God is a Triune Being, Three Persons in One. This passage will also serve to bring to light a hotly contested theological debate that some scholars like to call "the duality of scripture", we will cover this more extensively later on in the book.

In proceeding onward, the next obvious question should be: what could the word "weeks" represent? Are they literal periods of 7 days, or could they represent something else? In the Hebrew the word "weeks" can mean a literal "seven", or "to be sevened", or "to be completed", or "completion".

Initially, let's say for the sake of argument that these "weeks" cannot represent actual 7 day periods. Had they been literal days seventy weeks would have surely been comprised of a mere 490 days (70 x 7). Using a purely literal interpretation this would place the coming of **(v25) "the Messiah"** a paltry 1 year, 4 months, and 10 days to follow **(v25) "the commandment to restore and to build Jerusalem..."**; and this as we know according to scripture itself, as well as Jewish history, did not happen, and so goes the "day for a day" interpretation.

In actuality there would be a total of three decrees that would be given over a period of about 100 years well after the prophecy of Daniel concerning the reconstruction of Jerusalem. The only real question would become which one of these decrees would be able to act as the most qualified fulfillment of Dan.9. Logically, if we could determine which decree was best suited to fulfill the specifics of this prophecy, then this should go a long way in also determining the time interpretation of Daniel's "weeks".

It would eventually be Nehemiah that would rebuild the city and the walls (Dan.9:25) of Jerusalem, by the decree of King Artaxerxes in 444BC, as recorded in Neh.2:1-8; 6:15. With this information in hand, if we do the simple math of "70 weeks", or 70 x7, using the next available variable of "one day = a year" this would clearly leave us with a total of 490 years.

Counting down from 444BC this would place the coming of the Messiah somewhere in the vicinity of 46AD. Granted, by this reasoning alone I don't believe that we can properly determine with a certainty the exact year of Jesus' 1st coming, but this interpretation would serve to be exact in determining at least the specific "generation" of Christ's 1st coming as we know it today.

Now one could argue that this is precisely what God had intended us to know, when Jesus said in **Matt.24:34** regarding His second future coming, **"Assuredly, I say to you, this generation will by no means pass away until all these things take place."**

It should also be noted that for the sake of clarity we must make our calculation using the full seventy weeks as opposed to the 62 weeks or the 69 weeks. We must remember that at the time that Daniel received the prophecy he could not have known the specifics of Christ's sacrificial death at His first coming, the formation of the gentile church that would follow, or the second coming and the millennial reign that would follow that. He would have been extremely limited in his understanding of these separate time lines as he noted himself on multiple occasions in his own writings. One could probably safely surmise then that Daniel would have been greatly restricted to the more sensical interpretation of using only the seventy weeks, or the 70 x 7 approach.

At this time we must ask ourselves: does the Bible give us any scriptural proof to base this "year for a day" theory on? After all **II Cor.13:1** clearly states, **"In the mouth of two or three witnesses shall every word be established."** The question as I see it should clearly be: is there any post Biblical precedence in which for us to draw upon in our determining if this "year for a day theory" bears any validity?

Now let me just warn you ahead of time that this will be short and brief. I have no intention of veering off track from Dan.9 and getting bogged down with this premise that will only be thoroughly resolved in the end as we move closer to the conclusion of our study.

We touched earlier on **Num.14:34** where God announces to Israel, **"According to the number of the days in which you spied out the land, for each day you shall bear your guilt one year..."** (clearly a God given timeline representing a day for a year).

Next, we find in **Ezek.4:5-6** **"Lie also on your left side, and lay the iniquity of the House of Israel upon it. According to the number of the days that you lie on it, you shall bear their iniquity. For I have laid on you the years of their iniquity according to the number of days... (v6) "I have laid on you a day for each year."** Again, an indisputable usage by God Himself of "the day for a year" interpretation.

As a matter of fact, the Bible is full of scriptural references in which God uses an actual day, or days, to act as a shadow, or a type, of a futuristic prophetic event, that can carry with it a varied amount of multiples of the literal number. For example, a seven can be used as a literal seven, it however can be used as a multiple of 49; or 70; or 490; or 1,260; or 2,520; or even 7,000; a perfect example of this is the 7 day creation which many assert has a prophetic symbolic meaning representing 7,000 years, this would give us "a thousand years for a day" interpretation. This understanding would also serve to enlighten us to another of the definitions of the Hebrew word "weeks" which is "to be sevened" which we alluded to earlier.

Alright, hopefully by this time you are not thoroughly confused? Don't be, the point is actually very simple, there is ample basis to apply "the year for a day theory". In this case the "weeks" of Dan.9 can certainly represent years as opposed to a literal period of days.

For that matter, in **Dan.9:27** we read, **"And he shall confirm a covenant with many for one week..."** (Not much of a covenant if it's a literal 7 day covenant.) There are many other examples as well throughout scripture that we could cite to further make this point but that would only cause us to stray further from our original subject.

Simply put, what we can learn from all of this is that the "weeks" of Daniel are not literal days, but more in sync with the Hebrew translation "to be completed, or completion", considering that the actual time period of a "week" can carry a varied amount of multiples. Another fairly safe deduction we could make is that these "weeks" represent "completions of time".

We have tested the application of a "day for a year theory" and found it to be both Biblically plausible as well as historically accurate, at least to the actual "generation" of the first coming of Jesus. However, this discovery does little to explain the other

2 timelines of "69 weeks" and "62 weeks" that we find in Dan.9. It was this thinking that originally set me on a different course of research. It appeared to me that the "weeks" had to represent "a completion of time" that would cover all three timelines, spread over the course of many "generations", considering the amount of elapsed time that has already occurred between the two comings. Using this logic the question quickly turned to one of "could the weeks represent generations"? The test now would be to determine how many "generations" there had been from Adam to Jesus' first coming; and then, how many from His first coming to His second. This will be our focus in the next section. Naturally, we will allow the Holy Scriptures themselves to define for us what this generational countdown will look like. Again, how fitting it is, considering that the entire Bible is a genealogical record, an ancestral lineage, generation upon generation, of our Great God and Savior, The Son of man.

THE SEVENTY GENERATIONS

We should begin this section of our study by first clearly defining our objective before we move forward. We are seeking to understand the unknown variable that the Bible itself has assigned to the word "weeks" as it appears in Dan.9, this of course is of the utmost importance if we are to gain an understanding of the Messianic timeline that exists within Dan.9.

In our initial observations we have concluded that the use of a literal interpretation of 7 days to represent one "week" must be immediately ruled out as this would only constitute the briefest segment of time consisting of a mere 490 days.

Next we examined the plausibility of "the year for a day" theory; in this interpretation a day would represent a year and "70 weeks" would represent 70 x 7 = 490 years. In this application we substituted the use of a "week" for that of 7 years as a suitable candidate in arriving at the very least the "generation" of Jesus' first coming. However, this interpretation does little if anything to resolve the remaining two time frames of "69 weeks" and "62 weeks" that we also find in Dan.9. As the result of this finding alone, we have extended our search for an additional, more feasible applicant for the term "weeks", one that would act in a fully congruent manner in regard to all three time periods.

This brings us to our present course of study. In this section we intend to determine how many "generations" there were from Adam to Jesus' first coming, and then, how many from His first coming to His second coming. In this approach we will hope to verify a "week" as a Biblical "generation". Likewise, we will follow the strict guidelines of Scripture itself as the Bible can be the only true authority in defining these "generations" as they exist within the context of Biblical genealogies.

In order to begin our search we must immediately go to the only possible starting point, and that being the book of Genesis. It is in **Gen.5:1-31** where God emphatically records the genealogy of Adam: **(v1) "This is the book of the genealogy of Adam..."** It is in this listing that counting forward from Adam to Noah there is a clearly defined accounting of 10 generations, which is where the record pauses in order to tell the flood story.

It is not until **Gen.11:10-26** that we pick up the count from Shem, the son of Noah, as we find in **(v10) "this is the genealogy of Shem"**. If it is not obvious to you as to why we take up the count with Shem and not one of his brothers it is because the Bible strictly declares that the Messiah was to be the direct descendant of the Hebrew nation, and Shem was and is, the father of the patriarch's of the Hebrew's, his brother's are not.

Proceeding on through the passage of Genesis 11 once more we discover a grouping of 10 additional generations (including Shem of course). A simple addition of these 10 generations leaving off at Abraham and the 10 generations that we found in Gen.5 leaving off at Noah, and what we arrive at is a total of 20 generations from Adam to Abraham.

At this point we could continue on filtering through the several genealogies that are scattered intermittently throughout scripture, painfully searching for each one's location and then tirelessly pouring over them, name upon name, hoping for some grand payoff at the end; or for the sake of time we could fast track our research and just cut straight to the chase.

Remembering where we have left off with Abraham as the 20th generation let us now go to **Matt.1:17 "So all the generations from Abraham to David are fourteen generations; and from David until the carrying away into Babylon are fourteen generations; and from the carrying away into Babylon unto Christ are fourteen generations."** This passage clearly brings us home in our quest to complete our first stage of the genealogical record from Adam to Christ. A simple mathematical deduction leads us to arrive plainly at a total of 42 generations from Abraham to Jesus. Adding on the 20 generations from Adam to Abraham and what we have is a grand total of 62 generations.

By the use of this interpretation we have reached the first of Daniel's prophetic milestones that of Daniel's "62 weeks". Similarly we have located it in the ascending order that one might expect to find it, as it relates to Christ's first coming. This additionally carries with it an uncontested exactness that other interpretations fail to provide. How ingeniously simple that God placed this countdown in the 1st chapter of the New Testament, in the very genealogy that would herald the birth of His Beloved Son and His Gospel? Furthermore, the first verse of the chapter loudly proclaims in **Matt.1:1 "The book of the generation of Jesus Christ..."** This profound statement coupled with its preeminent placement as the Gen.1:1 of the New Testament, added to the unparalleled importance of its Holy inspired union with the Messianic timeline of Dan.9, and what we have is a testimony to the strength of God's desire to inform us of the coming of His Blessed Son.

Now, let us go quickly back to **Dan.9:26** where it reads **"... and after sixty and two weeks shall Messiah be cut off, but**

not for Himself." This passage makes it unmistakably clear that in this 62nd generation the Messiah would come and offer His life as a sin offering, "not for Himself" but for others; He would die, and that death as we now know would be for the sake of all mankind. Once more an exact fulfillment of God's given timeline. This also lends to add a deepened sense of understanding to what Jesus was attempting to teach us back in **Matt.24:34** when He said... **"Assuredly I say unto you, this generation shall not pass away, until all these things be fulfilled."** Jesus is pointing us to recognize that even as His first coming came precisely at the appointed generation, so shall His second coming be.

There were other such clues given throughout His teachings concerning His grave focus upon the generation of His day: In **Matt.3:7 "O generation of vipers..."; Matt.11:16 "How shall I liken this generation..."; Matt.12:39-45 "An evil and adulterous generation..."; Matt.16:4 "wicked and adulterous generation..."; Matt.17:17 "O faithless and perverse generation..."; Matt.23:36 "things shall come upon this generation..."; and Mark 8:12 " no sign shall be given unto this generation..."**; and several others as well. It becomes increasingly apparent that Jesus is addressing the generation of His coming in very specific terms. They have failed to recognize the prophesied time of His arrival despite the carefully laid out plans and purposes of the Father as they were recorded by Daniel in their very own Scriptures. What's more, there is the additional and equally devastating result of not understanding the sacrificial plan of salvation as it is also documented within the contents of the given timeline.

Another proof of this generational process is mentioned in the writings of Paul as he speaks of our very own salvation and the sanctification process, which he calls **"...the washing of regeneration, and renewing of the Holy Spirit"** in **Tit.3:5**. I could go on and on concerning how Jesus addressed the generation of His day, a continual indictment of how badly they had missed the mark in regard to their lack of response to the forewarning of the prophet Daniel.

Moreover, this would also solidify His response in **Luke 19:41-44** when He said in **(v44) "they will not leave one stone upon another because you did not know the day of your visitation."** They had the word of God to give them the timeline as well as the exact accounting of every generation leading up to that predetermined 62nd generation. Perilously though, they had ignored their own Holy writings given to them through the prophets. As a result Jesus offers this chilling rebuke in **Luke 11:29-51 "The queen of the south shall rise up in the judgment with the men of this generation, and condemn them...the men of Nineveh shall rise up in the judgment with this generation, and condemn it...that the blood of all the prophets, which was shed from the foundation of the world, may be required from this generation...I say to you, it shall be required of this generation."** Notice clearly that "the queen of the south" (Sheba) and the "men of Nineveh" both recognized the move of God as it related to their generations. I wonder if there were any in that 62nd generation that may have said to themselves: "We cannot know the time of His coming." It is certainly something to think about.

In addition, all of this establishes a strong argument as to why the wise men from the East we're so astute as to His coming. In **Matt.2:1-2** we read, **"Now when Jesus was born in Bethlehem...behold, there came wise men from the east to Jerusalem, saying, Where is He that is born King of the Jews? For we have seen His star in the east, and are come to worship Him."** These men are clearly in the possession of much more than just a timeline; they have a full confidence in who this person is that the time is attesting to, as proven by their response to "come to worship Him."

Apparently they had received the timeline of His coming from none other than Daniel himself. In the second chapter of Daniel, Daniel has just solved King Nebuchadnezzar's dream which the wise men and magicians of the kingdom could not solve. Earlier in **Dan.2:11-13** we read this, **"For this cause the king was angry and very furious, and commanded to destroy all the wise men of Babylon. And the decree went forth that the wise men should be slain; and they sought Daniel and his fellows to be slain."** Incidentally, this dream was also a timeline concerning the coming of the great King and His kingdom (the image with the head of gold), which would upon His arrival overturn all the kingdom's that were before Him.

As part of Daniel's reward for interpreting the king's dream, we read in **Dan.2:48 "Then the king promoted Daniel ....chief administrator over all the wise men of Babylon."** Also in **Dan.4:9** Daniel is referred to as *"Chief of the Magicians"*; and again in **Dan.5:11 "and king Nebuchadnezzar... made him chief of the magicians, astrologers, Chaldeans, and soothsayers"**.

These were the very men whose whole purpose in the Babylonian Kingdom was to learn and understand the interpretations of dreams, visions, enigmas, difficult writing's or prophecies, in order that they might grant the king skillful counsel when called upon. Even our modern day term for the wise men is sometimes substituted for the term Magi, which has been suggested to be an abbreviation for the word magicians; further lending to the strong possibility that Daniel's personal instruction of God's timeline given in Dan.9, in addition to the kingdom timeline of Dan.2, was taught directly by Daniel and received by the wise men. After all, the last time they got it wrong it nearly cost them their lives. In turn, they passed this knowledge down through the generations allowing for the king's of the east to be thoroughly prepared to greet the coming of the Messiah at the appointed time. Certainly something to ponder I would think.

Hopefully by now the scales are beginning to fall away from your eyes, those of you that may have entered into this reading believing that we cannot know when the Lord will return. But we have just gotten started. This all may be a perfect fit for the "62 weeks" of Dan.9, but lest we forget there are still two remaining timelines that we have yet to explore. Next, we will proceed on to the next logical timeline in its ascending order, that of Dan.9:25 and the "69 weeks".

THE SEED OF THE SPIRIT

In the previous section we have seen how the "62 weeks" of Dan.9 are a perfect match for the 62 generations from Adam to the first coming of Christ. This would leave us to take up our search of Jesus' second coming in Dan.9:25, the second timeline given to us of "69 weeks". Even as the first timeline would surely seem to represent "generations", so also we must naturally assume that the second timeline will also find it's fulfillment by the use of generations. Logically, we may also assume that this timeline will be one that will follow the first coming, which would exclude us from searching for it in the Old Testament. Further narrowing our search, I believe we could safely agree that this timeline will represent an exact 7 generations, no more and no less. In short, we are on the hunt for a genealogical record, to be found in the New Testament, which should be comprised of exactly seven generations, at this moment this is our mission statement.

To start the search, the genealogy of Matt.1 must be immediately eliminated as it concludes in (v17) with the first arrival of Jesus and goes no farther. The next genealogy to be found in the New Testament does not appear until Luke 3, but it too reveals nothing beyond the first coming of Jesus.

It would be here that our search will take a dramatic turn, as there are no other obvious genealogies in the N.T. to make our inquiry. In addition to that, let us place a high priority on the simple fact that Jesus died childless; this in itself adds a great complication in determining a genealogical lineage to follow His first coming. At first glance it would appear as if our search had abruptly ended before it even got started, that is unless we are going at this thing all wrong.

The truth is, it is impossible to find a physical earthly bloodline for Jesus because it simply doesn't exist. No children means no bloodline, and no bloodline means no genealogy. But what we can find is exactly what the Bible so loudly proclaims throughout the New Testament, Jesus' bloodline today can only exist as a spiritual bloodline.

Beginning our approach to this Biblical fact let it be said right off, this is not a metaphysical or philosophical bloodline. It is as real and tangible as any earthly bloodline, in fact, even more so. We read in **Heb.11:3 "Through faith we understand that the worlds were framed by the word of God, so that things which are seen were not made of things which do appear."** This verse boldly declares that the invisible spiritual world was first in its existence, and the visible, earthly, physical creation came later on as a result of that spiritual existence. It should be easy to see that the spiritual is every bit as tangible as the physical. In actuality the spiritual is superior to the inferiority of the physical.

Moreover, in **II Cor.4:18** it says, **"While we look not at the things which are seen, but at the things which are not seen: for the things which are seen are temporal; but the things which are not seen are eternal."** So not only did the spiritual world exist first, but it is eternal, it has no beginning or end. Simply put, the spiritual is preeminent in every way. God is Spirit, He and His angels, and His kingdom, are all spirit. We on the other hand are earthly, living in the confined space and limited reality of the physical, merely the creation of He who was, and is, before us. As Jesus so aptly put it in **John 8:53-58**

"Are you greater than our father Abraham... Jesus said unto them, 'Most assuredly I say to you, before Abraham was, I AM."

With this understanding in mind, we will see that what God has done in Christ Jesus has not only continued the genealogical record but has perfected it for all of eternity. This should add great weight to what Jesus said in **John 3:3-8 "Except a man be born again, he cannot see the kingdom of God... That which is born of the flesh is flesh; and that which is born of the Spirit is spirit."** The term "born again" speaks clearly to a "birthing or a begetting" into this spiritual ancestral linage which is fully documented in Dan.9.

In the book of **Deut.25:5-9** we read, **"If brothers dwell together, and one of them dies and has no son, the widow of the dead man shall not be married to a stranger outside the family, her husband's brother shall go into her, take her as his wife, and perform the duty of a husband's brother to her. And it shall be that the firstborn son in which she bears will succeed to the name of his dead brother, that his name may not be blotted out of Israel."**

This is precisely what occurred following the death of Jesus. He had died a premature death at the age of 33 without ever having any earthly offspring, He was childless. The disciples however as His brethren performed their duty and rose up a spiritual lineage to "succeed to His name", children that would be conceived by the Spirit of God just as Jesus Himself was conceived.

Jesus alluded to this very thing when He spoke to the "multitude" in **Luke 3:8 "...do not begin to say to yourselves, we have Abraham as our father. For I say to you that God is** able to raise up children to Abraham from these stones." This speaks to the unfathomable and unlimited capacity of God to "raise up" genealogical descendants as He would see fit.

This truth was never spoken more clearly than it was in **Ps.22:30-31 "A seed shall serve Him; it shall be accounted to the Lord for a generation. They shall come, and shall declare His righteousness unto a people that shall be born, that He has done this."** This passage is given at the very conclusion of perhaps the most extensive pictorial we have in scripture of Jesus' crucifixion. A detailed account of His sacrificial death, and His "seed" that shall follow Him as the result of that death.

The other challenger for the honor of being the most prolific word picture of His crucifixion is found in **Isa.53** and there we find also in **(v8) "And who will declare His generation?"**; and then again in **(v10), "He shall see His seed..."**; and still yet once more in **James 1:18 "Of His own will begat He us with the word of truth, that we should be a kind of firstfruits of His creatures."**

Finally we take a look at **Rom.9:6-8** which declares in **(v8) "...In Isaac your seed shall be called. That is, those who are the children of the flesh, these are not the children of God; but the children of the promise are counted as the seed."** This is a clear admonition that "the seed" of Christ is not "of the flesh", but one that would be "counted" as His seed as a result of true faith in Him, a spiritual seed.

With these few passages of scripture we have not even scratched the surface of all that God has said concerning Jesus' spiritual bloodline, but more shall certainly follow as we move forward in our study. The main importance for now is that we have laid a firm foundation so that we might be able to move forward and expand our search for the generations of Daniels "69 weeks."

With this criterion in mind (a spiritual bloodline) we have added the most instrumental of all our queries in order that we might continue our search. The genealogy must be in the N.T., in addition it must be an exact 7 generations, and lastly it will represent a spiritual genealogy as opposed to a physical one.

Once again for the sake of time we will leapfrog straight to that most amazing genealogy that God has preserved for us in His Holy Scriptures. Turn now to Rev. chapters 1-3. It is here that Jesus Himself has sent "His angel" (1:1) in a vision to the apostle John. He has come to John with a detailed message concerning the time of the end which would precede the 2nd coming of Christ. Once again we see God informing man of His timeline, this time using a series of events just as Jesus did in Matt.24 (the seals, the trumpets, and the bowls).

Equally reminiscent is Dan.9 where God sends the Archangel Gabriel to give His timeline to Daniel some 600 years earlier. So much for the theory that we can't know when the Lord will come. It should become more and more obvious that this timeline is very much on the heart of God and that He has gone to great lengths to share it with man down through the ages.

Immediately in **Rev.1:7** the angel makes it perfectly clear as to the purpose of this Divine visitation, **"Behold, he cometh with clouds; and every eye shall see Him, and they also which pierced Him: and all kindreds of the earth shall wail because of Him. Even so, Amen."** This is impossible to confuse, the entire purpose of this heavenly vision to John, and to all those that would read his writings succeeding down through the generations to come, is to make abundantly aware the circumstances surrounding the coming of Jesus upon His return.

It is also made unmistakably clear as to who this message is to be transferred to, in **Rev.1:4** we read **"John to the seven churches which are in Asia"**; and in **1:11, "What you see, write in a book, and send it to the seven churches which are in Asia; unto Ephesus, and unto Smyrna, and unto Pergamos, and unto Thyatira, and unto Sardis, and unto Philadelphia, and unto Laodicea."**

Now there are many things that could be said about this chapter but for the purpose of our study we will stay with the simplicity of that which is most obvious: a message concerning the 2nd coming of Christ has been given to John and it is intended for seven churches. With this as our focal point, let us move now to Rev. chapters 2 and 3.

The following 2 chapters are an explicit exposé singling out 7 churches of John's day, or are they? We know through historical records as well as through archaeological digs that these aforementioned 7 churches did in fact exist during the first century, or at the time that John received this message. What has been contested down through the years and has been the topic of much debate, is whether or not these churches have a much deeper hidden significance. The question has always been are they perhaps a foreshadowing of "7 church periods" that would proceed from the 1st century of John until the 2nd coming of Christ Jesus?

Furthermore, could they represent a prophetic glimpse into the spiritual bloodline of Christ Jesus? Is this the genealogical record we are looking for to complete our understanding of Daniel's "69 weeks"? One can only imagine the extreme significance that all of this would hold for us today if proven to be true? As you can see we have certainly got some sorting out to do, and with that said, we had best get started.

UNLOCKING DUALITY

At this moment in time we will need to take a brief detour in our study by way of the very nature of the question in which we are asking: Can the seven churches of Rev.2-3 have a multiple or dual interpretation? Can they represent simultaneously the seven churches of John's day (in the physical literal sense), while simultaneously representing a genealogical record of 7 church generations (in the spiritual sense)? This would be a prime case study for the quintessence of the much debated "duality theory".

To explore this theory further we must first take a look at what the Bible itself has to say about "duality" of Scripture. Does the Bible support this theory or does it denounce it? As with all of our findings the word of God must have the full authority and final say in the matter. If duality of scripture is a God given truth then we should be able to find that truth clearly stated in scripture.

It is my contention that within the book of Ecclesiastes lays the key that unlocks this controversial subject. It is an unusual observation that in my opinion serves as the fundamental building blocks of the heart and soul of Biblical "duality"; although as you will soon see, we will support our findings with a wide array of Biblical texts to support this conclusion.

Before we start our research let it be said that there are varying opinions as to who actually wrote the book of Ecclesiastes. However, for the sake of this study and holding down confusion we will ascribe its authorship to Solomon who is commonly agreed to as its author. Once more, how fitting it would seem that God would reveal this revelatory truth to he whom we commonly refer to as "the wisest man that ever lived", none other than King Solomon himself.

Another brief point which I would like to make before getting started, concerning this book which I find most fascinating, is that at its very onset it appears to be encased in a mystery. More precisely, the word "Ecclesiastes" is not found anywhere in the entire Bible other than as the title of this book. In every other book of the Bible (66 books in all), the title of that book would serve as an abbreviated depiction as it would relate to the contents of that particular book. Genesis is about the beginning of things, Exodus is about just that, the Exodus of Israel out of Egypt; Leviticus concerns the law as given to the Levites, and so on. However, in this case there is no neatly defined definition for this word in the Hebrew language. It has been translated down through the years to the closely comparative word of "qoheleth":- "one who addresses an assembly"; usually rendered into the English as "The Preacher". There is on the other hand a strong comparison and resemblance to the Greek word of the New Testament "ekklesia" which carries with it the English translation of our word "church".

In many circles the book is commonly referred to by the title of "the Preacher", but equally as odd the word "preacher" is not found in all of the O.T., with the exception of the 7 times it appears in this book. By in large the word "preacher" is and of itself a N.T. Word, at least by the Biblical standard. Nowhere except in this book is the word "preacher" ever used until we arrive at the N.T. in fact, some have even argued that the book would seem to have been written to the Gentiles.

By now you may be asking yourself ... "Where is he going with all of this?" I am merely attempting to draw your attention ever so briefly, to the possibility that this book was marked at its conception by the Holy Spirit for the N.T. church. If true, this would act as a huge example of "duality", as it would be encoded in the very title of the book. Additionally, this would lend to the suggestion that within the contents of this book lies a message not easily perceived until the arrival of the Spirit filled body of the Church. As amazing of a thought as all of this is, what would be the significance of this book to our modern day church if this is true?

I can only imagine the line that must be forming of those critics who would immediately find fault with this premise, but still I ask "What if...?" We'll come back to this later at the conclusion of this section, hopefully at that time we will be able to add considerable clarity to this assertion.

Without veering any further off course let us now proceed to **Eccl.1:3-7 "One generation passes away, and another generation comes... The sun also rises and the sun goes down, and hastens to the place where it arose... The wind goes toward the south, and turns around to the north; the wind whirls about continually, and comes again on its circuit... All the rivers run into the sea, yet the sea is not full; to the place from which the rivers come, there they return again."**

Here at the very beginning of Solomon's writings he makes his first observation in his attempt to answer the question that all mankind has been asking itself since the dawn of time... "What is the meaning of life?" Solomon puts it this way in **Eccl.1:13 "I set my heart to seek and search out by wisdom concerning all that is done under heaven; this burdensome** task God has given to the sons of man, by which they may be exercised."

In his initial finding, only 7 short verses into the book he discovers a most interesting principle: In a word, all of creation moves and flows under an orderly cyclical movement; or pattern; an unremitting cycle that repeats itself. It would not be until many centuries later that the enormity of the impact of this principle would be more thoroughly realized, again a clue that this book may have been written for a future time.

This principle as described by Solomon in Eccl.1:3-7 would seem to govern all of God's creation and would serve as the fundamental building block for the theory of duality, as duality in its most basic nature is in fact a cyclical continuum. Solomon is pointing us to the truth that "…all that is done under heaven" operates within the carefully constrained limits of a rhythmic cycle. Never finding its beginning or its end as with a circle; it is self-perpetuating under the restrictions so intricately set in place by none other than God Himself, a truly masterful demonstration to the entire physical creation of an Eternal God.

Ps.19:1-6 puts it this way: **"The heavens declare the glory of God; and the firmament sheweth His handywork. Day unto day uttereth speech, and night unto night sheweth knowledge. There is no speech nor language, where their voice is not heard. Their line is gone out through all the earth, and their words to the end of the world. In them hath He set a tabernacle for the sun, which is as a bridegroom coming out of his chamber, and rejoiceth as a strong man to run a race. His going forth is from the end of the heaven, and his circuit unto the ends of it: and there is nothing hid from the heat thereof."**

Now let me just add this...If this passage in any way indicates that the "sun" is an allusion to Jesus "The Son" of God, then this too is an example of duality, as the physically literal "sun" would act as a pictorial of the spiritually unseen "son". This is precisely the question that we are asking in regard to the 7 churches of John's day. Can they be a physically literal representation of an unseen spiritual genealogy of 7 church generations?

To further bolster Solomon's conclusion he adds this insight in **Ps.1:9-10 "That which has been is what will be, that which is done is what will be done, and there is nothing new under the sun. Is there anything of which it may be said, See, this is new? It has already been in ancient times before us."**

Now let's fast forward for a moment to our present day, with all of our modern science and technology we have thoroughly proven Solomon's conclusion to be true. Take for example what we have learned about our own galaxy. Within it we find carefully crafted circular objects (planets) rotating each one on its own individual circular axis, while simultaneously rotating cyclically in varied degrees around still another circular object (the sun). Add to all of this the cycles of the stars and the moon, and that at a great distance they all come together to form an even greater circular object (the galaxy). Not to mention this phenomenon repeats itself over and over again throughout our entire universe. Simply put, all of creation is operating under an immeasurable amount of interwoven cyclical cycles. A continual pronouncement that God is the creator and that He is Eternal.

Consider this fact that even the way in which we measure time is intricately linked to this exact same principle. Seconds go around and complete minutes, minutes complete hours, and hour's complete days. Days go around and complete weeks and then months, and eventually years, and so on. It too is a self-perpetuating cycle in the exact form of the creation itself. Ever growing from years, to decades, to centuries, to millenniums, to ages, and on into eternity.

Even our weather patterns are not immune to this principle: spring turns to summer, which turns to fall, which turns to winter, and eventually back to spring again. And with all of this the delicately interwoven balance of the geological systems of the earth, as well as the animal kingdom, on land, sea and air, all performing in unison their uniquely ordained migratory patterns. An utterly mind boggling intensive harmony operating within the constraints of this very same O.T. principle.

Even our food supply is entirely at the command of this principle. The trees and all of plant life as we know it, are all under the full sway of this governing principle of all of creation just as Solomon stated it.

Add to that, the sciences of the smallest known existing particles known to mankind, your microbes, your molecules, your atoms, your neutrons and protons, your quarks, etc; all ingeniously created to appear under the most powerful of microscopes as circular objects. Even down to the very D.N.A. that orchestrates the exactness of the creation of each and every living organism (man included) is in itself formed in the shape of a spiral, a cylindrical ladder when viewed beneath the most powerful of all technological eyes known to science.

This principle additionally is worked out in an uninterrupted fashion in the lives of every human being. For instance, a man comes into this life as a mere infant, unable to walk, talk, or do anything for himself, completely helpless and defenseless, and by the end of his life he has passed through the full cycle and back to where he began. Once more he is fragile and defenseless, and requiring assistance to accomplish the most basic and elementary of tasks. Even the physiological makeup of the human body is under the full dominion of this all encompassing cyclical principle. Moreover, when we realize the perpetual circuit that our blood supply engages in within our bodies we see our own heart acting as a virtual "sun" within the galaxy of the human body.

Now all of this brings me to my next point: even all of recorded history is no match for this principle. This principle has proven itself to be true time and time again. It is why we so vehemently agree that "history repeats itself". In fact, we scoff at the idea that this principle will not win over when we say, "The definition of insanity is to do the same thing over and over again and to expect a different outcome." Likewise, we employ a long standing adage of "What goes around comes around." It is in fact this very principle that provides the basis for historical repetition which in turn opens the flood gate for the existence of duality. The eventuality of being able to record a historical biblical event at the time of its initial occurrence, only to see it reemerge again in a slightly different form at a later time in history, this is the essence of duality.

In a nut shell, this cyclical principle revealed to Solomon and attested to according to all that we know today about everything, is the very "architectural blueprint of duality". As Solomon so boldly proclaimed in **Ps.1:9-10 "That which has been is what will be, that which is done is what will be** done... It has already been in ancient times before us." This is precisely why Jesus was able to make the following claims beginning with **Heb.10:7 "Then said I, 'Behold, I have come - in the volume of the book it is written of me"** The cyclical lives of the ancient fathers of the faith, ever winding through the cyclical events of time and history, ever pointing to the One and Eternal Creator of that principle, Jesus. He is both the originator and center of all. He is the centerpiece of "duality" It is not until one circle's back to the O.T. that this truth can be fully revealed. In **John 5:39** we read, **"Search the scriptures; for in them you think you have eternal life: and these are they which testify of me."**

And again in **John 5:46 "For if you had believed Moses, you would have believed me; for he wrote of me."** These statements by Jesus are declaring much more than that there are some scattered prophecies providing various clues about Him throughout the O.T., on the contrary, Jesus Himself is proclaiming that the whole of the O.T. is all about Him. This humongous statement would be completely impossible without the aid of "duality".

Paul the apostle spoke also of this in **Col.2:17** in regard to the law of feasts and holy days, **"Which is a shadow of things to come; but the body is of Christ"**. This would seem to be a definitive example of duality as an interpretive tool as used by Paul. In this example the "body" is the full reality, where the "shadow" is only a perception of that reality. By use of this illustration the 7 churches of John's day could merely be the "shadow" of the reality of the 7 church generations that would represent the actual "body"; which would also give additional weight to Paul's statement in **Rom.12:5 "So we being many, are one body in Christ"**

In **Heb.8:5** we read the writer's instruction concerning the priesthood, **"who serve the copy and the shadow of the heavenly things"**. This in itself is a powerful comparison to the truth that we are in search of. Here Paul is plainly telling us that the priesthood is merely a "copy" of something unseen at the time. This holds a direct relevance to our quest to determine if God might have assigned an unknown importance to the 7 churches of John's day.

And still again in **Heb.10:1 "For the law, having a shadow of the good things to come, and not the very image of the things."** By this verse we see that even the law is to conform to this concept of duality.

And once more in **Heb.9:8** it states, **"the Holy Spirit indicating this, that the way into the Holiest of All was not yet made manifest while the first tabernacle was still standing. It was symbolic for the present time..."** In (v23) it refers to these things as **"the copies of the things in the heavens"**. Even the tabernacle is not exempt from this governing principle. Over and over again we see the Holy Spirit indicating that the priesthood, the law, even the tabernacle itself, are all but "types" of a much deeper and more significant reality.

And once more in **I Cor.10:11 "Now all these things happened to them as examples, and they were written for admonition, upon whom the ends of the ages have come."**

And **James 5:10 "my brethren, take the prophets, who spoke in the name of the Lord, as an example..."**

And **Gal.4:24** Paul writes **"Which things are an allegory..."** Time and time again we see the holy ordained writers of God's own word using "duality" and teaching it to us.

Finally Solomon put it this way in **Eccl.3:11-15 "I know that whatever God does it shall be forever...That which has already been, and what is to be has already been; and God requires an account of what is past."** Here Solomon is making a direct link between God's Eternal Being and man's history. And why not? After all, it is the record of Jesus' history (or His story), not to mention His ancestral lineage.

Solomon continues in **Eccl.6:10** where he says, **"Whatever one is, he has been named already."** Again alluding to the fact that the origins of everything are found by circling backwards.

Also, in **Eccl.8:1, 7** Solomon continues his instruction to us, **"Who is like a wise man? And who knows the interpretation of a thing? .... For he does not know what will happen; so who can tell him when it will occur?"** Here Solomon is clearly stating that the hidden understanding is immovably blocked unless one applies himself to the spiritual cyclical principle that has been constructed by the ever Eternal God.

And again in **Eccl.7:23-25** Solomon states this, **"All this I have proved by wisdom. I said, 'I will be wise, but it was far from me. As for that which is far off and exceedingly deep, who can find it out? I applied my heart to know, to search and seek out wisdom and the reason of things."**

And finally, in **Eccl.12:9-10 "he pondered and sought out and set in order many proverbs..."** Solomon is clearly saying that this cyclical principle is the bedrock of all understanding, especially as it refers to those things which are most difficult, or even impossible to understand. Unfortunately for Solomon it would seem that even though he was right on track with his initial observation of this monumental principle, it was quite frustrating for him considering it bore little in the way of actual results. Just think of it, without the first coming of Christ to fill in all the blanks for us, we too would find ourselves in a likewise position with Solomon. Furthermore, for me this lends to add some additional support to my initial contention that the book of Ecclesiastes was primarily written for a later time; our time. It would take the Spirit filled church (ekklesia) that would not arrive for some 3,000 years later to make a full implementation of this principle as it refers to the interpretation of the Bible. And thus the title name Ecclesiastes or "Ekklesia", or "Church". Upon this understanding it would seem to be the possible equivalent of the opening salutation of a letter, or in this case... "Dear Church".

Not excluding the prophets themselves they put it this way: **Job 8:7-10 "Though your beginning was small, yet your latter end will greatly increase. For inquire, please, of the former age, and consider the things discovered by their fathers; for we were born yesterday, and know nothing, because our days on earth are a shadow, will they not teach you and tell you, and utter words from their heart?"**

In **Isa.40:4** we read, **"Who has performed and done it, calling the generations from the beginning? I, the LORD, am the first; and with the last, I Am He."** This title for God **"the First and the Last"** is repeated by Jesus, referring to Himself in both **Rev.1:8, 11** saying, **"I am Alpha and Omega, the Beginning and the Ending... the First and the Last"** Here too, this is an intelligible means of defining His Eternal Being by use of "the cyclical principle".

One can imagine a circle, and at any given starting point on that circle one may begin a full journey around the circle. Upon a full completion of the cycle an interesting phenomenon occurs. By arriving at the end of the cycle I have simultaneously arrived at the beginning. It is by this understanding that we see that the circle has no beginning or ending. This holds true no matter where I begin on that circle. In short, the end and the beginning are always going to be one and the same. By this knowledge all of creation and everything in it bears the reflection of God's Person-hood through the cyclical principle.

In **Isa.41:22** Isaiah writes, **"Let them bring forth and show us what will happen, Let them show the former things, what they were, that we may consider them, and know the latter end of them; or declare to us things to come."** Here is a prime example of God plainly saying that the past holds the key to understanding the future. Once more this is the construct of duality.

Moving forward to **Isa.44:6-8 "I am the first and I am the last... since I appointed the ancient people, and the things that are coming and shall come... have I not told you from that time, and declared it?"**

In **Isa.46:9-10 "Remember the former things of old; for I am God, and there is none else; ... declaring the end from the beginning, and from ancient times the things that are not yet done"**

In addition to all of this, time will not permit us to even remotely tap into the plethora of Bible events, one after another and their multiple fulfillments as they come to pass, time and time again in their repeated cyclical fashion.

There was Abraham's sacrificial offering of his son Isaac; the life of Joseph; David and Goliath; the ten plagues of Egypt; the first Passover, and the deliverance of all of Israel at the hands of Moses. All of these are extensive cases of duality, just to name a few. The simple fact is that duality is common place throughout the entire word of God. In truth, God Himself is a duality, equally distinct as the Father, the Son, and the Holy Spirit; and likewise unconditionally one God.

Finally, in **Hos.12:10** God speaks this with utmost clarity: **"I have also spoken by the prophets, and I have multiplied visions, and used similitude's, by the ministry of the prophets."** By all of this we must come to the undeniable truth, God is not just the author and creator of "duality", He is also a huge fan of its use.

In conclusion, duality of scripture is an invaluable tool which God has given to man to allow us greater understanding of both Him and the times in which we live as it relates to His plans and purposes. By the proper use of duality we can go back in time and reconstruct the events as they correlate to our lives today.

If you think about it, this is a common technique used today throughout the entire scientific world. In our modern age of the sciences it is simply called reverse engineering. When the solution to a problem is greater than the ability to grasp that solution, science immediately turns to the default mechanism of dissecting the problem backwards. By dividing the larger issue into smaller, more manageable bite size pieces, one can readily gain a more intensive knowledge of the inner workings of each isolated segment; and thereby providing a deeper and more enriched understanding of the thing as a whole. Where beforehand it had been an unapproachable task, now through the use of reverse engineering it not only becomes approachable but highly attainable.

This is the same methodology in which our entire modern day world operates today. Science, politics, religion, economics, law, all use the same general process of reverse engineering at one time or another when tackling the most complicated of problem solving. They all divert back to previous precedents that have already been set in the past in order to see their way forward in resolving the most difficult of issues. This is precisely how the Bible interprets itself.

By this time I rest my case, and will conclude with this final summation: Because God Himself is The Eternal Being, all that He creates comes out of Him and as a result is also eternal. Like the circle that has no beginning or an end, so is our God. His entire creation bears His Name and His fingerprints through these cycles, and gives witness to this eternal fact. Even His written Word is in its very nature cyclical, professing ever so loudly that God is eternal, and He is the Author; and in the case of Christ Jesus He is the Word. And it is for these reasons that "duality of scripture" in my humble opinion is not merely a "theory" it is an eternal fact. And therefore, it is more than highly probable that the 7 churches of Rev.2-3 most certainly can represent the missing 7 generations of Daniels "69 weeks." Similarly, it should also be noted under no uncertain terms, that the interpretation and understanding of all Biblical prophecy rests upon the proper use of this God inspired spiritual principle as it relates to all coming events.

WHY "SEVEN AND SIXTY TWO WEEKS" AND NOT SIXTY NINE WEEKS?

As we have seen there is more than sufficient proof that the 7 churches of Rev.2-3 can represent a great deal more than just the 7 churches of John's day. We have seen the Bible give its own witness that "duality of scripture" not only exists throughout God's Word, but that it is an invaluable method given by God Himself in helping us to see more clearly the difficult solutions to hard questions that lies beneath the surface of the Word. And perhaps, there is none more difficult than "when will Jesus return."

Furthermore, we have determined that the "seven weeks" that are missing from between Daniel's "62 weeks" of Christ's 1st coming, and the "69 weeks" of His second coming, must also represent generations just as the initial 62 generations. We have also made the clear observation that these generations cannot be represented in a literal physical form, but rather, they must represent a spiritual bloodline; which would lead us to believe that they may appear in some form through the use of "duality". They must also make their appearance somewhere in the New Testament for obvious reasons. And lastly, in our search through the N.T. for any genealogical record comprising of a strict list of 7, there is but one candidate, the 7 churches of Rev.

To start off with in the verification of this premise, I would just like to point out a few observations that I feel might help us in solidifying the path that we are now undertaking.

First, let us notice where we found the 7 churches. We found them as a prelude leading up to the message that would declare

Jesus' 2nd coming in Rev.2-3. In retrospect it makes perfect sense that the conclusion of this genealogy preceding His 2nd coming would show itself exactly there. Let us not forget where we found the final puzzle piece of the 42 generations that eventually qualified the first "62 weeks" of Daniel; we found them in an identical manner in Matt.1:17 immediately preceding the message of His 1st coming. In fact, the very next verse of **Matt.1:18** states this: **"Now the birth of Jesus Christ was as follows..."** For me this is a perfect match in the way of its location in the Word.

Another interesting point is that it is found in the primary book of all of N.T. prophecy. Why is that significant you might ask? Well, since we know that this genealogy must represent a "spiritual bloodline" consisting of 7 generations, and that at the time of John's writing the church was purely in its infancy, therefore one can easily deduce that anything he or any other apostle would have to write concerning the whole of the church would be futuristic. At best John and the Apostles would only have knowledge of the church of their day, or the 63rd generation. Therefore we could safely surmise from this that any writings concerning later church generations would have to fall within the parameters of prophecy. And thus, we find the genealogical record of the 7 churches in the most profound storehouse of all of N.T. prophecy, the book of Revelation. Once again a perfectly crafted location in order to insure that it is found by its future readers.

Next, consider this: John has just received a message revealing the 2nd coming of Jesus. As we have read earlier in the book, in Rev.1:11, John is instructed to deliver this message to the 7 churches of Asia; however, as we know Christ doesn't return during the time of these churches. This leads us to make a simple deduction, although the message was clearly involving them, and of central importance to them, it would not be for many centuries later that the dominate theme of the message (His return) would be of its most heightened importance. As a result, what John was actually commanded to do was to preserve the message by means of these 7 churches of his day.

In fact, Jesus Himself says it best in **Rev.1:19 "Write the things which you have seen, and the things which are, and the things which shall be hereafter..."** This is unmistakably speaking of the seven churches and their "dual" meaning; how can we be for sure? It really is quite simple, we read (v19) within the entirety of the full context of the passage. As **(v20)** is a continuation of **(v19)** we read, **"The mystery of the seven stars which you saw in my right hand, and the seven golden candlesticks. The seven stars are the angels of the seven churches: and the seven candlesticks which you saw are the seven churches.**

This is not just referencing a mere 7 churches that Christ has chosen to isolate in John's day. To cement the point, the very next verse begins the uninterrupted passages of Rev.2-3. So what we see is Jesus Himself preserving the message of His 2nd coming through 7 churches, for 7 churches that have not yet arrived. This provides an unbreakable link between them and us today; and for that matter every church that would follow them. This for me is an illuminating example of the true craftsmanship of "duality" as seen clearly in its actual creative formation. How ingeniously God?

This brings me to my next point: the wording of **Dan.9:25 "Know therefore and understand, that from the going forth**

of the command to restore and to build Jerusalem unto the Messiah the Prince shall be seven weeks and sixty two weeks..." Now I ask you: why did God state it this way? Why didn't He just say 69 weeks? Why the division, the separation, between the 7 and the 62? In my mind He is obviously creating an intentional distinction between the two. He is not only attempting to divulge a single period of whole time (69 weeks), but at the same time He is delineating the time in order to fully represent 2 separate and distinct times that come together to fully form the one. In my opinion He is isolating the 7 church generations of the New Covenant (the spiritual seed), from that of the 62 generations of the Old Covenant (the earthly seed), while simultaneously presenting them as one lineage of 69 generations.

In this He is attesting to the fact that though they represent separate periods of time, and separate aspects of His covenant, as well as separate people groups (Jews and Gentiles), by the virtue of Jesus they remain completely and perfectly one. It is all one genealogy under one finished covenant, and that genealogy belongs to Christ.

This should be startling information to all those who would wish to propagate the false doctrine that God has done away with His people Israel and that the church has replaced them. This is a damnable heresy and nothing could be farther from the truth. By the knowledge of Dan.9:25 we see one ancestral lineage comprising of both them and us. A confirmation of the one covenant, the first half to be made by the Father Himself in Gen.15:8-18, and the second half by His Son on the cross. These are not two covenants, so much as they are two ends of the same covenant. The first half looking forward to the One who would come, and the second half looking back at the One who has already come, and will come again; and all things pointing to the center who is Jesus the Christ. It is an exact replication of what we find in the strategic placement of the "weeks" in the genealogical prophecy of Daniel.

The sad fact of this whole truth is that neither we (the Church) nor they (the Jews) seem to be aware of this truth. Still today we too often think in terms of "them and us"; this is a great ignorance, there is only "us". This is the intricate construction of what Paul calls *"the one new man."*

In **Eph.3:15** he writes, **"Having abolished in His flesh the enmity, even the law of commandments contained in ordinances; for to make one new man, so making peace..."** This is more than just abolishing the enmity that had previously existed between God and man as a result of man's sin against the law; it speaks also to the barrier that has always existed between the nation of Israel and all the Gentile peoples of the world. The law was that barrier. It would eventually take the replacement of that law with grace in order to accommodate the unity of both Jews and Gentiles, as we find it in **Col.3:10-11 "And have put on the new man, which is renewed in knowledge after the image of Him that created him: Where there is neither Greek nor Jew, circumcision nor uncircumcision... but Christ is all, and in all."**

It is only through Christ, and Christ alone, that the "7 weeks" and the "62 weeks" can be combined to make the **"69 weeks"** of Daniel. A unified conversion of two ancestral lineages into one. This too was spoken of by the Apostle Paul in **Rom.11:15-32**, in **(v17)** we read **"And if some of the branches be broken off, and you being a wild olive tree, were grafted** in among them, and with them became a partaker of the root and fatness of the olive tree..."

It continues in **(v23) "And they also, if they do not continue in unbelief, will be grafted in: for God is able to graff them in again. (v24) For if you were cut out of the olive tree which is wild by nature, and were grafted contrary to nature into a good olive tree: how much more shall these, which are the natural branches, be grafted into their own olive tree?" (v25) "For I do not desire, brethren, that you should be ignorant of this mystery... that blindness in part is happened to Israel, until the fullness of the Gentiles has come in."** And finally **(v26) "And so all Israel shall be saved..."** This is more than just saying that all of modern day Israel shall be saved, on the contrary, it is saying "all of Israel shall be saved", meaning all of them (the Jews), and all of us (the Church) together will be saved.

Without getting into lengthy detail, this is a precise teaching of what we have found in Daniel 9. It even uses the analogy of a "tree" which is used to further illuminate the truth of the topic which is God's own "family tree"; additionally illustrated by the use of an "olive tree", which is a similitude for the "oil of His anointing" and the "Anointed One", the Christ that would accomplish this holy lineage by the power of His Holy Spirit.

Laying all of this aside for now, we must move on; however, there will be much more on these topics later. But for now my brethren, let us seriously consider this: how have we the church violated the commandment of God to "honor our father and our mother" (Israel); and for those of you that may call yourselves Jews, have you entirely rejected your own children (the church)?

In the words of **Mal.4:6 "And he shall turn the heart of the fathers to the children, and the heart of the children to their fathers, lest I come and smite the earth with a curse."**

THE MOUNT SINAI VISITATION

Now that we've constructed a strong foundation for this segmental divide which we find between the "62" and "70 weeks" of Daniel 9, let me point you to a fascinating example of this as it is found in the book of Exodus. In the passages we are about to take a look at Moses will act as a shadow and type of Jesus, providing a brief but compelling glimpse into the two distinct coming's of Christ as they were to occur much later in human history. This similitude will add additional credence to the conclusions and findings that we have already arrived at to this point in our study. It will also establish a thought provoking groundwork for where we are heading next.

Starting out, let me first say this: our examination of these passages must remain brief. We have not progressed to the point, as yet, where an in-depth study of this subject would be especially helpful. As our study goes on, and we have added one truth upon another truth, whatever is lacking will become more and more substantiated I assure you. With that being said, let us move on to **Ex.19:1-3,10-11; "In the third month after the children of Israel had gone out of the land of Egypt, on the same day, they came to the wilderness of Sinai."**

In this verse the children of Israel have completed their journey out of Egypt and have arrived at Mt. Sinai where they will soon meet their God at His glorious appearance upon the Mountain top. What I would hope to draw to your attention is the two underlined portions of this passage. God is clearly telling us something by the inclusion of this information and the preciseness in which it is worded.

Prior to their arrival at Mt Sinai in **Ex.12:18**, God had given Moses the strict particulars for the observance of the Passover Feast. At that time God announced that the Passover was to be continually observed on **"the first month, on the fourteenth day"**, this would also be the eve of the children of Israel leaving out of Egypt.

Now then, returning back to **Ex.19:1** we read, **"in the third month... on the same day"**, representing the exact day that Israel arrives at Mount Sinai. Through this comparison God is drawing our attention to the fact that Israel arrives at the mountain exactly 60 days from the exodus of Israel from Egypt.

Continuing to **Ex.19:2-3** we read this: **"So Israel camped there before the mountain. And Moses went up to God, and the LORD called to him from the mountain..."** In these next verses Moses ascends the mountain to meet with God, but what it doesn't tell you is how long Moses and the children of Israel waited at the base of the mountain before God called Moses up. It is not until 7 verses later in **Ex.19:10-11** that we read: **"... consecrate them today and tomorrow... and let them be ready for the third day, for on the third day the LORD will come down... in the sight of all the people."** By this God is definitively telling us that on the 63rd day from the Passover God would "come down" to the people.

Fast forward now to **Ex.24:16-18**, and we find Moses preparing to make another ascent up the mountain to God. In this account, God gives a different set of instructions: **"Now the glory of the LORD rested on Mount Sinai, and the cloud covered it six days. And on the seventh day, He called Moses out of the midst of the cloud... so Moses went into the midst of the cloud and went up into the mountain."**

By these passages God is clearly drawing our attention to two separate and distinct set periods of time. One period consists of 63 days, while the other period is 7 days. Looks an awful lot like Daniel's "62 weeks" and "69 weeks" does it not? There is of course an obvious discrepancy, there is clearly an inconsistency of 1 day in each case. Unless, we consider that the Passover Feast was to be observed on the "fourteenth day of the first month", and the Feast of unleavened bread (observed for 7 days) did not begin until the following day, which is the actual day Israel left Egypt. By this accounting the documented times of 63 days could be moved back a day to 62 days. Likewise, the second appearance upon the mountain top would additionally be moved back from 70 to 69 days, this would figure to reveal a perfect match of Daniel's 62nd and 69th weeks.

An alternative to this incongruity could also be as simple as the 63 days and the 7 days of the two ascensions of Moses are intended to carry with them an implied knowledge of Daniel's 62 and 69 weeks. They may represent an unspoken inference of the two. After all, this modification of its expression does nothing to lessen the truth that lies beneath the passage. On the contrary, it actually adds to that truth. Let me show you how.

Christ's crucifixion and resurrection, and eventual ascension unto the Father were the events that culminated Daniel's 62nd week, but simultaneously it was the specific moment of the dawning and birth of the 63rd week (1st church generation), precisely beginning with Jesus' ascension. Like the circle that has no beginning or end, these generations overlap one another, one ends at the exact moment another begins.

Equally, Daniel's 69th week will find its close with the glorious appearing of our great God and Savior Christ Jesus, while simultaneously ushering in the 70th week of Daniel and the Millennial Reign. In either case, we see plainly two separate time-frames representing two separate and distinct visitations of God, serving as an identical match to that of Dan.9. And unless we should forget, this is all occurring some 1,000 years before Daniel's timeline.

Another perfect illustration of the same time divide as that of Dan.9 is found in Gen.46:8-27. Jacob, his wives, and all of his sons, and their families are on their way to enter into the land of Egypt to meet up with Joseph. In this passage of scripture God gives us a detailed listing of all the names, as God would count them, of all the family of Jacob that would make this incursion into Egypt. Upon a closer look at this passage we see that God has divided this census into four distinct groups according to the children of Jacob's four wives. The four groupings consist of 33 persons; 16 persons; 14 persons, and 7 persons. Without unnecessarily complicating this matter, let me just jump to some obvious conclusions: The first two groupings of 33 and 16 added together total 49 (Dan.9 70 x7); add to that the third grouping of 14 and you have 63 (as we found in the ascension of Moses), an implied shadow of Daniel's "62 weeks". Lastly, add to that the final grouping of 7 (as we found in Moses' other ascension) and we end up with a grand total of 70, equally lying within it the hidden inference to Daniel's "70 weeks".

Once more this is a seemingly obvious allusion to the Daniel timeline which occurs some four generations even before that of Moses at Mount Sinai, demonstrating still again the divisional breakdown that we find in Dan.9. Furthermore, how appropriate of God to construct this picture of the prophetic ancestral lineage of the "Messiah" of Dan.9, and place it precisely within the origins of Israel's ancestral forefathers, whom by the way were on a journey to meet up with Joseph who is without contradiction one of the most prolific shadow types of Jesus in all of Scripture, and thereby completing the synchronicity between the stage-mental timeline with that of the life and ministry of Christ Jesus. By now the hair on the back of your neck should be standing at attention as you are profoundly witnessing the authenticity, inerrancy, and immutability of God's Holy Word.

To summarize all of this, God is using the ascensions of Moses as a pattern of witness of the two future appearances of the coming of our Lord Jesus. Additionally, He is distinctly drawing an illustration of the two appointed set periods of time of Daniel 9, even though the prophet Daniel would not even write Dan.9 for another 10 centuries.

And as an additional point of reference, in Ex.40 He concludes the book of Exodus with God's glory falling upon the newly constructed tabernacle (a third visitation). This is the culmination of Daniel's "70th week" and the conclusion of His 1,000 year Millennial Kingdom on earth (Rev.21), at which time God the Father Himself will come down and abide with His children forever. Last but not least, let it be clearly understood that without the God given instrument of "duality" it would be utterly impossible for us to comprehend any of this.

Now I realize of course that I am throwing a lot at you right about now. My showing you all of this, at this time, may be entirely premature. We are still very early on in our study of this subject, and this type of conclusion on my part deserves a great deal more of an explanation than I have offered as yet. However, I will say this: the further that we continue on in this study, the more you will be able to look back with an increased sense of clarity and understanding and see that this conclusion is exactly what God was intending us to see by His structuring of the wording of these passages. For now, I would just ask that you take it all in, if for nothing else as an intriguing finding, and allow me the opportunity to solidify its truth with further proof as we move forward; although I am most certainly hoping that you will find it to be much more than that.

CHAPTER TWO

A HISTORICAL OVERVIEW
OF THE CHURCH AGE

Before we move ahead let me just quickly explain the meaning of my usage of the word "age" as it appears in the title of this section. As simply as I can put it, the word "age" is merely the next larger period of time following the time period of a "generation". As an example: the 7 churches of Revelation do not represent 7 church ages (as some might suggest), but on the contrary, they are representative of 7 "generations" as Daniel 9 prophecies them to be. It is the total accumulation of those 7 generations that makes up and forms the one "church age".

In terms that are easily understood today, it is our equivalent of 10 "decades" to form a "century", or 10 centuries to form a "millennium". Paul used this same distinction in Col.1:26 where he wrote, "Even the mystery which has been hid from "ages" and from "generations", but now is made manifest to his saints." Now that I have said all of this in an attempt to hopefully clear up any confusion that I may have caused with the use of this word let us now proceed to look at what many might consider to be a very basic and somewhat generic generational breakdown of the church age, or otherwise known for the sake of this study as the "7 weeks" to directly follow Daniel's "62 weeks".

Right off, let me confess openly that I am by no means a historian by any stretch of the imagination. I am not in possession of an acute historical knowledge that has at its ready access an accomplished mental database for spurting out times and dates, and the names of this one and that one. Additionally, you will find no extensive use of historical nomenclature or terminology in much of my references. In my defense however, it should be clearly understood that a deep and specific detailing of the historical past is not necessary for the purpose of our study, in fact it would only serve to clutter the true issue.

I will however attempt to point out the ridiculously obvious, that which is readily known and widespread as the most basic of knowledge as it pertains to these 7 suspected time periods. If my task going in is to draw a simplistic parallel of the past 2,000 years of church history as it aligns itself to the messages given to the projected 7 church generations of the book of Revelation than my lack of historical refinement should be adequately sufficient. Again, and as always, let the Spirit of God be the judge.

EPHESUS

It stands to reason that if the "7 weeks" leading up to Daniels prophesied "69 weeks" are representations of the 7 church generations of the church age than we should be able to verify this by means of comparison. We should be able to methodically and accurately match the details of Christ's messages in Rev.2-3 to the past 7 individual churches generations, using the actual historical record as it details the past 2,000 years of Church history.

Putting this method to its initial test we will begin our comparisons with the church of Ephesus (Rev.2:1-7), which would represent the 1st of these 7 generations and likewise will also be the same church generation of the 12 Apostles.

Early on as Scripture records these great men and women of the faith had taken up the mantle left to them by Jesus at His departure. They had been divinely commissioned by none other than Christ Himself (Matt.28:18-20). Not long after that they would receive their conception by the Holy Spirit in Acts 2 in the "upper room", 120 persons in all would be "filled with the Spirit" of God just as Joel 2:28-29 had prophesied many centuries earlier. It would be this small assembly of believers that would initially become the nucleus of this infancy stage of the entire church age to come.

This is a church generation that would start out in the dawning of its early years at a fast and furious pace, with the teachings and experiences that they had lived out with Christ still fresh in their minds, and the newly revealed empowerment of the Holy Spirit coursing mightily through their hearts and souls they launched out with feverish zeal and fervency to propel the message of salvation forward to a lost and dying world.

As we begin in Rev.2:1-7 we see Jesus at the outset commends this 1st church for their "works... labor" and "patience...", as well as for their defense of the church itself against "evil" that would desire to creep into the congregations by means of stealth and potentially bringing with it a gross perversion of the truth. This commendation of Christ would seem to clearly address the early stages of this 1st generation as it was headed by the apostles themselves.

This was a golden time for the church as they labored tirelessly to spread the truth of the Gospel at home and abroad. The book of Acts is packed full of their exploits as they continuously extended themselves beyond the limits of their earthly capabilities. The challenges were unquestionably great and yet they fought fearlessly forward in their Spirit driven desire to win the souls of those that were lost. They endured the severest of hardships as they traveled on missionary journeys into foreign lands, preaching and teaching the Gospel of Christ, and all along the way building churches and constructing newly formed assemblies of true worshipers of God.

Likewise, they braved the continual attacks of idolatry, false religion, and tyrannical rulers, and murderous and corrupt governments. They fought unceasingly in the face of every type of satanic opposition and yet their labors were richly rewarded as the grace of God emboldened them time and time again. The church was growing at an unprecedented rate of speed as people were being healed, even raised from the dead, as a witness and testimony to this great message of salvation by faith through grace in Christ Jesus. This was truly the early legacy of the 1st church generation, but it would not last.

It would not be long before these same pillars of the faith would eventually be removed through the persecutions of their day. James the brother of Jesus would be beheaded in Jerusalem, and Simon Peter and Paul, would meet their end soon after. One by one this first generation of steadfast believers would dwindle down, eventually even to the passing of the Apostle John himself who may have been the last of his companions to close his eyes and rest.

It would be at this time that the 1st church generation would begin its earliest intermediary phase. The baton would be gradually passed to the men and women that would soon make up the next succeeding generation. With the absence of those early church fathers there immediately becomes a dangerous and ominous void, a spiritual vacuum that is eerily reminiscent of **Judg.2:10 "And also all that generation were gathered unto their fathers; and there arose another generation after them, which knew not the LORD, nor yet the works which He had done for Israel."**

As the first generation of the church rapidly passes into a transitional leadership it is also at this time that we see Jesus' earlier affirmation of the church of Ephesus turn to one of rebuke and correction as we find in **Rev.2:4-5 "...you have left your first love... remember from where you have fallen, and repent, and do the first works..."**

The church had previously staved off accusations and attacks by those that would have desired to give entrance to the heresies and false doctrines that would harm the church. It was through the staying power of those men and women who had received the teachings directly from Christ Himself that had held strong as a buffer between the church and its enemies. With the gradual passing of these champions of the faith those that had previously been held at bay were now flooding into the church. The church by this time has been inundated with all manner of lies and deceptions, greed, corruption, strife and self-promotion; and thus, much deserving of the harsh rebuke of our Lord.

Adding to all of this the fact that a great judgment has befallen all of the children of Israel in 70 AD. Jerusalem is no more, and likewise the temple itself has been utterly destroyed. At this time the church has become steeped in fear and confusion and through it all Jesus has still not returned, which was broadly expected by this 1st church generation.

What we find is a church that has in varying degrees given up on this hope of His soon return and has gradually shrunken back into the complacency and normality of the world, just as Jesus had warned them back in **Matt.24:48-49 "But if that evil servant says in his heart, 'my master is delaying His coming, and begins to beat his fellow servants, and to eat and drink with the drunkards, the Master of that servant will come on a day when he is not looking for Him, and at an hour that he is not aware of, and will cut him in two and appoint him his portion with the hypocrites."**

It is this very state of degeneracy and deterioration of the church that would provoke the Lord to warn this first generation with the chilling words of **Rev.2:5 "... or else I will come unto you quickly, and will remove your candlestick out of his place..."** As we know, in 70 AD this is precisely what would occur at the hands of the Roman Empire.

At best this is a purely elementary look at the church of Ephesus as it relates to that 1st church generation. It should also be noted that I have not, nor will I venture to provide any exact time frames for these generations as they may very well overlap one with another as one transitions into the other. For me this would be a mute point. In its finality the 1st church generation historically speaking bears an absolute and uncanny resemblance to that of the message given by Christ to the church of Ephesus.

Let me also say that as it is the way of "duality" it can offer multiple fulfillments. Even as the 7 churches of Revelation offers a literal interpretation of the churches of John's day, and likewise, as we are now finding out represents a prophetic historical account of the 7 generations that would form the church age to come, at the exact same time it carries with it a **very** personalized interpretation for each and every individual believer that would ever be borne by the Spirit of Christ including that of us today.

Bearing this truth in mind we must ask ourselves: which part of that 1st church generation best represents me? As with most newly born Christians we start out fast and furious for Christ. We are on fire for our Lord as our works, labor, and confession all vehemently attest. But just as that 1st church generation, time passes, persecutions and trials come, and the lure of the world begins once more to lay hold of us. Have we too grown apathetic and indifferent to the dying world around us? Have we also become disillusioned with the bedrock principles of church, prayer, and the reading of God's word that so delighted us in the beginning? It is precisely at this time that we should realize whether or not, if we too have lost our first love; and if so we must hurriedly "repent". We should each one search ourselves carefully lest we also be found to have "fallen" from the foundations of our early faith, and in turn be found greatly deceived just as the 1st church was.

SMYRNA

Next, we will move on to the second church generation synonymously known in Revelation as "Smyrna". At this time we pick up the church as it moves into the 2nd and 3rd centuries. The gospel message has been rapidly spreading across the entire Roman Empire for quite some time now. The church is growing with immense velocity and is becoming so widespread that it has gained the attention of the ruling elite in Rome. The church has provoked such a great societal and economic change that the very allegiance of the people has become in question as Rome sees it. For fear that the people may share a greater loyalty to Christianity than to the empire it has been perceived by the Emperor of the day that Christianity is an unacceptable threat to the very governance of its territories.

With the stability of the status-quo in doubt edicts are hurriedly issued, ordering by Roman law the banishment of all church buildings, church gatherings of any type, private or otherwise; as well as a strict prohibition against any and all persons that would even call themselves Christian. These edicts were enforced with the utmost of swiftness and cruelty, punishable by confiscation of all Christian owned businesses, lands and possessions, and to follow that imprisonments, and as a newly instated capital offense: death by execution.

At this moment in history Christianity is officially marked empire wide as a grievous crime of sedition and insurrection. It would be the kingdom's attempt to root out and to rid itself of every vestige of the faith in its entirety, in all of its forms no matter where or how it might exist. By the end of the 3rd century under the Emperor Diocletian the severity of the persecution would rise to such a feverish pitch that it would later become known as "the Great Persecution". This would also be the church generation that would be fed to the lions in the Roman Coliseum for the entertainment of the blood thirsty public.

Let us now take a look at **Rev.2:8-11 "I know your works, tribulation and poverty... and I know the blasphemy of them which say they are Jews, and are not, but are the synagogue of Satan. Fear none of those things which you shall suffer: behold, the devil shall cast some of you into prison, that you may be tried; and you shall have tribulation ten days: be faithful unto death..."**

There are many points that could be made here but the truth is: this passage speaks overwhelmingly to this 2nd church generation and the immense suffering it would be forced to endure. I will add only three additional points to further illustrate this.

First, when it speaks of "them which say they are Jews, and are not", this is a direct reference to a church that has been forced underground, they have gone into hiding for fear of their lives. It is a church that has been given a devastating ultimatum: recant your faith or be martyred. Many were "faithful unto death" as we know, but many others were not. There were many at this time that renounced their faith in order to save their own lives. When given the choice they chose to reject their savior and His church for the comfort and safety of the Roman Empire. They were "tried" and purged out of the church, they were found out not to be of the true faith despite their confession to be otherwise. The term "synagogue of Satan" is a clear definition for those that would appear at least on the religious surface to be members of the body of Christ, but more of a truth, their father is not the God of Abraham. It was at this time that a cleansing was taking place of all the heresies that had filtered into the church at the latter end of the previous generation leaving only those who were true to the faith.

Secondly, the point that I would make regards the statement "and you shall have tribulation for ten days". These "ten days" have been understood by many to represent a series of exactly ten separate and distinct persecutions that would arise over this bloody period at the behest of successive Roman Emperor's. This too is historically accurate and extensively documented.

Thirdly, there is the reference of "the devil shall cast some of you into prison, that you may be tried"; this is a clearly defined use of the agent of evil that will be used to carry out this horrible carnage. Laying aside the obvious responsibility of Satan himself for these heinous acts, it is also a fact that throughout scripture Satan has always used the wickedness of man to perform his destructive tasks. It is for this reason that I believe that this statement bears a direct reference to the murderous emperors that would inflict this great persecution upon the church.

Albeit an extremely abbreviated comparison, once more we see Jesus' message to the 2nd church generation (represented by Smyrna) to be fulfilled with striking precision.

Again we must ask ourselves at this time: "On which side of the fence do I fall?" Have I become offended by the Gospel in some way that I have chosen unconsciously not to commit? And has the church itself been the possible cause of that perceived offense? Or has some trial arisen in my life that has caused such a deep and lasting wound that I have withdrawn from my faith in Christ altogether? Or perhaps I have become so dependent of the things of my own life and this world that I have quietly and secretly faded into the shadows of what used to be a vibrant faith in the Lord. And possibly the question might be: am I fearful of what others might say about me or what they might think? Am I not invested as I should be, but rather lying in the weeds at a distance while all the time maintaining the uncertain pretense that I am a true Christian. These are all hard questions for sure, but even as the 2nd church generation had to endure many things as they too were brought into question concerning their own faith, Jesus is now asking us today to learn from them.

PERGAMOS

As the church now moves into the 3rd church generation, or "Pergamos" of Rev.2:12-17, we find ourselves in the 4th century. The devastating persecution of the previous generation has slowly subsided largely impart to the miraculous re-growth of the church. The new Emperor is Constantine and it has become obvious to him that the Christian movement will not be stamped out of its existence as his predecessors had hoped. Just as a tree that is freshly pruned the dead wood has been removed and newly formed branches have taken its place. The tree is once more vibrant and alive and teeming with new life. The persecution has run its course and has done its dubious business and the church has come out on the other end, bigger and stronger than before the persecution had begun. The blood of God's faithful martyrs has watered the field and harvest has come. Once more I am reminded of the words of Joseph in **Gen.50:20 "But as for you, you thought evil against me; but God meant it for good".**

It is at this time that the Emperor Constantine takes a revolutionary approach to the church. He has seen the church blossom into a burgeoning power economically and socially under his reign. It has infiltrated every level of society, ascending even unto to the highest echelons of business and politics; immersing itself thoroughly throughout the four corners of the Empire. There will no longer be any thoughts of its eradication that time has passed. It is here where Constantine makes the momentous decision to officially integrate Christianity within the Empire.

Was Constantine converted many have asked? I don't think that anyone can say for sure, but what we do know is that it had become politically advantageous for Constantine to fully assimilate the Christians if he was to retain his rule.

Furthermore, he had become increasingly aware of many foreign threats that were arising at every border of his empire. He realized that if he were to be successful in defending and maintaining its vast territories he would need two things: First, he would need an army of considerable size to ward off these ever increasing threats, and in order to obtain such a necessary military force he would have to enlist the swelling population of the Christians.

Secondly, he would need stability and loyalty from within. This would not be the time to take on additional enemies within the internal populace of the kingdom. It was these concerns primarily which made it most crucial for him to resolve the Christian issue.

In any case, Christianity would now become the state sponsored religion of the entire empire by direct decree of the Emperor himself. This marks the historical end of Rome's long existing pagan roots and the beginning of its religious fervency that will eventually give rise to the Papacy, and what we now call Catholicism.

As this 3rd church generation would progress the unification of church and state would present its own unique set of problems. The church by this time has now become heavily embroiled in the politics of the day. It has transitioned from hiding in the underground shadows to that of being a major power player throughout the Roman Empire, and with this newly attained prestige, power and authority, comes the much expected pride, greed, and authoritarianism, ever increasingly becoming more entrenched in both the pews and pulpit.

The personal and intimate faith that had once existed between a man and his God has now been self-delegated to the establishment of a governmental body and a commercialized church, an organizational overlord of the hearts and minds of the people. The church is no longer simply a community of selfless believers, rather it is has morphed into a self-appointed empirical overseer of all faith, something to be feared rather than adored. By this, evil men have once more entered in, not for the love of Christ, or His church, but rather for power, wealth, and lavish living.

The concern has greatly shifted from that of complete allegiance to God to one of unfettered allegiance to the Holy Roman Empire and the Mother Church. This will begin a very long period of spiritual depravity that will result in the slaughter of many and extend even to the very desecration of the written word of God itself, and all to be done at the hands of this so-called church. It is here that Jesus addresses the church of Pergamos.

Now let us look at **Rev.2:12-17** beginning in **(v12)** where Jesus gives a threatening introduction of Himself to this church: **"These things says He who has the sharp two-edged sword..."** And again in **(v16)** **"Repent; or else I will come to you quickly, and will fight against them with the sword of my mouth."** These are unmistakably words of war that one might speak of an enemy. This is clearly a church that has seriously provoked the Lord to anger.

As a quick comparison to further emphasize the point let us quickly look at a similar response as found in **Rev.19:15 "And** out of His mouth goes a sharp sword, that with it He should smite the nations... and He treadeth the winepress of the fierceness and wrath of Almighty God."

By the previous statement in Rev.2:12-17 as it relates to Christ's reaction to the church of Pergamos, we can see that Jesus is plainly telling this church that if they don't repent they will meet the same fate as all of God's enemies upon His Return. Additionally, it should not go unnoticed that this is an obvious statement that this church will still be on the earth, still practicing these same evils of the past, still storing up the wrath of God at the time of Christ's return.

Going back to **Rev.2:13** we read, **"I know your works, and where you dwell, where Satan's throne is... where Satan dwells."** This is a church generation that has found itself immersed in the midst of Satan's own headquarters, even to his actual earthly throne room. It would appear that he (Satan) has ensconced himself as the ruling power over this church, and as such, has implemented his own church "doctrines" as we find in **(v14-15) "...you have them there that hold the doctrine of Balaam, who taught Balak to cast a stumbling block before the children of Israel, to eat things sacrificed to idols, and to commit fornication. So you also have them that hold the doctrine of the Nicolaitians, which thing I hate."**

One only has to read Num.22-24 and Num.31:1-16 to properly understand the "doctrine of Balaam". Balaam was in the simplest of terms a prophet for hire, wealth and personal honor was all that concerned him. He was in fact, for sale to anyone that could offer him the appropriate wages. On the surface he presented himself as a man of God, that had some knowledge and understanding of God, however, the actual truth was that his heart was wicked. And when he realized that he had no power to destroy Israel by means of cursing them, he changed his approach to one of creating an environment in which they would destroy themselves. This environment would be to lure them into the intermingling and assimilation of their enemies. It would be by this absorption that they would commit a type of spiritual fornication through idolatrous practices with the gods of that land, and thus God would become angered with his people.

This is exactly what we know occurred in the 4th century. The Roman Empire had abandoned its hope of ever destroying Christianity outright, and as a result it changed its approach to that of tolerance and assimilation. This produced the desired effect as Satan would have it, and as Jesus attests to by His verbal chastisement of this church.

In regard to the "doctrine of the Nicolaitians", what we do know is that this was a heretical group whose teachings and practices were first introduced back in the first century, and were a troubling element to that 1st church generation as well (Rev.2:6). The startling difference being, that the 1st church fought back and resisted these heresies, while by this time the 3rd church has been thoroughly infiltrated and become fully compliant with the hateful doctrine.

Once more we see a precise foretelling of the events to come. Through Jesus' message to the church of Pergamos we find a unique and generally specific outline of the 3rd church generation just as history would record it.

As with the other churches that we have looked at leading up to this point, we must now ask ourselves again: How does this pertain to me today? Is it possible that I too may have fallen prey to a faith, or a local body of the church that is deceptively steeped more in religion than in an actual personal relationship with Jesus? Have I gone the way of ritual and traditions made by man over the true doctrine of intimacy with Christ Jesus through prayer, and His word, and by His Holy Spirit? Have I committed or delegated the responsibility of my faith more so to man than to God Himself? These are all questions that we must ask, and when we answer them we must answer them truthfully. It is my earnest desire and heartfelt petition that the God of all of heaven and earth open the hearts and minds of us all.

THYATIRA

As we move forward into the 4th church generation the church finds itself as a slave to the master of religion, and as all religion does it prides itself on the futility of external practices and offers little in the way of actual internal transformation. It is cold and calloused, only bearing an appearance of the true church while in the Spirit there is no resemblance at all. As Jesus would put it best in **Matt.23:27 "Woe unto you, scribes and Pharisees, hypocrites! For you are like whited sepulchers, which indeed appear beautiful outward, but are within full of dead men's bones..."**

This church is a progressive continuation of the third generational church that had birthed it. It will be a time of war between the Roman Empire and the invading Germanic tribes. The start of the 5th century will see the fall of Rome to the Visigoths, and later the sacking of Rome by the Vandals. It is a bloody time for the empire. It will also be during this time that the plague will cut the population of Europe in half, but through all of this upheaval one thing shall remain constant: the Holy Roman Church.

The 5th and 6th centuries will be the coming of age of Papal supremacy and the construction of a priestly hierarchy that will exalt itself above all men and God. It will set its own authority even above the Word of God. It will change "times and laws" that have been otherwise prescribed by God's law, and this to all be done in an attempt to shake off the remnants of its Jewish roots in favor of the paganistic culture of the Roman Empire in which it has ever so comfortably crawled into bed with. With great arrogance this church will then crown itself as God's only ordained representative on earth. It will set the diabolical policy that would result in the confiscation of the Word of God, and place its knowledge and instruction behind the heavily fortified walls of the religious elites. This is the satanic time of the dark ages.

With its pervasive power grab in full implementation all that would remain would be to bring the rest of the known world to its knees in homage to this, the self-professed "only true church of Christ." This church would enforce a strict doctrine of compliance and submission, not to God, but to the church itself; and as it had learned from its murderous and bloody bed fellows of the past it too would invoke violence and fear as its methods to insure the adherence of all. It would be this church and its generational successors that would institute the cruelest of all the persecutions that the faithful of Christ would ever have to endure. A time of martyrdom that would far surpass anything that the true church had ever known. And finally, with the rise of the Islamic religion in the east, Christianity would soon find itself in a new paradigm shift, and that of "the holy war".

It is here that we turn our attention now back to the book of Revelation. Before we start it must be understood that in the light of all that we have learned about this particular church generation, this is foremost **a time of two churches**. There is the one that I have gone into some detail concerning, but there is clearly another that is unwaveringly steadfast in their devotion to the truth and our Lord Jesus Christ. It is to them that Christ initially addresses in **Rev.2:18-29. In (v19) "I know your works, and charity, and service, and faith, and your patience, and your works; and your last to be more than the first.**

Likewise, He speaks of the other so-called church in **(v20)** **"Notwithstanding I have a few things against you, because you allow that woman Jezebel, Which calleth herself a prophetess, to teach and to seduce my servants to commit fornication, and to eat things sacrificed unto idols."** In this text Jesus is clearly exposing this supposed church as a perpetration of the truth and forcefully likens its true nature to that of a Biblical villain named Jezebel.

The Bible documents the person of Queen Jezebel in 1 Ki.16-19, and again in 2 Ki.9. In short, she was a wicked woman who had married into her position of royalty by means of a treaty that was fostered by her father, just as this church generation had come to its prominence through a purely political agreement made between the state and church in the previous church generation.

Jezebel would then begin her conquest of usurping the authority of the kingdom at the permission and negligence of her much weaker husband. This would be an identical illustration of the Holy Roman Church superseding the authority of the empirical empire as it was found in a weakened and vulnerable state. The woman Jezebel would then make herself the enemy of the true and faithful of God by murdering their prophets and striking terror into their hearts. She would then set up her own perverted priesthood and demand the blind obedience of all the subjects of the kingdom to give homage to her idolatrous practices. These are the charges that Jesus has brought before the church of Thyatira, the similarities are undeniable.

This is the 4th church generation of Thyatira as intricately detailed by Jesus some 6 centuries earlier in His message to the churches of Revelation. In **Rev.2:21-29** Jesus continues,

(v21) "And I gave her space to repent of her fornication; and she repented not." This is a direct reference to a church that has been given a substantial period of time to repent. So much time in fact, that the remainder of this message is centralized on addressing this same church that will still be in existence at His actual 2nd coming. **(v22) "Behold, I will cast her into a bed, and them, that commit adultery with her into great tribulation, except they repent of their deeds."** This is clearly an end time reference that singles out this church as the "Mother of Harlots" of Rev.17:1-6.

Finally, in **(v24)** we read, **"But unto you I say, and unto the rest in Thyatira, as many as have not this doctrine, and which have not known the depths of Satan, as they speak; I will put upon you none other burden."** Here Jesus identifies the "doctrine" of this church as being **purely satanic** in its origins.

To best understand the doctrine of Satan one only needs to read **Isa.14:13-14**. In the words of Satan himself he proclaims his own doctrine: **"I will ascend into heaven; I will exalt my throne above the stars of God; I will also sit on the mount of the congregation, on the farthest sides of the north; I will ascend above the heights of the clouds, I will be like the Most High."** It is plain for all to see that this church has truly exemplified this doctrine point by point. Moreover, this is a far cry from the words of Jesus as He spoke them in the garden of Gethsemane in **Matt.26:39 "...not as I will, but as thou wilt."**

There is obviously a great deal more that could be said on my part but hopefully I have made the point that this is once again a clear representation of another church generation in the line of 7, as it is intricately aligned with the historical past.

It is at this time that I must ask what might be possibly the hardest question yet: With the knowledge that we now have concerning this church and how God Himself views it, can we with a pure conscience continue to lend our support to such a church? Or will our lifelong allegiance to this church be greater than our actual love and devotion to God, and His truth? Will our faithfulness and loyalty to this church supersede our actual commitment to the thoughts and feelings, and admonitions of our Lord?

Let us not forget what Jesus says in **(v20) "Notwithstanding I have a few things against you, because you allow that woman Jezebel..."** Could it be possible that we have actively participated in the sins of this church without even realizing it and thereby making us culpable as well in the eyes of God? Or just maybe I should ask: Am I in denial? God grant us that we might have eyes to see, and ears to hear; and I would add this: strength to respond with obedience.

I will close this section with the words of Paul as recorded in **Gal.4:16 "Am I therefore become your enemy, because I tell you the truth?"**

SARDIS

By this time we come to the 5th generational church of Revelation's seven churches, we find this church located in Rev.3:1-6. This is a period of church history that has been well documented by the writings of many that had experienced it first-hand. Over the course of several centuries its barbarous acts would defy the human imagination. One excellent and well known written account of this time period is *"Foxe's Book of Martyrs"*.

As I stated earlier this church is yet a further progression of the church generations before it, and its horrific steepened slide into depravity. The Holy Roman Church has become a mockery to the word "holy", it is in every respect reprobate and it has become the personification of evil on earth. Power and lust of conquest will propel it into the bloody massacres of the Crusades. Hatred and oppression are her common practices and delight. Greed and corruption she will wear as a crown, and of all of those that may be of a dissenting opinion she crushes with the fiercest of cruelty. We have entered the time of Papal persecutions and the inquisition. All told, she has raised her fist at God and done all in the name of Christ.

This is the height of the Dark Ages and there is no other force on earth that has done more to bring this period to pass. Satan himself is her general, and her orders are clear: steal, kill, and destroy.

It is here that we find Jesus in His address to them in **Rev.3:1-6 (v1) "I know your works, that you have a name that you are alive, but you are dead."** This is a church that has been pronounced "spiritually dead" by none other than Jesus Himself despite the earthly applause of men.

In **(v3) "If you will not watch, I will come on you as a thief, and you will not know what hour I will come upon you."** Here Jesus is clearly warning this church once again, that if they will not repent their fate will be the fate of the condemned. This is the exact language the Apostle Paul uses in 1 Thess.5:1-8 where he clearly distinguishes between the saved and the unsaved at the time of Christ's return. Jesus is blatantly cautioning this church, that to this point they have warranted upon themselves the judgment of the lost and ungodly. Furthermore, not to be lost in the threatening tone of our Lord, is a staggering example of the mercy of God that He still pleads with them to repent. How truly blessed and gracious is our Savior.

In **(v4)** He continues: **"You have a few names even in Sardis which have not defiled their garments; and they shall walk with me in white, for they are worthy."** This passage cannot be mistaken, out of an entire church generation there remains but "a few names" that have been found righteous in the eyes of God. These are His faithful martyrs and devoted ones, men like John Huss, John Wycliffe, Jerome, and the Waldenses of France; and the untold countless numbers of all the men and women that went to their deaths and suffered imprisonments in the defiance of this great evil.

Once more let us now look at this church as it appears in its end time state as recorded in **Rev.17:1-6 (v4-6) "And the woman was arrayed in purple and scarlet color, and decked with gold and precious stones and pearls, having a golden cup in her hand full of abominations and filthiness of her** fornication: And upon her forehead was a name written, MYSTERY, BABYLON THE GREAT, THE MOTHER OF HARLOTS AND ABOMINATIONS OF THE EARTH. And I saw the woman drunken with the blood of the saints, and with the blood of the martyrs of Jesus..."

Rev.16:6 put it this way: "For they have shed the blood of saints and prophets, and you have given them blood to drink; for they are worthy."

By this time we should be able to see that the seven churches of Revelation are definitively speaking to 7 church generations. They are a remarkable point by point declaration of the entire church age that will follow the 1st church of the Apostle John.

As this section closes I have but one question to ask: Does God have a short memory? Let us remember the words of Jesus at His first coming as He spoke to the wicked and sinful religion of His day: **Luke 11:37-54 (v47-48) "Woe unto you! For you build the sepulchers of the prophets, and your fathers killed them. Truly you bear witness that you allow the deeds of your fathers: for they indeed killed them, and you build their sepulchers."**

As a purely curious point of interest, at the time of the writing of this book it was just 1 short month ago that the pope himself paraded out the supposed bones of Saint Peter buried in a sepulcher beneath the Vatican itself and made a public media spectacle out of them.

Continuing on in **Luke 11:49-52 "Therefore also said the wisdom of God, I will send them prophets and apostles, and some of them they shall slay and persecute: That the blood of all the prophets, which was shed from the foundation of the world, may be required of this generation. From the blood** of Abel unto the blood of Zacharias...It shall be required of this generation. Woe unto you, lawyers! For you have taken away the key of knowledge: you entered not in yourselves, and them that were entering in you hindered." Once more I now ask the same question as I did earlier: Does God have a short memory?

PHILADELPHIA

As we begin our look now at this 6th church generation I am compelled to point out how exactly this following reference in **Rev.3:7-13** so pervasively and thoroughly defines them. Beginning in **(v7)** **"...He that has the key of David, He that opens, and no man shuts, and shuts, and no man opens." (v8) "...I have set before you an open door, and no man can shut it, for you have a little strength, and have kept my word, and have not denied my name."**

This passage has a direct reference to Luke 11:52 which we just read at the conclusion of the last section. Even as the scribes and Pharisees were guilty in their day of "taken away the key of knowledge" and hindering the people from "entering in" to the true faith of God, so also the previous churches of Pergamos, Thyatira, and Sardis would all be eventually defined by the same evil and cruelty, this time at the hands of the Holy Roman church.

The "Dark Ages" by the time of its ending had lasted more than five centuries, but with the arrival of this Philadelphian Church all that would gradually come to a close. This passage written to the 6th church generation begins with this amazing proclamation, announcing boldly that it would be during this period of church history that God would intervene mightily. He would reinstate "the key of knowledge" as it would concern the truth of His Holy Word. He would fling open the door that would allow many to enter in to a true relationship with their Savior by faith through grace. And likewise, He would slam shut the door on those which for so long had separated the children from their Father with their lies and hypocrisies.

What we have here is Jesus' foretelling of the Reformation Movement that would occur in this 6th church generation of the church of Philadelphia.

By now the church has moved into the 15th and 16th century and the evidences of the opening of this great door are too numerous to cover them all; so for the sake of time I will just point out a few that I feel are of the utmost significance to this transformative generation.

To start with, Johannes Gutenberg invents the printing press in 1450. This will open a floodgate to the printing and publication of the word God as never before. Until now the word of God has been confiscated and kept privately hidden from the masses, being exclusively held fast by the religious elite. For many centuries it had been a crime to be even in the possession of a Bible outside the walls of the church. In turn, this would give the church great leeway to manipulate the interpretation of its text and thereby control and oppress the common man. With the invention of the printing press this great sin would over time see its end.

Soon after in 1517 a man named Martin Luther would post his thesis containing 95 points upon the door of the local church, calling into account the governing church body for its grievous hypocrisies and distortions of the word of God. This would be the actual moment of the inception of the Protestant Reformation (the word "Protestant" to derive its meaning from the English word "protest").

It would be at this instant in church history that would later give rise to the newly discovered doctrine of "salvation by grace". No longer would "he who thirsts for righteousness" be held at bay by the teaching of fruitless works of the flesh as prescribed by the impostor church, but rather, the true doctrine of **"salvation by grace, through faith, as the free gift of God" (Eph.2:8-9)** would become the battle cry of the faithful in Christ.

Jesus Himself who is **"the Door" (John10:7-10)** would fling open the door of intimate and personal relationship with the Father through faith in Him, and by Him; and not by a church, and not by a religion, and not by good works, not even by a pope or a priesthood; but by faith in the Son of God alone.

The church and its lies were becoming exposed for the first time and many were being set free at last. A great spiritual revival was spreading like fire across the whole of Europe as it did once before in the earlier days of the Apostles. This would be the time of great men and women of God rising to the challenge of spreading the truth of God to the trodden masses. Men like John Calvin, and William Tyndale, and countless others; many who would pay the ultimate price to preach publicly the truth even at the threat of the loss of their own lives at the hands of a wicked and vengeful church, ever clinging to the hatred and violence of its inception.

Translations would be made from the Latin and Greek to the varied languages of the common man, and eventually to English giving an easy access to all who would desire to know the truth of God's word for themselves. The fraudulent church and all of its institutions would see its heinous death grip on its many false doctrines slowly slipping away from its grasp. It would be at this time that it would mount up for one final period of death and destruction in a futile attempt to maintain its savage control over its enslaved subjects. This would give rise to the Spanish inquisition in 1542, and later in 1572 the

Saint Bartholomew's Day Massacre where 50,000 Protestants in France were slaughtered for their faith. Despite it all, for all of the church's desperate attempts to cling to its sins of the past, the door has been finally opened and no man can close it now.

It will not be until the 17th century that we would see the emergence of the Authorized King James Version of the Bible in 1611; and in 1620 a group of Pilgrims will drop anchor at a place called Plymouth Rock in search of a land free of religious tyranny. It would be the rise of this new land (America) that God would use to spread the Gospel of His Beloved Son Jesus and to evangelize the world.

It is at this point that once more I feel the need to apologize to all of those that may read this very inept attempt of mine to summarize the history of this church generation. There are literally libraries that are filled with the books of those much more qualified than I to bring to light this period. However, with the obvious task in mind, I have attempted to once more illuminate the precise correlation between this historical time period and the references made by Christ concerning this 6th church generation of Philadelphia.

Here is where we must also take notice that this church generation is not just the 6th out of a grouping of 7 (as listed in Rev.), but equally, it would be the 68th generation overall, and herein lies our dilemma. We know from Dan.9 that Jesus will come again in the "69th week", and with no clear method in which to determine the exact length of time of this 6th church generation of Philadelphia how are we to know if we are still currently in the 6th generation (68th week), or if we have moved into the 7th and final generation of Rev.2-3 and Daniel's 69th week?

Bearing all of this in mind, we are left with the only alternative of proceeding on to the 7th church generation of the Laodiceans with the most crucial of missions on the forefront of our minds: Does this 7th church generation represent us today? The consequences of our getting this wrong are immeasurable as we know from Jesus' first coming, **Luke 19:41-44 "... they will not leave in you one stone upon another; because you did not know the time of your visitation."**

By now shouldn't we be asking ourselves: Why has Jesus gone to such great lengths to inform us so extensively of His 2nd coming? It would be nonsensical if He didn't want us to know, or as so many love to assume that "we can't know".

In the next few sections we will explore the most monumental of all church generations, as well as hope to resolve what might be perhaps the most crucial of all questions that should concern us today: Does God in precise detail give us that final clue that will mark the end of Daniel's 68th week and pinpoint the exact beginning of the 69th week that will see Jesus' 2nd coming?

THE LAST TIMELINE

Now then, before we rush immediately into our look at the Laodicean church let us first examine rationally what we have already found up to this point in our study.

Jesus Himself, when confronted with the question of His return back in Matt.24:3 pointed the disciples to what may have seemed to be an obscure passage of scripture in the book of Daniel the prophet (Dan.9:27). Upon our search of this chapter we discovered a clear timeline consisting of what Daniel referred to as "70 weeks" (Dan.9:24-27). In addition to this finding, we discovered that these "70 weeks" would be broken up into 3 separate and distinct periods of time, indicating multiple "visitations" of the coming of the Messiah, the first to occur at the "62nd week", the second to occur at the 69th week, and the 3rd and last one to occur at the "70th week".

Continuing on from there we examined some genealogical records of the O.T., on the hunch that these "weeks" of Daniel were actually representative of Biblical "generations". We obtained this foresight from Jesus Himself in Matt.24:34, along with many other references He made to the "generation" of His day. What we eventually found was undeniable proof of the Bible documenting a genealogical record from Adam to Jesus' first coming, consisting of exactly 62 generations just as Daniel had prophesied nearly 500 years earlier.

It was at this point that we modified our search for the next 7 generations leading up to the "69th week" of Daniel. At the beginning it was obviously clear that this generational record of 7 could not have a physical origin as Christ died without ever conceiving any naturally born children. From this we surmised that if Jesus was to continue His own lineage it would have to be of a "spiritual" nature as the term "born again" clearly attests to.

We then began our search of the N.T. looking for this very concise genealogical record consisting of both a "spiritual bloodline", and an exact accounting of 7 generations. We found only one plausible candidate in Rev. 2-3.

At the conclusion of our historical overview of the first six churches of church history, from the 1st church of the Apostles to the 6th church of the Reformation we found an unmistakable likeness and similarity between the generational prophecies of Jesus given nearly 2,000 years ago in Rev.2-3 with that of the 6 periods of church history that we have examined. And thus we find ourselves at the 7th and final church generation of the Laodiceans; which in turn marks the second phase of Daniels timeline prophesied of "69th weeks".

By now the question has surely shifted, it is not so much a question as to whether or not the Laodicean church represents the fulfillment of Daniels "69th week", it does; but rather, when does this final generation begin?

We have seen our search take on a very precise and methodically well planned route as God Himself has orchestrated it. However, without the exact predetermined time frame of the start of this last and final generation, our search no matter how fruitful would end with vagueness and obscurity. It would leave even the benefactors of this last generation to ponder and debate as to whether or not they were in Daniels prophesied 69th generation; does that sound familiar?

There would remain a constant uncertainty, and from everything that we have learned leading up to this moment that would seem to be a dreadful inconsistency on the part of God. On one hand we have followed a course that has been surgically mapped out for us throughout scripture by no less than the very Hand of God, only to arrive at the end of the most crucial of all generations leaving us to scratch our heads in confusion and ambiguity. This is not the ways of the God we serve I assure you as we have bore witness of Him through the course of this study.

This brings us now to Matt.24:34 where Jesus once more will define even this, the most crucial of all timelines for us. As I have stated earlier He did not leave the disciples around the corner of His return, nor down the block, nor in front of the house, no! He would walk them all the way to **"the door"** of His coming **(Matt.24:33)**.

THE "PARABLE OF THE FIG TREE" (MATT.24:30-34)

Let us now look at **Matt.24:30-31** **"And then shall appear the sign of the Son of man in heaven: and then shall all the tribes of the earth mourn, and they shall see the Son of man coming in the clouds of heaven with power and great glory. And He shall send His angels with a great sound of a trumpet, and they shall gather together His elect from the four winds, from one end of heaven to the other."** It is in these two verses that Jesus specifically answers the first of two questions that His disciples had asked Him back in **Matt.24:3** **"...what shall be the sign of your coming, and of the end of the age?"**

It should be equally noted as well, that within this same question is the parallel statement "and of the end of the age". This presents an unmistakable link between Jesus' return and the end of the church age. Just as we have uncovered in the prophecies of Daniel 9, Christ's return will autonomously bring to pass the end of the 7 church generations, or church age as a whole, and thereby concluding Daniel's "69 weeks".

It will be in Jesus' further response in **Matt.24:32-34** that He will answer their other question asked earlier in **(v3)** **"Tell us, when shall these things be?"**

Jesus continues in **(v32-34)** **"Now learn this parable from the fig tree; when its branch has already become tender and puts forth leaves, you know that summer is near. So you also, when you shall see all these things, know that it is near, even at the doors. Assuredly, I say to you, this generation will by no means pass away, until all these things be fulfilled."**

Jesus in this passage is clearly linking "this parable" with the "final generation" preceding His return. Simply put, if we can learn and understand this parable than we can know the time of the final generation, or the 7th and final church generation of the Laodiceans; and moreover, the "69th week" of Daniel's chapter nine prophecy.

Equally important to the wording of this passage is: "Now learn this parable..." Jesus is not merely asking His disciples to learn the parable, on the contrary, He is telling them to learn it. Just as we had earlier assumed, given all that God has so intricately provided for us until now going as far back as Gen.5, it would have been completely implausible to think that God would not likewise provide the final puzzle piece that would so perfectly bring us to "the door" of His Son's second coming. As this relates to us so imperatively today, we have a mandate from Christ Himself to learn this parable. With this understanding in the forefront of our minds let us get started.

In order for us to begin our research on "the *"Parable of the Fig Tree"* we should first ask ourselves: what relevance did these words immediately inspire in the minds of the disciples as they first heard them spoken by Jesus? What would have been their initial thoughts concerning this parable? Would it remind them of a previous parable that they may have heard Jesus teach? Would it have represented a parable that may have been of common knowledge to the Jewish culture of their day? Where would their thinking be immediately diverted to upon hearing the words *"Parable of the Fig Tree"*?

Consider this: It was only hours earlier before these words were spoken to them that they witnessed in amazement a fig tree dried up at the roots and withered away (Matt.21:18-20) following Jesus' cursing of that same tree the day before. It would seem totally impossible to me that their thoughts would not immediately revert back to the startling event that had just occurred only hours earlier that same day concerning the fig tree. It is here that we shall begin our search for understanding of the parable.

The episode of Jesus' cursing of the fig tree only appears in two of the Gospels: Matthew 21 (as listed above) and Mark 11:12-14, 19-20. In each case the central theme of this event is one of Jesus' being on His way to Jerusalem when suddenly He comes upon a fig tree, this comes at a time in which He is hungry and would desire to partake of some of its figs to eat. The tree although appearing from a distance to be ready to fulfill the Lord's need, upon closer observation is merely an illusion that disappoints. Yes, the tree is bushy and green, and full of leaves, but there's one major problem: the tree has no fruit upon it, and thus it is unable to satisfy the Master at His moment of request. It is at this time that Jesus curses the tree and immediately from that moment on it begins to wither away and dry up from its roots.

It would be the following day as Jesus and His disciples were once more on their return to Jerusalem, as they spent their nights outside the city's outskirts, that they would notice that the curse had performed its task just as Jesus had spoken it. They marveled at how quickly the tree had met its fate. This would be the event that would be foremost in the minds of the disciples upon hearing Christ's mention of "the *"Parable of the Fig Tree"* only hours later.

What the disciples didn't know then was that this would be yet another use of Scriptural "duality", this time by Our

Savior Himself. The fig tree in this case was a clear and direct representation of the children and nation of Israel, who upon the arrival of their long awaited Messiah were caught unprepared just as the fig tree had been, or as Jesus had put it in **Luke 19:44 "...you did not know the time of your visitation."** Although they appeared to the external eye to be pious and religious by their outward appearance, upon the closer examination of their hearts they were found to be fruitless, and thereby bringing the judgment of God upon themselves just as the fig tree itself had been found to be thoroughly inadequate upon the Lords scrutinizing inspection.

What Jesus is emphasizing here through His use of the *"Parable of the Fig Tree"* is that there would be a time of judgment that would befall the people of Israel as the result of their neglect to recognize the coming of their God and Messiah. By their clear rejection of Him God in turn would likewise be forced to cast a bitter and harsh dispersion upon His people. Even as the fig tree would suffer the extreme consequences of its untimely neglect of the Savior so also would the nation and people of Israel be treated in like manner.

Similarly, there remains in the second half of the fulfillment of the parable as given by Jesus the clear admonition that God's anger would not last indefinitely, but rather there would come a set time in which the nation of Israel would surely receive it's healing and restoration upon being brought back and restored to its native homeland. Furthermore, it is this 2nd part of the fulfillment of the parable that would act as the decisive sign that would loudly and boldly proclaim the arrival of that generation that would soon usher in the 2nd coming of Jesus. In short it would be this very public and historic event that would provide the definitive timeline for the start of Daniel's 69th week.

It would not be many years afterwards that Jerusalem would be utterly destroyed by the Romans in 70 AD and the remnant of God's children would be scattered to the four winds of the earth. Every vestige of the nation of Israel would be withered away and dried up at the roots, just as the fig tree had become. As we shall come to know the further we progress in our study, this would serve to be only the first half of the interpretation of "the *"Parable of the Fig Tree"*. The second half of its interpretation would come nearly 1,900 years later as it would relate to the 7th church generation of the Laodiceans.

For now, let us fast forward to 1948. The end of World War II has been removed by a space of three years. It is a time of healing and restoration for all of the nations and people of the earth, but there is none in a more dire need of healing than the Jewish people themselves who have been decimated by the atrocities of the Holocaust. They are a people that have been devastated to the point of near extinction. There has never been a people in all of the history of mankind that has suffered so much tragedy, for so long, and yet have steadfastly maintained their existence as a people.

Since that fatal generation of 70AD they have been a people without a homeland, barely clinging to their own ancestral identity, but forever holding on to the singular promise of all the prophets that had came before them: **Ezk.38:21-22 "Thus saith the Lord GOD; Behold, I will take the children of Israel from among the heathen, wherever they be gone, and will gather them on every side, and bring them into their own**

land; And I will make them one nation in the land upon the mountains of Israel"

On May 15th 1948, the second half of the interpretation of "the *"Parable of the Fig Tree"* would take place. It would be on this date in history that the nation of Israel would be reconstituted. By the setting forth of an international mandate by the United Nations, borders would be drawn up and the ancient land would be given back to the Jews. For the first time in over 19 centuries Israel would once more become a nation, and its children the Jews would once more return to their native homeland just as God had promised. It would be nothing short of a miraculous resurrection from the dead, and an exact fulfillment of the words of Jesus in **Matt.24:32-34 "Now learn a *"Parable of the Fig Tree"*; when his branch is yet tender, and puts forth leaves, you know that summer is near."** Jesus was prophesying of the day that the fig tree (Israel) would sprout back to new life. He would also go on to say in **(v34) "Surely I say to you, this generation will not pass away, until all these things be fulfilled** (Jesus' return).

The prophet Job spoke of this as well thousands of years earlier: **Job 14:5-9 "Seeing his days are determined, the number of his months are with you, you have appointed his limits that he cannot pass: Look away from him, that he may rest...For there is hope for a tree, if it is cut down, that it will sprout again, and that its tender shoots will not cease. Though its root may grow old in the earth, and its stump may die in the ground; yet at the scent of water it will bud and bring forth branches like a plant."**

Remember **Daniel 9:24 "Seventy weeks are determined upon your people and upon your holy city..."**) Not only does

Job give a precise account of both the start and finish of the *"Parable of the Fig Tree"*, but likewise he drives home the point that its fulfillment will be as a result of a "determined" timeline, which we now know is Daniel 9; and this lest we forget was written thousands of years prior to these events. Just imagine how truly astonishing this all is!

If all of that is not mind blowing enough than add this as well: How fitting it would seem that the first half of the interpretation of the parable would occur in the 1st church generation, only for the second half of its interpretation to conclude as the landmark event that would trigger the 7th and final church generation. It would appear that the parable is equally linked to both the Jews and the church, just as Daniels "70 weeks" are a clear amalgamation of the two; and as exactly as Christ Jesus had intended it to be when He spoke it. How truly amazing are the ways of God.

If your mind is not teetering on tilt yet then let's throw another log on the fire: Consider that the countdown of the first timeline of Daniel's "62 weeks" involves the first return of the Jews to Jerusalem (Ezra and Neh.) and ends with the eventual 1st coming of the Messiah. Likewise the second timeline of Daniel's "69 weeks" also consists of a second return of the Jews to eventually include Jesus' 2nd coming. This is duality that explodes the mind! If you've ever wondered if the word of God was truly inspired by God, this hopefully should put that doubt to rest.

The prophet Ezekiel wrote this: **Ezek.36:8 "But you, O' mountains of Israel, you shall shoot forth your branches, and yield your fruit to my people Israel, for they are about**

to come." This again bears a striking similarity to the wording of the *"Parable of the Fig Tree"*.

And yet once more the prophet Hosea said this: **Hos.9:7-10 (v7) "The days of visitation has come..."**, and in **(v10) "...I saw your fathers as the firstripe in the fig tree at her first time..."** This is God Himself directly referencing Israel's "fathers" as ripe fruit "in the fig tree", an unmistakable linkage of the terms given in the *"Parable of the Fig Tree"*, with the additional inclusion of the words "the days of visitation", drawing a unique comparison to the subject of Christ's parable (the fig tree) with that of the "days of visitation" (Christ's return).

Furthermore, upon reading the passage in its entirety we find these statements... **(v7-9) "the prophet is a fool, the spiritual man is mad,... but the prophet is a snare of a fowler in all his ways,... they have deeply corrupted themselves,... He will visit their sins."** This clearly speaks to the lack of ability and knowledge of the prophet of this looming day to discern the time and properly warn God's people. Sounds an awful lot like our end time church of today, does it not?

As impressively convincing as all of this might seem, one still might ask: is there any precedent in the Bible for the symbolic use of a tree as a representation for a nation? The answer to that question is an emphatic and overwhelming yes!

Just to briefly share a few examples with you, turn now to **Dan.4:10-27.** Daniel once more is interpreting a dream for the king of Babylon (King Nebuchadnezzar). In **(v10)** we read, **"I was looking, and behold, a tree in the midst of the earth..."** Later, in **(v20-22)** Daniel gives the interpretation of the dream, **(v20) "The tree which you saw which grew and became strong..."** **(v22) "...it is you, O king"** Here Daniel is

111

plainly giving us God's own interpretation of how He sees the kingdom of Babylon, He likens it to a tree.

In **Isa.6:11-13** we read the account of Isaiah's commission as a prophet as it is given to him through a direct and personal heavenly consultation between him and God, in the very throne room of heaven. Upon receiving this ministerial calling God immediately proceeds to announce the nature of the prophet's message as he would have Isaiah to deliver it to the Northern Kingdom of Israel. It is in these verses that God likens the remnant of His people **(v13)** "**... as a teil tree, and as an oak... when they cast their leaves**"

Turning now to the prophet Jeremiah, we read this in **Jer.11:9-18** "**The LORD called thy name, a green olive tree, fair, and of goodly fruit... For the LORD of hosts, that planted thee,**" In this passage God once again is definitively drawing the parallel of a nation (this time the Southern Kingdom of Judah) with that of a tree.

Additionally, we find the prophet Ezekiel referring to the children of Israel as a tree in **Ezek.17:1-24** using such terminology as "**Took the highest branch of the cedar... he placed by great waters, and set it as a willow tree. And it grew and became a spreading vine, and brought forth branches, and shot forth sprigs.**"

Likewise in **Isa.61:3** we read "**... that they might be called trees of righteousness, the planting of the LORD**"

In **Psalms 1:3** there is this pronouncement "**And he shall be like a tree planted by the rivers of water, that bringeth forth his fruit in his season; his leaf shall also not wither**"

Additionally in **Rom.11:17** the Apostle Paul says this, "**And if some of the branches be broken off, and you being**

a wild olive tree, were grafted in among them, and with them partakers of the root and fatness of the olive tree," In this entire chapter of Rom.11 both the people of Israel as well as the church itself are both simultaneously likened unto an "olive tree".

Even Jesus when referring to the church draws this comparison in **John 15:1-6 "I AM the true vine... every branch in me that beareth not fruit He taketh away; and every branch that beareth fruit, He purgeth it, that it may bring forth more fruit."**

The actual truth is I feel a bit silly sharing all of this with you, as the Bible itself is packed full of these types of representations, and not just of the nation of Israel but as they relate to all the nations of the world. Over and over again we see God likening a nation and its people to that of a tree, it really is a mute point. This is precisely what Jesus was alluding to when He spoke in **Luke 21:29 "Behold the fig tree, and all the trees; when they now shoot forth, you see and know of yourselves that summer is now nigh at hand."**

As an equally important issue, it should be clearly stated at this time that within the passages of Scripture that I have just provided there are varying types of trees used as illustrations of Israel; however, this should not become a point of confusion for the reader. We must always remember that at the time of Jesus' giving the *"Parable of the Fig Tree"* to His disciples, He was unmistakably addressing the typology of the fig tree that He had recently cursed, of which His disciples were fully aware.

Finally, if for any reason you are still on the fence as to whether or not the nation and people of Israel (the Jews) represent "the fig tree" in this parable I have but one final fact to share with you: In the entire Bible there are but 31 passages in which the word "fig" appears. Excluding the two passages of Matthew and Mark which addresses the parable itself we are left with 29. Of these 29 only 4 times does the passage represent an actual literal fig tree; leaving 25 passages. Of these 25, 24 of them are direct statements pertaining specifically to the land and the people of Israel.

Only once in the whole entirety of scripture is the word "fig" ever used outside of its relationship to Israel (with the exceptions of its literal use); in Nah.3:12. In this passage it is used as a symbol of God's judgment against a foreign people that have done harm to Israel.

Furthermore, it is a proven fact that throughout the Word of God the "fig tree" is listed as a type of national symbol that represents the prosperity and blessing of the nation of Israel. If the Bible itself interprets itself, than I say that by this foundational understanding it has spoken loudly.

In summary: *"the fig tree has blossomed"*, the parable has run its course as of 1948 and we and the whole world have seen it. By this knowledge there should be no doubt that we are living in the 7th and final church generation. Likewise, that would simultaneously place us squarely in the midst of Daniel's 69th week, and as we know Jesus is preparing to make His 2nd visitation as prescribed by His prophet Daniel.

In closing, Isaiah put it this way: **Isa.27:6 "He shall cause them that come of Jacob to take root; Israel shall blossom and bud, and fill the face of the world with fruit."** Jesus Himself, and His Kingdom is that fruit!

THE LAODICEANS
(OR OTHERWISE KNOWN AS "US")

Now that we know that the message that Jesus gave to John for the church of the Laodiceans is equally a personal message to those of us today who are called the church, let us examine that message carefully and take its meaning to heart. I have intentionally left this message to the Laodiceans temporarily off to the side, hoping to first prove that we are that church by means of the *"Parable of the Fig Tree"*, as Jesus plainly drew the correlation Himself between the last generation and that parable.

My intention was simple, by delaying our study of the Laodicean church until this truth could be fully brought out into the open it should command at that time an exponential emphasis to our study of this 7th church generation as we move forward, and that time is now.

Bearing in mind where we had left off at the Philadelphia church (or the 6th church generation), the church was undergoing a huge resurgence as the rise of the Reformation Movement had taken root and quickly spread throughout the down trodden masses across all of Europe. Eventually it would be the result of this metamorphosis that would create a splintering off of a new branch of the church being formed (the protestants) that would eventually extend across the ocean to the west and be planted in the new land (America). A new world and a new freshly revived church had been born, and this should be instrumental in our understanding going forth of the 7th church generation.

With this being said, we must clearly realize that this message to the 7th and final church generation is not just a message of rebuke to the Catholic church as it has come down through the generations, it is in fact a letter which addresses both Catholic and Protestant alike, otherwise we would see a clear delineation between the two distinct churches in Christ's message, and we do not, as you will soon see.

At the start, I would like to make one quick point regarding the meaning of the name of the church of Laodicea. The word "Laodicean" by its original Greek definition means "judgment", or "judgment of the people". This name and its meaning is just what we might expect for a church generation that would see the coming of the Lord, as we know that prior to His return there will be a great time of severity for the entire planet and all of its inhabitants concluding with the great and final judgment of our God.

The name itself of the Laodicean church is still yet another confirmation of the magnitude of the time in which this church will be in existence. This further builds upon what we already know regarding the 7 churches as prophetic time periods leading up to Christ's return. As we move forward with our study of this generation let us never lose track of the fact that what we are learning has a direct relevance for us today. What we will see is a candid portrait of the Christian church of our time, as seen through the eyes of God Himself. With this as the centerpiece of our understanding let us now begin.

Getting right to the message let us turn to **Rev.3:14-22**, starting at **(v15-17) "I know your works, that you are neither cold nor hot; I could wish you were cold or hot. So then, because you are lukewarm, and neither cold nor hot, I will**

vomit you out of my mouth. Because you say, 'I am rich, have become wealthy, and have need of nothing; and do not know that you are wretched, miserable, and poor, and blind, and naked."

Jesus' immediate response to this church generation is very interesting, it is one of diagnosing an affliction that it is readily suffering from. Jesus in this message is exposing a condition that has plagued the entire body of the church. Like a cancer this final church has a fatal disease, and if this state goes untreated it will unquestionably bring about its certain death, and a spiritual death at that.

Right off we must take notice that this church is nothing like its sister churches that have preceded it. This church has not been found blatantly guilty of the usual sins of the past, it is not being openly charged with the polluted stench of corruption and false doctrine as its predecessors were, nor is it indicted for the standard practices of manipulation or oppression, even though all of these are fully applicable to her as well. No, this is something different, something new to the church age as a whole. So new in fact that the word which Jesus uses to describe its condition is only used this once in all of Scripture. This one solitary mention of the word "lukewarm" is not found anywhere else in the entire Bible, it would almost appear as if this is a diagnosis that is totally exclusive to this end time church only.

Upon searching out the Greek definition for the word "lukewarm" we find the word: "tepid", it gives no other meaning whatsoever. However, extending our search by looking up the word in the Webster's English dictionary we find these additional meanings: "moderately warm, tepid, lacking conviction, halfhearted". Going a bit further, the word "tepid" itself means: "marked by an absence of enthusiasm, conviction, or interest."

In essence what we are seeing through these definitions is a church that is riddled with apathy, it is unfeeling, unemotional, disinterested, unconcerned, and indifferent, which should immediately lead us to the next question of why? Additionally, in this passage Jesus clearly states the cause of this malignant tumor that has infested this church, it is because its nature has become selfish, self-seeking, and self-absorbed, that it has become completely unattached. It is materialistic and worldly, setting its own security and comforts as its highest priority, and as a result it is self-diluted and self-deceived. This is a lethargic church that is on the borderline of being totally spiritually asleep. This is not a church undergoing the hardships and persecutions of the past, but rather a church that has grown fat as it rests in a numbing state of ease and laxity.

And if all of this was not bad enough, this is all happening at the absolute most critical time in all of human history. This is the church generation that will see the coming of the King and His Kingdom. This is a church that is in danger of finding itself on the wrong end of every parable that Jesus ever taught about the coming of the Lord. Jesus in His statement "I will vomit you out of my mouth" is offering the sternest of rebukes to a church that is so distracted with "self" that it finds itself dangerously at risk of not knowing the time of their visitation, and unless we forget that church is us.

Now I am not unaware that this message may be offensive to some Christians which would point to all the good that the church is obviously doing throughout the world today; the many local and community bodies that do labor so vigorously to uphold the name of Jesus, and to be a light in a darkened culture and society. And I would be the first to say that they are to be greatly commended for all of their strenuous efforts, and deep love and conviction for those that they shepherd, as well as for those that are lost. Let me just add this: this critical indictment from our Lord was never intended for them. As with every church generation that had gone before the Laodiceans, there was always the remnant which had not succumbed to the common practices of the evils of the church of their day. What I do understand this text to mean, is that by in large, and as a whole this church generation is seen by our Lord as unfit and negligent of their responsibilities to the faith.

Neither do I believe that this message is purely intended for the corporate body of the church only, far from it. It would seem overwhelmingly apparent that this admonition and reproof is of a very personal and individualistic nature as well. Each and every one of us must conduct a complete and thorough search of the true motivations and intents that lie within the deepest recesses of our own hearts and minds.

Now there are those undoubtedly that might say that I am being too harsh with my assessment of this church especially considering that this is an evaluation of the church as it exists today; well I would just say to that: this is exactly why I am being so transparent with my appraisal, it is because this is exactly what I see infecting our church body today. Ours is a church that looks good at a first glance; we've perfected the illusion of looking like a church, but even the world itself sometimes sees us better than we see ourselves. They can't take us seriously, neither can they find themselves desiring what were offering, and the reason? They know were behaving just like them.

Oh sure, we say all the right things, but do we practice them? Were quick to announce our love for God, but our lives tell another story. We believe in mercy, and forgiveness, and giving, and service to our Lord, but just not enough to implement any of it on a continual daily basis. Were convinced of the authority of God's word, but not enough to read it, let alone obey it. Were sold on the idea of the power of prayer, but just not enough to get on our knees and actually pray. We love to share our own testimonies with other Christians about how God has blessed our lives as long as it doesn't involve actually witnessing to the lost.

We have become consumed with our own personal lives, our priorities are the same priorities that the world shares: our family, our home, our job, our money, our car, our clothes, our food and our entertainment. We are fixated with all things "me". All of our labors are spent on either maintaining what we already have, or the upgrading of something bigger, something more. All of our thought process is exasperated with our own fears, our own worries, our own doubts and concerns, while all of our time and energy is being drained into the cesspool of "self". By in large we are takers, and what suffers most from all of this personal obsession? Our faith!

Let us not forget, this is the very instrument that Satan and his emissaries are planning to use against the entire world in order to bring it under his subjection and rule: **Rev.13:16-17 "And he will cause all, both small and great, rich and poor, free and bond, to receive a mark... And that no man might buy or sell, except he that has the mark"**

By this passage Satan's master end time strategy is plainly revealed, his is to go after the house, the car, the job, the money, the food, and everything else that seems to be the preoccupation of this final church. Isn't it ironic that the very things that Christ deems as having plagued this 7th church generation is the very things that Satan plans to use to bring this same church into his fold?

In any case, the intention of all of this is not for me to be a finger pointer, but rather to point out that despite how we might see, or think, or feel about the church today, Christ has made it perfectly clear what His position is. Perhaps the most fearful part of the entire admonition are these words, "...and do not know that you are wretched, and miserable, and poor, and blind, and naked." It's the "and do not know" part that should alarm us all.

As one might easily imagine it could be awfully tough, even near impossible to set a course correction if one doesn't even know that he needs one. It is for this reason that Jesus out of His goodness, mercy, and love, comes to us through John's writings to inform us of our condition, this is the necessary first step in initiating our healing.

Continuing on in **Rev.3:18-19** He proceeds to write the prescription for our medicine that will bring about our speedy healing and recovery: **"I counsel you to buy of me gold tried in the fire, that you may be rich; and white raiment, that you may be clothed, and that the shame of your nakedness does not appear; and anoint your eyes with eyesalve, that you may see. As many as I love, I rebuke and chasten: be zealous therefore, and repent." Behold, I stand at the door, and knock:**

if any man hear my voice, and open the door, I will come into him, and will dine with him, and he with me."

In this passage Jesus is administering a five part plan that would be sure to restore His patient to a perfect bill of health. There is a lot here for us to unpack, so let us take it slow and address this point by point as we go, as we realize that this Holy "counsel" is specifically intended for you and me.

Beginning with step one, Jesus counsel's us to "...buy of me gold tried in the fire". At the first this would seem to be a very ambiguous statement to say the least. However, using the Bible's own prescribed method of interpreting itself let us turn immediately to **Isa.55:1-3 "everyone that thirsts, come to the waters, and you who have no money, come buy and eat; yes, come, buy wine and milk without money and without price. Why do you spend money for what is not bread, and your wages for what does not satisfy? Listen carefully to me, and eat what is good, and let your soul delight itself in abundance. Incline your ear, and come to me, hear and your soul shall live; and I will make an everlasting covenant with you..."** A total of four times in this passage Jesus is prophetically calling to the reader to "come" and to "buy" from Him. He uses the most basic of all necessities (food and drink) to explain our most foundational need, and He is that need.

In **John 6:53-55** Jesus declares **"Except you eat the flesh of the Son of man, and drink His blood, you have no life in you. Whoever eats my flesh, and drinks my blood, has eternal life... For my flesh is meat indeed, and my blood is drink indeed."** Once more Jesus draws us the parallel of food and drink as the most fundamental of man's fleshly and earthly needs, with that of His body and His blood as being man's most preeminent need. As these are the staples of the communion table (I Cor.11:23-26) in which Christ Himself instructed us to partake, by this we can acknowledge that through His wording He is calling us to "come" to the unique intimacy of covenantal communion with Him.

He then continues to make the point that He may be purchased "without money and without price." This is to say that the purchased exchange that one makes with Him is essentially free to the buyer. The cost has already been paid, and that price is more precious than "gold" (His blood; His life); "tried in the fire" of His suffering (His cross); only to come out on the other end of His resurrection as the purest of all sacrificial payments. All that remains now is to "come" and receive "what is good" and "let your soul delight in abundance" as He will freely give you.

In addition to this he questions the reader "Why do you spend money for what is not bread, and your wages for what does not satisfy?" This is a clear admonition that the things of this world cannot fulfill our deepest need, they cannot offer any satisfaction to the need of "your soul". Also, within this text one can sense the gentleness and patient hearkening of His invitation to "come", ever lovingly beckoning unto us all that we should draw near to Him.

This passage is primary in understanding the failure of the Laodicean church. They have said, "I am rich, and increased with goods, and have need of nothing..." Jesus is saying that we need to change our view of what we find important, our priorities must encounter a shift from the things of this world and we must re-focus them on the one thing that our soul "thirsts" for, and that one thing is Him.

It is a curious bit of counsel in one respect: isn't Jesus speaking to the church as He bids them to "buy of me" in Rev.3:18? Is it possible that within this church there are those who have yet to "come" to Him and make this purchase? Even more startling than that, isn't He saying that this illness has over taken the church as a whole, that by in large a vast number of this church generation has not yet "come" to Him?

Remember in Matt.24 how Jesus addressed His disciples concerning His return, and the generation of His return. In a continuation of these instructions He immediately goes into a parable of "Ten virgins" in **Matt.25:1-13**. In **(v8-9)** it reads **"And the foolish said unto the wise, give us of your oil; for our lamps are gone out. But the wise answered, saying, not so; lest there be not enough for us and you; but go ye rather to them that sell, and buy for yourselves."**

It would seem that the outstanding issue of this parable is not merely those that have oil and those who do not, but more foundationally significant, those who have already bought, and those who did not buy. Jesus is warning us that at the time of His return there will be those within the church who have not yet purchased from Him, and not just an isolated number of a few people, but He uses a 1 to 1 ratio analogy emphasizing that for as many as are prepared there is an equal amount of those that are unprepared. This is a frightening development considering the words of Christ when He said, "and do not know".

In the end the parable comes to a dreadful conclusion: those that did not buy had waited too long to buy as **(v10-12)** clearly indicates: **"And while they went to buy... the door was shut. Afterward came also the other virgins, saying, Lord, Lord,** open to us. But He answered and said; surely I say unto you, I know you not."

Likewise, we find in **Matt.13:44-46 "Again, the kingdom of heaven is like treasure hidden in a field, which a man found and hid, and for joy over it he goes and sells all that he has and buys that field. Again, the kingdom of heaven is like a merchant seeking beautiful pearls, who, when he had found one pearl of great price, went and sold all that he had and bought it."**

Jesus' 5 point prescription for what ails this final church generation begins with point 1: We must re-adjust our priorities from that of this world to being certain that we have made Him our foremost priority. We must exercise the same conviction, enthusiasm, and commitment to Him as we have done in our pursuits of the things of this world. And we must not delay, we must make this priority shift immediately while there is still time, while the door is still open we must "come" to Him.

Point 2 of this illustration in **Rev.3:18** is a continuum of point 1: **"buy of me gold tried in the fire, that you may be rich, and white raiment, that you may be clothed, and that the shame of your nakedness does not appear..."** Here Jesus is further explaining that we need to be clothed by Him as well. This is not the latest designer clothing that the world has to offer, no, this is spiritual clothing that comes only by being "in Him". It is by our being "in Him" that we are clothed with the "raiment" that he is clothed with.

In **Mark 9:3** we read **"And His raiment became shinning, exceeding white as snow; so as no soap on earth could whiten them."** This signifies His purity, holiness, and glory; this is the substance of His clothing, and it is this clothing that we also must put on. Now there is not one of us that can adorn ourselves with such a garment. For us this garment does not exist, but for Him this garment is the perfect reflection of His character and His person. He pleads with us once more to allow Him to give unto us this "His raiment".

Rev.7:14 may offer the greatest description of this garment and how we must appropriate it: **"These are they which came out of great tribulation, and have washed their robes, and made them white in the blood of the Lamb."**

In **Rev.3:4-5** Jesus makes this promise to His church: **"You have a few names even in Sardis which have not defiled their garments; and they shall walk with me in white: for they are worthy. He that overcomes, the same shall be clothed in white raiment..."** This passage makes another crucial point, that in fact there are those who have on garments that are defiled. What is this defiling of their garments which Jesus indirectly speaks of?

Jude tells us in **Jude 23 "...hating even the garment defiled by the flesh."**

And there it is: our need to be clothed by Him is out of our need to rid ourselves of the garments we are currently wearing, that have been defiled by the flesh. Jesus is saying we must make an exchange with Him. Our sinful and defiled garments for His perfect and righteous garment. This is the foundational pillar of Justification by faith. It is by our faith in Him as the complete and total payment for our sins that He becomes able to put away our defilement and uncleanliness and clothes us with His Righteousness, Holiness, and Purity.

It would seem to stand to reason that if our complete and total trust in the finished work of Christ as the full payment for our sin is what is required in order that we might obtain His garment of Righteousness, than likewise, if we do not fully submit and yield ourselves entirely to His finished work upon the cross, but rather choose to produce our own righteousness by the many means of our own performance, such as church attendance, giving to the needy, reading our Bible's, and even prayer itself, that is divisively intended to produce our own righteous, than we may find ourselves to have fallen victim to the defiled garments of the flesh.

This is precisely what Paul was attempting to convey by his statements in **Eph.2:8-9 "For by Grace are you saved through faith; and that not of yourselves: it is the gift of God: not of works, lest any man should boast."**

Once more we see Christ addressing His church with the admonition that there are those within its walls that have still yet to fully put off these garments of the flesh. They are in the pews and the pulpits, but they are not in the body of our Lord.

In **Matt.22:1-14** Jesus again speaks a parable that illustrates His return in **(11-14)** we read this: **"But when the king came in to see the guests, he saw a man there who did not have on a wedding garment; so he said unto him, 'Friend, how did you come in here without a wedding garment?' And he was speechless. Then the king said to the servants, 'Bind him hand and foot, take him away, and cast him into outer darkness, there will be weeping and gnashing of teeth.' For many are called, but few are chosen."**

These words are startlingly reminiscent of the parable of "the ten virgins." To be caught unprepared at the crucial moment of His return will be inexcusable. This should be an alarming revelation for all of us who find ourselves in the midst of this 7th and final church generation. Jesus is making it abundantly clear that this church generation is currently in great danger of finding itself in a state of unpreparedness. We should all take great warning and become sober minded concerning the realities of our own individual faith.

Finally, I leave you with the words of **Isa.61:10 "...for He hath clothed me with the garments of salvation, He hath covered me with the robe of righteousness"**.

Moving forward to Point 3 in **Rev.3:18 "...and anoint your eyes with eyesalve that you may see."** This is Christ's solution for the root of this churches problem: it cannot see. Backup one verse to **(v17)** and we read: **"...and you do not know that you are wretched, and miserable, and poor and blind, and naked."**

Jesus is demanding an honest self-evaluation of the condition of this church on the part of itself, but until now it is unable to do so. It is disconnected from the truth as it is ill-equipped in regard to its lack of the anointing. This should come as no surprise considering what we have already learned about its precarious standing as it concerns true faith and actual salvation. There cannot be one without the other: no salvation, no justification, no justification, no Anointing of the Holy Spirit. This should add great clarity as to why this church is so disposed to the things of this world, this is a church by name only. It is fundamentally unsound.

In the *"Parable of The Sower"* of **Matt.13:3-23** Jesus defines this condition with remarkable transparency: **(v13-15) "Therefore I speak to them in parables: because they seeing see not; and hearing they hear not, neither do they understand. And in them is fulfilled the prophecy of Isaiah, which said, 'By** hearing you shall hear, and shall not understand; and seeing you shall see, and shall not perceive: For this people's heart is waxed gross, and their ears are dull of hearing, and their eyes they have closed; lest at any time they shall see with their eyes, and hear with their ears, and should understand with their heart, and should be converted, and I should heal them."** If one did not know better this passage would almost seem to have been written exclusively to this Laodicean church.

And what is the primary cause for this diluted and self-deceived condition? We find the answer in **(v22) "He also that received seed among the thorns is he that hears the word; and the care of this world, and the deceitfulness of riches, choke the word, and he becomes unfruitful.** These words should be terrifying for this Laodicean church generation. After all, we remember what happened the last time Jesus came looking for fruit and found none.

In **Luke 21:34** Jesus gives us this statement: **"Take heed to yourselves, lest at any time your hearts be weighed down with carousing, drunkenness, and cares of this life, and that day come upon you unexpectedly."**

And then again in **Luke 18:8** Jesus asks this stunning question: **"...when the Son of man cometh, shall he find faith on the earth?"**

By this message of Christ to His end time church we must sit up and take a dramatic look at ourselves. We cannot downplay the extreme urgency of the things that we have learned in this study. We must become awakened out of our sleep, bearing in mind that there is entirely too much at stake if we don't.

Which brings us to point 4 in **Rev.3:19 "...be zealous therefore, and repent."** In the Greek language the word "repent" carries this definition: *Strongs Concordance (#3340)* "to think differently; reconsider; morally feel compunction; to transform; (literally or figuratively "metamorphose"); change; transform; transfigure; compunction for guilt; reformation; reversal of decision."

There is not much that I could add to this definition, it is fairly self-explanatory and direct. Jesus is counseling this church to make a striking and thorough course correction. We must take Jesus' assessment of this church over that of our own. We cannot make this imperative judgment on our own. We cannot take the mistaken position that this warning does not pertain to me or my church. Jesus is not instructing some isolated pockets of Christianity, He is making a sweeping and pervasive analysis of an entire church generation as a whole. We must each one individually, as well as corporately, take this message with the utmost of seriousness and importance. With that being said, we will move to point 5 where we will see what more this correction involves.

Point 5 is found in **Rev.3:20 "Behold, I stand at the door, and knock: if any man hear my voice, and open the door, I will come into Him, and will dine with him, and he with me."** Simply put: hear the message, believe the message, and respond to the message. Jesus is saying in this text that until now He has been on the outside looking in. He has been kept out by means of a closed door. He has not been invited in. He is knocking in order that He may gain entrance, but no one has answered the door. His desire is to set up residence in the hearts and minds of us all, but we ourselves have prevented Him from doing so.

To "dine with us, and us with Him" is to forge a new life of intimacy and deepened relationship with Him, and thusly He will do the same with us. A meal shared among friends, family, or guests, in ancient Jewish culture was an event that evoked the strongest sense of close association, suggesting an informal warmth or privacy, a very personal and familiar connectedness, a unity and a oneness. This is in fact what Christ is calling us to. To shake off the chains of apathy and lethargy, and to enter in to the freedom and fullness of intimacy and relationship with Him. Not in some temporary or artificial sense, but with the driven purpose of His continual presence in our lives, day by day, moment by moment. We must also share His disdain for the "lukewarm" attitude that has for too long plagued our lives and our church. "To open the door" is to make the conscience decision to yield all of ourselves, with all of our entirety. It has been said that "He is either Lord of all, or no Lord at all." Which is He in your life today?

As Paul so aptly put it in **II Cor.13:5 "Examine yourselves, whether ye be in the faith; prove your own selves."**

A SUMMATION

As we conclude this chapter of our comparisons of the 7 churches of Rev. 2-3 with that of Church history, I would just like to add once more that I am fully aware that my simple analysis on this topic has been purely generic at best, but as I have stated earlier at the onset of our examination my goal was not to provide an all encompassing and exhaustive account of church history as I am clearly unqualified to do so. There are many others much more qualified than I to make those most intricate and explicitly defined comparisons. However, for the sake of our study it is my hope that what I have shared is more than adequate in making the desired point, and most emphatically.

It is my contention and has always been throughout this study that the 7 churches of Revelation are clearly representations of 7 church periods of history, or 7 church generations as prophesied many centuries earlier by the prophet Daniel in his writings of Dan.9.

Furthermore, it should also be noted that this additionally gives answer to another much debated theory that many scholars would seem to subscribe to: "The Gap Theory". This too is an erroneous misconception that would suggest that God has become prophetically silent over the past 2,000 year period of the current church age.

As a matter of fact, "duality" is unanimously present in almost every place where men might suggest the presence of the gap theory, and that what they are actually looking at, and missing, is God's delineations of time as He is openly exposing the mysteries of "duality". There are countless examples that I could use to make this very point of which there is no time to touch upon at this moment.

As we have seen through our research of the first "69 weeks" of Daniel everything is in order and fully accounted for. There is not the mysterious silent "gap" that many do assert, following the 1st coming of Christ, and extending into this the "Age of Grace". On the contrary, the church is not only listed in the genealogy of Christ but methodically spelled out by the use of Christ's own prophetic teachings in Rev.2-3. Again, a further example of God's own willingness to withhold nothing from His children in the way of His plans and purposes.

And as we conclude this chapter I would just like to make this final observation concerning the obvious dual nature of the prophecy of Dan.9, as we find yet another startling fulfillment in Daniel's "seventy weeks" that to this moment we have not yet addressed.

Given what we now know concerning Jesus' 1st coming at the "62nd week" of Daniel, we may also attribute the coming of the Holy Spirit as a dual fulfillment of the "seven weeks" to follow Daniel's 62nd week. This would be equally applicable to the first calculations which we made earlier on in the book involving the "day for a year" interpretation that likewise brought us snugly to the exact generation of Christ's first coming.

These "seven weeks" in-between Daniel's 62nd and 69th weeks would mathematically hold a calculation of $7 \times 7 = 49$ (this time by the use of a literal "day for a day" interpretation), and as we know the Holy Spirit would come precisely following the fulfillment of those seven weeks. Even Jesus' ascension to the Father 7 days before the Pentecost event, would act to perfectly illustrate the remaining (7days or 1 week) of Daniel's 70th week and final week.

This is precisely why God chooses to illustrate the two ascensions of Moses on Mt. Sinai after 63 and 70 days, while studiously causing them to coincide with the day of Pentecost. God is ingeniously pointing us to the weeks of Daniel and its multiple fulfillments, and all of this to be done centuries before Daniel would even be born.

Moreover, it is even noted in Ex.34:22; Lev.23:15-21; Num.28:26-31; and Deut.16:9-19, where the Feast of Pentecost is literally called "the Feast of Weeks" (as in Daniel's 70 weeks).

Additionally, it would be the fulfillment of this aspect of the prophecy that would equally set the stage for the same seven weeks to then be reapplied (in the form of Biblical duality) to the more extensive fulfillment of the seven church generations immediately following the arrival of the Holy Spirit. This is duality at its absolute finest.

You see, one interpretation does not nullify the other, they are perfectly and intricately harmonized into one and the same, while simultaneously remaining unmistakably distinct just as the Creator of the timeline Himself is a three part harmony. Like the swelling ripples of a pond after a stone has been cast in, so is our Lord "the Rock" who was dropped into the pool of humanity, and His expanding ringlets continue to swell evergrowing outwardly to this day. Another monumental proof of the complex beauty of scriptural duality as God so brilliantly illustrates it through the genealogical lineage of His Blessed Son (Dan.9).

Hopefully about this time, you have followed this study carefully and found the evidence presented to be compelling at the least, if not thoroughly persuasive. If you are one that came into this reading with the mindset that "we can't know the time of the Lord's return", my greatest hope is that as of now that opinion has forever been erased from your thinking.

Or maybe you are one that entertained the thought that "what difference does it make if I know or not? After all, all that should really matter is that I'm saved and living a sanctified life." My hope for you is that you have seen that it makes a great deal of difference. This understanding is bigger than you, or your life. There is a whole world out there, and they do not know what you now do, and many of them are unknowingly sitting in the pews next to you every Sunday. What about them? Do you feel an increased swelling of responsibility to do what you can to help them to get prepared? Has the sense of urgency set in yet, as we realize how short the time actually is?

As Moses best stated it in **Ps.90:12-13 "So teach us to number our days, that we may apply our hearts unto wisdom. Return, O LORD, how long?"** These are my hopes and prayers for us all.

CHAPTER THREE

HOW LONG IS THE 69TH GENERATION?

All that we have learned leading up to this point in our study has gradually, step by step, brought us to the 7th and final church generation of Jesus' 2nd coming, and which has simultaneously brought us to today. By now we should have a much keener understanding as to what Daniel's message of the "70 weeks" was intended to convey to the reader. We have attempted to answer some very hard questions for sure, and we have found that within the Scriptures there is no question which is too hard for the Lord.

There is of course the matter still remaining of Daniel's final 70th week and we shall cover that as well later on in this book, but first for the sake of logical progression we cannot move forward until we examine first, the question that may be foremost on the hearts of many about this time. As helpful and vitally necessary as all of this information has been in determining our specific place in the prophetic timeline, it still leads us to ponder yet another extremely significant question, quite simply: "How long is this final 69th generation?"

Let's face it, it is pretty eye opening to realize that we are alive today in the "69th week" of Daniel's prophecy, the very generation that will see the soon return of Jesus Christ.

However, as riveting as this truth obviously is, it too loses something in its impact if we consider within our own hearts that this generation could last hundreds of years before it too is completed. This just further emphasizes our need to get to the bottom of this truth as well. We must know what the Bible says concerning the length of time of this 7th and final church generation. If there's one thing that we have seen, time and time again throughout our study, is that the answers are all there, it is simply up to us to uncover them through the guidance and direction of the Holy Spirit as He chooses to reveal them.

For that matter, without this information we may find ourselves in danger of falling into the same snare that **2 Pet.3:1-4** speaks of: **"...I stir up your pure minds by way of reminder, that you may be mindful of the words which were spoken before by the holy prophets, and of the commandment of us, the Apostles of the Lord and Savior; knowing this first, that scoffers will come in the last days, walking according to their own lusts, and saying, Where is the promise of His coming? For since the fathers fell asleep, all things continue as they were from the beginning of creation."** To say the least, this would be a very unenviable position to be in preceding the time of His return.

This topic itself has been the subject of much debate among many biblical scholars for a very long time. Many varied theories have been offered by many learned men, over the course of many years, and much study and research. Now I do not pretend to know more than all of those that have come before me, but what I do know is what I have been taught, and by whom I have been taught. In this section, I will do my best to share this instruction with you.

Let me now say at the start, I am not a date setter. I am not presenting this information with the intention of pinpointing the exact time of Jesus' return. I am however sharing this revelation with you as it was shared with me, and if you are able to take away anything from this study let it be exactly the same thing that overwhelmingly commanded my attention at the first, and that is: how seriously short the time really is before our Savior returns.

In the end, and as always, it will be the work of God's Holy Spirit to confirm this knowledge, or disavow it within the hearts and minds of each individual reader. As we move forward, all that I would ask is that the reader be pliable to the truth. It is most imperative that we release any of the dogmatic and preconceived notions that we may have formerly held. Our opinions, philosophies, or even former theological training's may only add to our reluctance to accept the truth as it shall be laid out before us. And with all of this being said, once more let us begin.

I have thought long and hard as to how to begin with the presentation of this message. This is surely a case where the message is much greater than my natural ability to teach it, as could be said of this entire book. There is no quick and conveniently easy way to share this information. As with constructing anything that will be strong and durable it must begin with the strenuous work of laying a firm foundation first. Without the sturdiness of this foundation, all that one has is an edifice that looks good on the outside, but at its core it is flimsy at best.

Likewise, this will take time to construct properly, and it will require the reader to be patient and studious as the study progresses. Let it also be said, that when the study is completed, it will yield the ripest of fruit. It will affirm the authenticity of God's word once more as never before realized. It will also provide a glimpse into the incomparable wisdom of God, and remove long existing veils that have for too long shrouded us from the end time plan and purposes of God. And finally, it will glorify Him greatly, once we see more clearly His unfeigned love for us, that He would not withhold anything from us, but rather treasures us so much as to divulge all in regard to His Beloved Son and His momentous coming. And with this, let us begin to lay the first bricks.

It has become my confidence over time that there is no better starting place to appropriately begin this foundation than in Isaiah chapter 7, this is precisely where we shall begin. May the Spirit of Christ give us His grace to proceed.

ISAIAH 7

To set the stage for the events of this chapter we must begin at **Isa.7:1 "And it came to pass in the days of Ahaz... king of Judah, that Rezin the king of Syria, and Pekah... the king of Israel, went up to Jerusalem to war against it"**

At the beginning, what we see here is a time in which the tribe of Judah, and the 10 tribes of Israel, are separate and distinct nations from one another. Previous to the events of this chapter the children of Israel had suffered a great division among themselves, and as a result they have become two nations ruled by two kings. From this historical moment forward they shall be known as the Northern Kingdom and the Southern Kingdom. This can be studied more in-depth by the passages of I Kings 11:9-13; 29-36 and I Kings 12:1-24; as well as II Chr.10:1-19.

The events of this split could be best understood by the modern day equivalent of what had nearly transpired between the northern and southern states of America during the time of "The Civil War".

Returning back to the 7th chapter of Isaiah, we see the northern 10 tribes rising up against the southern tribe of Judah in warfare. Shamefully the northern tribes have conspired to take away the capital city of Jerusalem from their brethren with the aide of an alliance which they have formed with the gentile nation of Syria. Multiplying their sin, this was to be done in the direct defiance of the will of God, as God had clearly stated earlier that Jerusalem was to remain the possession of the tribe of Judah after the separation of the now two nations, as recorded in the passage of I Kings 11:13, 32, and 36.

Moving forward to **Isa.7:3-7 "Then said the LORD unto Isaiah, Go forth now to meet Ahaz, you and your son Shearjashub... and say to him, Take heed, and be quiet; fear not, neither be fainthearted... because Syria, Ephraim** (10 tribes), **and the son of Remaliah** (King Pekah of the 10 tribes), **have taken evil counsel against you, saying, Let us go up against Judah, and vex it...Thus says the LORD God, It shall not stand, neither shall it come to pass."**

Here God is clearly intervening on the behalf of Judah and its capital city of Jerusalem. He has sent His prophet Isaiah to go to the king of Judah with a message. This message is perfectly clear; God Himself will defend Judah against the intruding parties. What is not so obvious however, is that God has an unusual instruction for Isaiah, he is not to deliver this message alone, but he is to take with him his son Shearjashub, which begs one to ask: what could this be about? We will come back to this point in one moment, but first let us continue on with Isa.7:8-11 and the rest of God's message for king Ahaz of Judah.

In **Isa.7 (v8-9)** we read, **"For the head of Syria is Damascus** (capital of Syria), **and the head of Damascus is Rezin** (king of Syria), **and within 65 years shall Ephraim** (10 tribes) **be broken, that it be not a people. And the head of Ephraim is Samaria** (capital of the 10 tribes), **and the head of Samaria is Remaliahs son** (Pekah, king of the 10 tribes).

In these verses God is clearly identifying the guilty culprits, furthermore, He is pronouncing a judgment upon the king, the nation, and the people of that nation, consisting of the 10 tribes called Ephraim.

Once again we see God providing a timeline leading up to the impending judgment of His people. In this text God is announcing a grace period of "65 years" that will precede that judgment, at which time afterwards, "Ephraim (10 tribes) shall be broken, that it shall not be a people."

This judgment would eventually be carried out exactly as the LORD had said that it would come to pass, as the Bible records it in II Kings 17:5-6. Historically, this would be the conquering of the northern kingdom of Israel by the Assyrian Empire in 722BC. It would be this event that would cause the nation to be taken into captivity, and for the next 2,600 years the 10 tribes of Israel would go virtually unknown as a people, just as God had commanded through His prophet.

This brings us now to **Isa.7:10-14 "Moreover the LORD your God spoke again to Ahaz** (king of Judah)**, saying, Ask a sign of the LORD your God; ask it either in the depth, or in the height above... Therefore the LORD Himself shall give you a sign; Behold, a virgin shall conceive, and bear a son, and shall call His name Immanuel."**

Here God is speaking through the prophet Isaiah, and saying, that He Himself will provide "a sign" that shall act as the confirmation of all that He has spoken to King Ahaz, that the judgment of the northern kingdom would surely come to pass.

Likewise, this sign would serve as an alarm that would sound loudly, the drawing near of the fulfillment of the "65 years" that God had earlier prophesied. Once the sign was fulfilled, this would signal that the 65 years had nearly expired and judgment was looming at the door. Here again we see God preparing an avenue, and going to great lengths to do so, to alert His people of the time in which they live, always mercifully clinging to the hope that His children would turn back to Him and repent, and thereby prevent the prophesied catastrophe.

Moreover, God is plainly saying that the sign in which He will provide will be "a virgin birth of a son", this sign will mark the surety of the destruction of the tribes of Ephraim at the close of the "65 years".

Now, before we proceed, there may be some among you who are saying, "Wait a minute, this prophecy is speaking of Jesus and His future birth." And you would be absolutely correct of course, but this does not eliminate the literal context in which the prophecy was given. This is a perfect illustration of Biblical duality. On one hand it is most certainly a prophetic utterance of the future birth of our God and King, Jesus. On the other hand, within the literal context of the time and events that it was written, it is clearly speaking to the generation of Isaiah and the northern and southern kingdoms of Israel. This should be incontestable. This too will become more abundantly clear as we move ahead in our study. For now, let us proceed forward and see if this sign was actually fulfilled in the time of Isaiah.

We will now move only verses ahead to **Isa.8:3-4**, where we read, **"And I went unto the prophetess** (the virgin)**; and she conceived, and bare a son** (the sign)**. Then said the LORD to me, Call his name Mahershalalhashbaz. For before the child shall have knowledge to cry, My father and my mother, the riches of Damascus** (Syria) **and the spoil of Samaria** (Ephraim) **shall be taken away before the king of Assyria** (the conquering empire)**."**

This is a direct fulfillment of the prophetic sign given back in Isa.7:14, even to the exact details of **Isa.7:16 "For before the child shall know to refuse the evil, and choose the good, the land that you abhor shall be forsaken of both her kings**. This should be enormously clear, the sign as God Himself would designate it, is precisely fulfilled in these verses. I promise you that Isaiah could not have understood these unfolding events as anything else. As you can see this is a perfect example of duality of scripture at its finest.

Now you might ask, what all of this has to do with our study of "How long is the last generation?" Well first of all, we have learned that these passages are far more expansive in their meaning than what we might have otherwise thought by just a mere casual reading. In fact, these passages of scripture are deeply connected and intertwined with the revelatory knowledge that we now know exists within the prophecies of Dan.9, as well as Matt.24. Let me show you what I mean.

Remember back in Isa.7:3 where God tells Isaiah to take with him his son "Shearjashub?" This name of "Shearjashub" in Hebrew means: "A remnant will return". By the very name of Isaiah's first son we see an exact representation that would speak of a coming exile, and then the eventual gathering back of a remnant later to be fulfilled. I submit to you now, that this is God giving Isaiah's generation a form, a shadow, a typology, of the *"Parable of the Fig Tree"* prior to His carrying out of the pronounced judgment.

As a similitude, the events of Isaiah's day would beautifully illustrate the coming events of Jesus' 1st coming. As a perfect parallel before Jesus' arrival there would also be an exile, this time to occur in 586BC, followed then by the return of a remnant as recorded in the books of Ezra and Neh., and likewise, depicted by the name of Isaiah's son "Shearjashub". At the same time it would be this return of the Jews to their native homeland that would also signal the beginning of the countdown to the 1st coming of Jesus, as we learned in **Dan.9:25 "Know therefore and understand, that from the going forth of the commandment to restore and to build Jerusalem unto the Messiah..."**

Even more fascinating is the fact that the exact time-frame of the fulfillment of the *"Parable of the Fig Tree"* would be repeated again in a cyclical fashion, "65 years" after the birth of Christ (virgin birth), according to the prophecy of Isa.7:14, this time with the destruction of the city of Jerusalem in 70 AD by the Roman Empire. Additionally, by this reasoning we can further surmise that Jesus would have been born in the exact year of 5AD, according to the exact same O.T. prophecy that would proclaim His future birth. His birth would be the second fulfillment of the same prophecy given to Isaiah.

As concerning the first fulfillment of Isaiah's day, "the sign" would be the birth of a son as well. This son as we have already learned would be born to Isaiah in Isa.8:3 through "the prophetess" (the virgin), and would be named "Mahershalalhashbaz". In discovering the meaning of the name of this 2nd son of Isaiah, we find this Hebrew definition: "speed the spoil, hasten the booty".

Here God is using the name of this 2nd child to convey the fulfillment of the second half of the *"Parable of the Fig Tree"*; that is, with the birth of this son, the time of the prescribed judgment would be speeded up and hastened as it was with the nation of Israel in the time of Jesus birth.

Exactly as it occurred with the northern kingdom of Isaiah's day it would likewise be for the generation of Jesus; same prophecy, same illustration of the *"Parable of the Fig Tree"*, same timeline of 65 years, same fulfillment of an exile and a return of a remnant, even to the point of the words of Isa.7:8 "shall no longer be a people." In both cases they are conquered by the prevailing empire of the day, scattered into captivity, and left without a nation or a land, and from that time on they would no longer be a recognized people group as nations go.

Later, it would be Jesus Himself that would tie this same prophecy of Isa.7 to our generation today as a third and future fulfillment, by His use of *"the "Parable of the Fig Tree"* in Matt.24. Although He is not openly giving mention to the Isaiah passage itself, He is clearly using the *"Parable of the Fig Tree"* to represent a coming exile of the Jews (70AD), to be followed later in the "the last days" with the return of a remnant, which would additionally serve as "the sign" to "speed the spoil and hasten the booty" (both names of Isaiah's two sons).

And all of this to precede the final end time judgment as foretold in the book of Revelation, to follow shortly soon after. As it did with Ephraim in Isaiah's day, and likewise, as it did with the Jews at the 1st coming of Jesus in Daniel's 62nd week, so also it shall be done at the 2nd coming of Christ in Daniel's 69th week

So as we see, Jesus was actually repeating the parable that had already been fulfilled once in Isaiah's day, and would be fulfilled a second time not soon after His departure concluding His 1st coming, and then would eventually be fulfilled again, a third time in the last days as it would "speed and hasten" the return of His second coming as well.

By all of this it should be readily apparent as to why we would search this same passage of Isaiah 7 for possible clues to the length of time of this final end time generation of Daniel's 69th week. Now I ask you: is your mind completely blown by now, or what? I know mine is just trying to adequately explain it all. All glory and praise be to our God!

Alright, at this time let us go back to Isa. chapters 7-8, where we shall attempt to approach this passage of Scripture in a slightly different manner. Considering all that we have learned in regard to the first two fulfillments of this prophecy, it should only stand to reason that within the prophecy of Isa.7-8 we should also find evidence of the third and final fulfillment within its text.

Furthermore, if we do find within its content a third fulfillment as it relates to Christ's second coming, than we must also accept that lying within this text is additionally a timeline to the prescribed judgment, as it did for the first two fulfillments. And for the sake of our stated goal of determining "how long is this final church generation?" this would seem to be the perfect place to advance our search.

We have just read in Isa.8:3-4 how "the sign" of the birth of a son was fulfilled by the birth of Isaiah's son Mahershalalhashbaz. It is in the following verses of (v6-18) that we read a detailed account of the coming destruction upon the northern tribes as God had promised. It is also within this text that we see the message take an unusual turn, in more ways than one. Within this short passage there are multiple points that give witness to this shift, however, for the sake of time I will just touch on a few of these points that I have found most compelling.

First point: Although the text begins most assuredly addressing the time and events of Isaiah's day, there is a very subtle change in the tone of the message that takes on a futuristic fulfillment not of Isaiah's day. In **Isa.8:13-15** we read, **"Sanctify the LORD of hosts Himself; and let Him be your fear, and let Him be your dread. And He shall be for a sanctuary; but for a stone of stumbling and for a rock of offense to both the houses of Israel, for a trap and a snare to the inhabitants of Jerusalem. And many of them shall stumble, and fall, and be broken, and be snared, and be taken."**

This portion of the message can in no way be referring to Isaiah's day. Remember, the initial point of Isa.7-8 was to deliver a message to the king of Judah that God would deliver Judah and Jerusalem from the plot of its adversaries. Scripture itself would later bear out this fact in Isa.37. This chapter occurs after the Assyrian Empire has conquered both the Syrians and the northern kingdom of Israel, just as God had spoken earlier through Isaiah. In addition to this, Judah has been spared by the hand of God as promised.

In Isa.37 the Assyrian Empire in its own arrogance now makes the fatal mistake of prolonging its conquest by means of attempting to take Jerusalem as well. It is in this chapter that we see God send "the Angel of the Lord" in (v36) who enters the camp of the Assyrians, and destroys in one night 185,000 Assyrian soldiers causing the defeat and withdraw of its remaining army. Once more a fulfillment of the message that God gave to Isaiah for the king of Judah, that God Himself would deliver Judah and Jerusalem.

Now, going back to **Isa.8:13-15** we read something very different in **(v14)** "**...a stone of stumbling and for a rock of offense to both the houses of Israel** (Ephraim and Judah), **for a trap and a snare to the inhabitants of Jerusalem.**"

Here in this same message is a foretelling of a time in which "both houses of Israel" (northern and southern), and "Jerusalem" will suffer judgment. This as we know did not occur in Isaiah's day, as Judah and Jerusalem were spared as we just read. Additionally, it cannot fully represent the destruction that fell on Jerusalem and the Jews in 70AD at Jesus' 1st coming, because the northern kingdom of Ephraim was no longer in existence at that time. This is obviously referring to a future third fulfillment at the end time of Jesus' 2nd coming.

The Apostle Paul confirms this interpretation in **Rom.9:33** "**As it is written, Behold, I lay in Zion a stumblingstone and rock of offense: and whosoever believes on Him** (Jesus) **shall not be ashamed.**" This passage confirms that Jesus is the focal point of (Isa.8:13-15) and thereby making it impossible to be related to the days of Isaiah. In short, there should be no question at all that Isa.7-8 is a definite example of "duality" bearing multiple fulfillments throughout its text.

Second point: Because this message, initially given to the king of Judah, would have an additional significance for generations to come, God in **Isa.8:1** commands Isaiah to "**Take a large scroll, and write on it with a man's pen concerning Mahershalalhashbaz.**" In other words, God is telling Isaiah to record the message so that it might be preserved. Later, as the message nears its end, we see God give this command in **(v16)** "**Bind up the testimony, seal the law among my disciples.**" Here God is commanding that the meaning or understanding of this message be "sealed" for a particular group of persons and for a later date in time, which He calls "my disciples". This is unmistakably reminiscent of **Dan.12:4 "But you, O Daniel, shut up the words, and seal the book, even to the time of the end..."**

Furthermore, the word "disciple" or "disciples" is only used this one time in all of the Old Testament, it is never used again. It is with a certainty speaking to the New Testament believers that are still yet to come. This preserved message is preserved for them, another strong confirmation of the dual nature that lies within this passage.

Finally we come to the third point: In **Isa.8:8** we read **"And he shall pass through Judah; he shall overflow and go over, he shall reach even to the neck; and the stretching out of his wings shall fill the breadth of thy land, O' Immanuel."**

Remember the sign given to **Isaiah** in **7:14 "...a virgin shall conceive, and bear a son, and shall call His name Immanuel."** The name "Immanuel" means "God with us" in Hebrew. As this name would unmistakably refer to the first coming of Christ, who is without any debate God in the flesh (John1:1-14), it likewise is used in another context as it appears in Isa.8:8. As it is spoken in this passage, it is clearly referring to the land and the people of that land. Here Isaiah bestows the very name of the promised child "Immanuel" on Judah itself, emphasizing that she would only be preserved as the result of "God being with" the nation.

Only two short verses later in **Isa.8:10** we read: **"Take counsel together, and it shall come to nothing; speak the word, and it shall not stand; for God is with us (Immanuel)."** Here God is speaking exclusively of the land and the people of the land of Judah by His own use of the definition of the word Immanuel. Moreover, in this context we are looking at the possible third fulfillment of this prophecy.

In this fulfillment as with the others, yes, there will be an earlier exile (70AD); and yes, there will be a remnant that shall return (1948); and lastly, there shall be a virgin birth of a son (the virgin land itself shall give birth to the people of modern day Israel: the new nation of Immanuel), which shall act as the sign that the time is drawing near to its end.

Now some of you may be struggling right about now with this interpretation as I have offered it, so let's just let the book of Revelation clear this up for you.

Turn to **Rev.12:1-6 "Now a great sign** (Isa.7:14) **appeared in heaven; a woman** (a virgin) **clothed with the sun, and the moon under her feet, and upon her head a crown of twelve stars** (both houses)**: and she being with child cried, travailing in birth, and pain to be delivered** (shall conceive)**... and, the dragon stood before the woman which was ready to be delivered, for to devour her child as soon as it was born. And she brought forth a man child** (and bear a son)**, who was to rule all nations with a rod of iron; and her child was caught up unto God** (Jesus)**, and to His throne. And the woman** (the virgin) **fled into the wilderness, where she has a place prepared of God that they should feed her there 1,260 days."**

Now I ask you, who is this woman? Who or what does this woman represent? Clearly this is the third fulfillment of Isa.7:14 where the woman is getting ready to give birth to a son, as a great sign, which is end time Israel (Immanuel).

Israel here is in the process of being "born again" by the Spirit of God as stated in Rom.11, it is likewise the moment of conception for "the one new man" of Eph.2:14-16. As with any birth the precise time of delivery for the woman is signaled by the "water breaking", this is also the time of the "latter rain" of Joel 2:23, 28-29, in which the Church and Israel will be joined together as that one new man, which additionally explains why the woman simultaneously resembles both the natural people of Israel, while at the very same time the Church of Christ.

In this prophecy of Rev.12 the birth as it is mentioned is not one of Jesus' being born physically a second time into the earth, neither is Mary in labor again in the last days, but rather, the nation of Israel and the Jews are being born for the 1st time by the Holy Spirit. In this passage the land of Israel is the virgin, and the Jews are the son Immanuel. God is clearly tying in the events of Jesus' prophesied birth in Isa.7:14 with the end time birth of Israel, as a multiple and third fulfillment of the prophecy given to Isaiah.

Still not convinced? Over and over again the Bible calls the land of Israel, or Jerusalem, "a virgin daughter". Likewise, over and over again, the people of Israel are called "God's son". Unfortunately time will not permit me to prove this out with any great detail, but it is a well known truth on both accounts for anyone who studies the word of God extensively. One only has to do a simple word study of the words "virgin" and "son" throughout scripture, by use of a *Strong's concordance*, and these claims as I have stated them will be fully verified. I will, however, just leave you with a few: Ex.4:22-23; Jer.31:9; Hos.1:10; Isa.37:22, Jer.31:4-21; Lam.2:13.

As a final proof that I will offer, I will give you one more that should hopefully cement the issue for you: **Isa.66:7-10 "Before she was in labor she gave birth; before her pain came, she delivered a male child. Who has heard such a thing? Who has seen such things? Shall the earth be made to give birth in one day? Or shall a nation be born at once? For as soon as Zion was in labor, she gave birth to her children. Shall I bring to the time of birth, and not cause delivery? says the LORD. Shall I who cause delivery shut up the womb? says your God. Rejoice with Jerusalem, and be glad with her, all you who love her."**

In this passage what we see through the use of its symbolism is a definitive reference to the actual physical birth of the nation of Israel in 1948 following nearly 1,900 years of exile. It can also have an additional fulfillment as we have just read in Rev.12, where it references the coming spiritual birth of the nation that will be fulfilled prior to the 2nd coming of Jesus' return. One represented by the first son of Isaiah, and the other by the second son. In either case, it clearly depicts the land as the virgin that shall give birth to the nation of Israel; which only further solidifies our earlier interpretation that within Isa.7-8 there is a clear reference to a third fulfillment in which the end time nation of Israel shall "be conceived", and in turn be called "Immanuel".

With all of this presented, we are now left with what to do about the timeline ("65 years"), lest we forget that there is also a precise timeline given within this same passage that was equally and explicitly relative to this prophecies first two fulfillments.

In each of the first two fulfillments the timeline was carried out exactly as promised. So precisely in fact, that there is a little known portion of this prophecy that has gone virtually unnoticed and it too was fulfilled to the letter.

In **Isa.7:16** it states, **"For before the child shall know to refuse the evil, and choose the good, the land that you abhor shall be forsaken of both her kings."** God once more reaffirms this promise in **Isa.8:4**, literally the very next verse following the birth of Mahershalalhashbaz: **"For before the child shall have knowledge to cry, 'My father, and my mother, the riches of Damascus and the spoil of Samaria shall be taken away before the king of Assyria."**

This is Gods way of plainly saying that very soon after the birth of this prophesied son the judgment would be carried out. In the case of Isaiah's son Mahershalalhashbaz, he is never mentioned again throughout all of scripture following his birth in Isa.8:1-3. This leaves us the assumed indication that after his birth there was nothing left of major importance to record concerning him, for just as the prophecy would declare, judgment became the central theme of scripture at that point. His birth had served its prescribed purpose as "the sign", and as such his work was thoroughly done.

As this same prophecy relates to the life of our Lord Jesus Christ at His first coming, it is a well known fact that He lived a very short time on earth. The popular belief is that He lived some 33 ½ years, and even shorter still was the actual length of His ministry, a mere 3 ½ years. This would act as a second fulfillment of the same prophecies of Isa.7:16 and 8:4.

Considering that Jesus lived a sinless life and was not born into the sin nature of man, it would be entirely proper to suggest that He would have undoubtedly lived an unprecedented length of years, had He of not of course offered up His life willingly as our sacrificial offering. As the perfect replica of "the first Adam" of I Cor.15:45, prior to the fall, we know that His life would have far exceeded that of the 930 years in which Adam lived.

Scripture makes it clear that "the wages of sin is death" (Rom.6:23), likewise, where there is no sin there is no death. Therefore, if He had not offered up His life as the full payment for the sins of all mankind, He would most certainly still be alive on the earth today. By this comparison, we can surely see that His life would have been cut off in its mere infancy, following only 33 ½ years of life. At the same time, it would be very soon afterwards, following His death and resurrection, and eventual ascension to the Father that Judgment would fall harshly upon the Jews even as the prophecy would declare.

Furthermore, as this prophecy additionally relates to the third fulfillment of Isa.7-8 and "the end times", we must also conclude that the nation of Israel would likewise be in a comparative state of its infancy at the time that the final judgment of Revelation would be rapidly approaching. This is no way lends us to the belief that this "69th week" of Daniel, or the 7th and final church generation will see any extended or prolonged waiting period before the judgment comes to pass, just as the *"Parable of the Fig Tree"* so specifically illustrates when Jesus says these words: **Matt 24:34 "this generation shall not pass until all these things be fulfilled."** Jesus is plainly referring to the same exact generation that shall see the birth of the nation of Israel, shall likewise see the coming of "the Son of man". This interpretation would surely present the nation of Israel to be in a symbolized state of infancy at the time of Christ's return, and once more, for the third time, act as a perfect fulfillment of the prophesy of Isaiah.

These two previous fulfillments of Isaiah should cause us all to sit up in our chairs and take notice. If the third fulfillment is in progress now, and has been since the forming of the nation of Israel in 1948, than according to this portion of the prophecy there would be a 65 year timeline, and then the spiritual re-birth of God's own son Israel, and soon afterwards, the judgment of Revelation immediately preceding the return of Christ.

In short, this leaves absolutely no wiggle room for the skeptic to assume that this final generation could last hundreds of years, or stretch on for any lengthy period of time into the future. No, on the contrary, it says the complete opposite. It tells us emphatically that we are rapidly approaching the end of this final grace period. So much so, that even now, at the time that I am writing this we are currently in the 65th year since the physical birth of Israel in 1948. This would place us at the dawning moments of the spiritual birth of the nation of Israel, and the coming judgment soon after. For now, however, let us just briefly move ahead, and we shall leave this all temporarily as food for thought. We will undoubtedly return to it later, once we have made our foundation surer as we shall endeavor to continue to build upon this premise.

At this moment, let's briefly summarize what we have learned from Isa.7-8. This passage of scripture is clearly upon closer examination, revealing three separate and distinct fulfillments. One of Isaiah's day, one of Jesus' first coming, and a third fulfillment for the end times nation of Israel, prior to Christ's second coming. We also see within its context a timeline of 65 years that will precede a great judgment of God. This clearly leaves us with a monumental question: How does this 65 year timeline pertain to the third and final end time fulfillment of Isaiah's prophecy, which just so happens to be the exact same period of time in which we find ourselves living today?

Believe me when I tell you that I wish that the answer to this question could be easily shared with you. But consider this, look how much instruction we have had to persistently endure just to get to this point in which we currently find ourselves. God for His own purposes has intricately disguised this information, and concealed it beyond the natural abilities of any man to discover it, let alone disclose it. It is only by the inspiration and instruction of the Holy Spirit that it can be brought forth to light and revealed.

Now I am not saying this to project myself as anything that I am clearly not. I am only stating this openly to give the proper glory to God for His immeasurable wisdom, and secondly to ask those of you who have remained with me through this study thus far, to please continue to remain patient and bear with me. The knowledge when it is done will reward you mightily, I assure you, and that reward of course will be none other than "the truth".

Before we set off on a new course of study let me make it abundantly clear that we are not leaving this question of the 65 year timeline. What we are doing is approaching it from a fresh vantage point. We will now begin to examine this same subject through the use of alternative perspectives, using various other passages of Scripture to assist us in our resolve to gain a more deepened sense of clarity and understanding.

Leading into this approach we know that the word of God is consistently congruent from Genesis to Revelation, with a perfect synchronicity and continuity throughout. It is through this method of our examination that we will sure-up the foundation that we have begun to build. Once we have further advanced our construction of this assertive premise, we will then revisit Isa.7-8, and hopefully at that time be able to tie it all neatly together.

A GENERATIONAL LIFE SPAN

The first point that I would like to make as we begin this next section of our study, is in regard to this final generation that will eventually see the ushering in of Christ's return, and His kingdom. There has been somewhat of a controversy involving the question of "how long is a biblical generation", and there are clearly a variety of theories offered as a response to this question. I however, believe with great certainty that we are asking the wrong question. Let me briefly explain what I mean.

At the time of Adam, we know that he lived 930 years according to Gen.5. Adam was of course the first generation of man (Daniel's 1st week). Similarly, Adam's descendants and their life spans are equally spelled out for us in Gen.5. Seth lived 912 years; Enos lived 905 years; Cainan lived 910 years; Mahalaleel lived 895 years, and so on. By using this most basic of information as our guide, we could make the simple deduction that a generation would have to be estimated somewhere in the vicinity of 900 to 1,000 years. However, the problem with this course of thinking becomes obvious when we consider that the further that we go down the genealogical ladder, the life spans of Adam's descendants become increasingly shorter as we go.

By the time we get to the 20h generation of Abraham in Gen25:7-8, we read that Abraham's life span is concluded after a mere 165 years. Continuing even further down the family tree of man we come to Moses in Deut.34:7, where we read that he dies at 120 years. Then in Ps.90:10 Moses further complicates the issue with these words: "The days of our years are seventy; and if by reason of strength they be eighty years..."

Add to all of this the conundrum of the "wilderness generation" that clearly lasted only 40 years, as described in Num.14:30-35, and what we are left with is a multi-varied hodge-podge of inconsistent periods of time in which to gage the actual length of time of a "generation" in general. However, there is another way of seeing all of these generations in a way that would provide complete integrity and continuity as a whole.

In examining the definition of the word "generation" as given in the *Webster's dictionary*, we find this: "a body of living beings constituting a single step in the line of descent from an ancestor; which each one holds only for a limited period; the average span of time between the birth of parents and that of their offspring."

More simply put, a generation does not carry within itself any set period of time in which it can be measured in reference to the generations that have gone before it, or shall come after. The truest definition of a generation is the actual life span of the persons living in that generation. By this definition all of the generations that were aforementioned are synonymous with one another in this one singular way: they each represent the average life span of the people that lived in those specific generations.

The actual proof of this simplistic finding is in Dan.9 itself. The "Seventy weeks" that are representative of 70 generations, with each generation lasting a different length of time, they are not counted by set periods of time as they occur individually, they are in fact, 70 life spans of the individuals which are counted. By this we must also conclude that the final generation of Daniel's "69th week", leading to the second coming of Christ, would also be appropriately measured by the general life span of that final generation.

Examples of this assertion would be the judgments that fell on the generation of Noah, almost immediately to occur, within the precise year in fact, following the generation of his grandfather Methuselah.

Likewise, with the judgments that fell on Sodom and Gomorrah, which simultaneously coincided within the exact life spans of Abraham and Lot, and copiously occurred within the exact same time-frame of a single year from that of the birth of the son of promise, Isaac.

The same could be said of Moses, and the judgments that befell his generation. As a perfect illustration, the judgments of Egypt, as well as those of the wilderness journey would seem to have unanimously run their course within the impeccable timing of a singular year from that of the deaths of Miriam, Aaron, and Moses himself.

As an additional proof, the generation that suffered the great judgment of 70AD at the hands of the Romans, was also the same generation (1st church generation) that saw the interrupted life span of Jesus at His first coming. It was not witnessed by another generation to follow, but by the very same generation of His day.

The same would hold true of the judgment of the northern kingdom of Israel in 722BC, or the generation of Isaiah; and likewise, the southern kingdom of Judah in 586BC, as represented through the prophet Jeremiah and his generation. In both cases the judgments fell during the life spans of the people that had originally received and documented the fatal warnings.

By all of this we should clearly see how irrational and ill-logical it would be to suggest that this 7th and final church generation could go on for any lengthy period of time. That could only be true if the general life span of our generation was 150, or 200, or 300 years. After all, the entire purpose of the *"Parable of the Fig Tree"* is to bring to the attention of the reader that **"this generation shall not pass until all these things be fulfilled" (Matt.24:34)**, with the additional knowledge that this will also be the same generation that shall see the return of the Lord.

Using this logic, we not only discover a complete cohesiveness between all past generations, but at the same time we see more clearly how the timeline of the "65 years" in Isa.7 could be a sensible fit for our generation today, as it may find its prophetic dual fulfillment in our lifetime.

There are so many Biblical examples that I could use to provide additional evidence of this truth, but once again for the sake of time it is best that we move on. Hopefully though, I have adequately explained myself, albeit in a much abbreviated way. Again, this is only a singular brick laid, with many others to follow. We shall touch more on this subject as we go on, I assure you.

ZECHARIAHS WITNESS

In the next few sections we will begin to explore some parallel passages of Scripture that should provide additional insight and offer some much needed support for what we have already learned. Our first stop on this tour will be the prophet Zechariah.

As an opening observation, I would just like to say that anyone that has ever read the book of Zechariah closely, would have to most likely agree with the following statement: This book is clearly a companion book to the prophetical books of both Daniel and Revelation. The topics addressed, and the points made throughout the writings of Zechariah are overwhelmingly referring to a futuristic time called the "end of days", which in turn qualifies it to speak pointedly to our generation today, and that is of course the generation of Daniel's "69th week".

Time of course will not permit me to make this point as extensively as I might wish, with a detailed verse by verse examination of the book, however, I would highly recommend its reading by anyone following with me in this study, in your own private time, as you will surely see for yourself that the parallels are undeniable. Of course it should also go without saying that if one is not equally familiar with the reading of the books of Daniel and Revelation then there will be nothing in which to draw from in order to make the necessary comparisons.

However, at this time, for the purpose of our study we will do a very brief and simplistic survey which should be more than adequate to consolidate the point in which I would hope to make as we will draw near to the conclusion of this section.

Beginning our brief survey starting with **Zech.1:8-11** we see this: **"I saw by night, and behold, a man riding on a red horse... And behind him were horses; red, sorrel, and white. Then I said, My lord, what are these? So the angel who talked with me said to me, I will show you what they are... these are the ones whom the LORD has sent to walk to and fro throughout the earth."** In this opening chapter we can very early on see clearly an unmistakable likeness to that of the "four horsemen", or otherwise known as the first four "seals" of Rev.6:1-8.

It will be later on in Zech.6:1-7 that we shall see these same four horses mentioned again, this time as they move out in their pursuit of fulfilling their individual purposes, as similarly demonstrated by the opening of the first four seals of the book of Revelation.

In **Zech.6:2** we read: **"In the first chariot were red horses; and in the second chariot black horses... (3) "And in the third chariot white horses; and in the fourth chariot grisled and bay horses... (v5) "And the angel answered and said unto me, 'These are the four spirits of the heavens, which go forth from standing before the LORD of all the earth."** In my opinion, it should be an uncontested fact that what we are undeniably looking at here is a perfect similitude of the "Four Horseman" of the book of Revelation.

Returning now, back to **Zech.2:1-7** we read this: **"Then I raised my eyes and looked, and behold, a man with a measuring line in his hand. So I said, Where are you going?**

And he said to me, To measure Jerusalem, to see what is its width and what is its length."

Once again, as a perfect contrast we see a striking similarity in **Rev.11:1-4 "Then I was given a reed like a measuring rod. The angel stood, saying, 'Rise and measure the temple of God, the altar, and those who worship there. But leave out the court which is outside the temple, and do not measure it, for it has been given to the Gentiles. And they will tread the holy city (Jerusalem) under foot for forty-two months."**

It should additionally be noted, as concerning the passage of Zech.2, that it is a fact that Zechariah is writing this book at a time following the captivity of Judah, which means Jerusalem as well as the temple of God of his day have both been totally destroyed some 70 years earlier in 586BC, as stated in Zech.1:12. This would most certainly lend to the opinion that Zechariahs vision and writing could only be relative to a future time. Yes, the temple would be rebuilt as well as the city of Jerusalem, but what I am proposing here is that what we are actually witnessing is a perfect example, and a clear cut case of prophetic Biblical "duality", which makes its many comparisons to the book of Revelation even that much more compelling.

Continuing on now to **Zech: 2:6-7**, we also read of a reference to **"the daughter of Babylon"**, as it bears a direct relationship to that of **Rev.17** and **"Babylon...the Mother of Harlots"**. In this case, one would seem to be most obviously the "offspring" of the other. Again, a definitive inference of an existing prophetical relationship between the two passages of the two books.

Moreover, in **Zech.3:1-10** we read of the **"high priest"** of Israel (of Zechariahs day) being commissioned and given authority in a vision by a heavenly court, as a prophetic shadow of the "end times", as likewise recorded in **Dan.7:9-10,22,26-27**, in which a heavenly court there also makes the following judicial pronouncement: **(v22) "...and judgment was given to the saints of the Most High; and the time came that the saints possessed the kingdom... (v27) And the kingdom and dominion, and greatness of the kingdom under the whole heaven, shall be given to the people of the saints of the Most High"** Once more what we see here in both passages, is a heavenly judicial ruling being passed down in the favor of the children of God, in the very throne room of God itself; remarkably and prophetically adjacent to one another.

Furthermore, within this same text in Zech.3:8 there is the precise prophetic allusion to Jesus Himself ("the BRANCH"), and again in Zech.6:12, as He is the perfect fulfillment of this heavenly court and its seeding of authority to the saints of God through the Divine coronation of its King. Once again, these are undeniable references of the intricate link between the book of Zechariah and the "last days".

Moving ever forward, we come to Zech.5:1-4 which alludes to a "flying scroll" which has been opened already, again a precise comparative passage to the opening of the 7 seals of **Rev.5:1-9; 6:1-17; 8:1-2**, containing **"the curse that shall go out over the face of the whole earth"**, with writing on both sides of the scroll, just as it appears in Rev.5:1; which equally represents the "trumpets" on the one side and the "bowls" on the other. Again, an identical prophetical match.

Additionally, in Zech.5:5-11 we see the prophetic reference of "the Great Harlot of Mystery Babylon" of **Rev.17**, as **"a woman sitting inside the basket... when it is ready the basket will be set there on its base."** Again, a subtle yet profound example of the events of the "end times" preceding the 2nd coming of our Lord, as demonstrated by the writings of the prophet Zechariah.

Next is **Zech.6:1-7** where the book returns back to **"the four horseman"**; and once again in **(v9-15)** we see the **"heavenly coronation"** of the **"high priest"** as a clear representation and type of Jesus, which clearly states: **"...the man whose name is the BRANCH"**

And in addition to all of this, we see in **Zech.10:1-12** the **"latter rain"**, and then in **Zech.12:1-14 "Jerusalem a cup of trembling"**, as well as the actual appearance of Christ to the nation of Israel; and all of these as the prophetical "end time" staples that they are, and on and on the parallels go.

Later in **Zech.13** we see Jerusalem as the staging ground for the battle of **"Armageddon"** as seen in **Rev.16:16.** And finally, in **Zech.14** we have **"the return of the Lord"**, the final judgment of God, as well as several passages throughout the book which clearly pertain to the "Millennial Reign" of Christ. And all of these are but a few of the key highlights and clearly most critical events that distinguish the book of Zechariah as a definitive end time book; which also uniquely and unequivocally qualifies it as a pictorial of the conclusion of Daniel's "69th week", and the 7th and final church generation, lest we forget.

As one final but exactingly precise similitude, that may not be so obvious, Zechariah and his companion the prophet

Haggai, are themselves shadow-types and forerunners of the **"two witnesses"** of the book of Revelation **(Ezra 5:1; Zech.4:1-14; Rev.11:1-4)**.

Alright, what is the point that I am trying to make you ask? As simply as I know how to put it: There should be no denying that the book of Zechariah is an end time book, although, at the exact same time it clearly offers glimpses of the time, and events, and the people of Zachariah's own day, intricately interwoven with the prophetic fabric of the events of the "last days" (unmistakable duality).

With this clear understanding in mind, I refer you now to **Zech.1:12 "Then the Angel of the LORD answered and said, 'O LORD of hosts, how long will you not have mercy on Jerusalem and on the cities of Judah, against which you were angry these seventy years."**

Here also we find another precise prophetic shadow of the book of Revelation as it relates this time to the "5th seal", as **Rev.6:9-10** records it: **"And when He had opened the fifth seal, I saw under the altar the souls of them that were slain for the word of God, and for the testimony which they held; and they cried with a loud voice, saying, 'How long, O Lord, holy and true, do you not judge and avenge our blood on them that dwell on the earth?"** In both instances the wording of the question asked remains the same: "how long"; and in both cases the question immediately follows the unmistakable descriptions of "four horsemen", this holds a direct correlation to the "5th seal".

As a separate matter, but of equal importance, isn't it curious that within these 2 texts we see in the passage of **Zech.1:12 "the Angel of the LORD"** asking this question of "how long"; and then in the other text of Rev.6:9-10 we find it being asked by "the souls of them" which are "under the altar"? My point is this: What we are seeing here are the angels of heaven, as well as all of those saints which have gone before us, all asking the same question that we today find our own selves asking: "How long?" Apparently, they too haven't gotten the memo that says "we cannot know the time."

I ask you now, is it possible that this verse of Zech.1:12 could also be of a prophetic significance to the end time generation in which the rest of this book clearly addresses? Here in the very midst of the four horseman; the harlot of Babylon; the two witnesses; Armageddon; and the second coming of Christ; the final judgment, and the millennial reign, which simultaneously perfectly aligns itself with that of the 5th seal, we find a definitive time period which states that 70 years have elapsed prior to all of these events.

As I have stated earlier, God is clearly using various people and events of Zechariah's time to draw these prophetic comparisons. In this case He is clearly referring to the 70 years in which Judah has been in captivity following the judgment that fell upon them in 586BC. My question is whether or not it might be equally possible that this same 70 years is also a creatively and strategically placed illustration of "Biblical duality" as it may refer to the "end time" period in which the rest of the book so vehemently describes? Could this be a disguised glimpse into the actual time-frame of the "69th generation" of Dan.9, and likewise the measurement of time that will make up the "fig tree" generation of Matt.24 preceding the coming of the Lord?

Now granted, it is not the perfect fit of 65 years that we found in Isa.7:8, but it is certainly close enough that it should merit our attention. One obvious conclusion that we could make, is that these two periods of time could definitely fall within the same generational time period, or qualify as being within the same general life span, as they are separated by only 5 years. Now I know that as we are nearing the end of this section of the book we are left with more questions than actual answers, but it cannot be overstated that what we have done is created a construct, a premise in which to continue our research, and to base it upon.

At this time let me just add this: I am not attempting to write a mystery novel, but as I have already stated, there is no benefit in short cutting the process. Realizing this, I am doing my best to share this knowledge with you the same way that I believe that God has shared it with me. Trust me when I tell you, if I jumped ahead of myself and just gave you the solution to this inconsistency as it relates to these two separate and distinct periods of time, many of you would not receive it without the scriptural proof, as well you shouldn't. Remember we are building a foundation, and for this cause, once more I must ask you to remain patient. As we move forward now, we will file away in our mental data-banks two seemingly very contradictory timelines: one of 65 years, and one of 70 years. I promise you, this will all become amazingly clear as we continue on.

"WITHIN" 65 YEARS OR 70?
(ISA.7:8)

In our earlier study of Isa.7:8 we found a God given timeline of "65 years" to precede the judgment of the northern kingdom of Ephraim. Upon further research we also discovered that this prophecy would have multiple fulfillments, including a third fulfillment which would be marked for the "end time" generation of Daniel's "69 weeks".

At the time that I learned of these "65 years", and its obvious connection to the coming of our Lord, it was very unsettling for me. In all of my prior research on the topic of a timeline I kept on finding 70 years not 65. As you might imagine this created quite a confusion for me. I knew that the 65 year time table was very significant, and as such, it was much too important to just ignore, no matter how many times I kept finding 70 years throughout other passages of scripture. Nonetheless, there was this nagging inconsistency that would have to be resolved before I could broaden my understanding more fully of the timeline in general.

I can't remember exactly how it came about, but through my continued studies of the book of Isaiah a startling revelation had begun to unfold for me. The initial wording of the passage in Isa.7:8 is what struck me the most, "...within 65 years Ephraim shall be broken". It was this use of the wording of "within" which stayed with me incessantly in a way that I cannot describe, it was as troubling for me as was the actual inconsistency of the 65 years itself, and it never left my mind.

This continued on until one day while I was studying **Isa.16:14** that I read these words: **"But now the LORD has**

spoken, saying, 'within three years, as the years of a hired man, the glory of Moab will be despised with all that great multitude, and the remnant will be very small and feeble."

Suddenly there was that word again, this time it would say "within three years". Almost immediately it became obvious to me that this was another prophetic timeline, and there was that same word "within", that had troubled me so much from the Isaiah 7 passage.

In this case, the verse of Isa.16:14 presented a timeline that was also intended to pronounce a similar impending judgment to that of Isa.7, although intended for a different people group all together, that being the people of "Moab"; but for me the same question came to mind: what would be the event that would trigger the countdown for these "three years"? After all, in Isa.7 we are clearly given "a sign" ("the virgin shall conceive and give birth to a son") that was to mark the beginning of its 65 year countdown, but here in Isa.16 no such sign was given.

It would not be long after before I would begin asking myself if these two timelines were somehow connected. Could this verse of Isa.16:14 be a continuation of Isa.7, and could these two timelines actually be one and the same? Could this passage of Isa.16 be saying to us that this timeline of "within three years" would follow immediately after the "within 65 years" of Isa.7?

For me the answer would be easy to arrive at if this was true, at least in theory. If these two passages were actually meant to be linked as one overall timeline than there should still be another missing part of the timeline which would consist of "two years" somewhere yet to be discovered in Isaiah; this would complete the "70 year" timeline that I had kept finding all over the Scriptures; just as the one that we have just previously discussed in the book of Zechariah.

Furthermore, once the multiple parts of this timeline were all in plain view a common sense approach would dictate that they could not exceed a total of 70 years, it would have to be exact if my theory was correct. Any additional timelines that might extend the overall count beyond 70 years would immediately prove my theory to be wrong.

However, I wouldn't have to wait long for the pieces of this puzzle to begin to fall into place. In the very next three verses of **Isa.17:1-3**, immediately following that of **Isa.16:14**, I would get a partial answer: **"The burden against Damascus. Behold, Damascus will cease from being a city, and it will be a ruinous heap... The fortress will also cease from Ephraim. The kingdom from Damascus, and the remnant of Syria, they will be as the glory of the children of Israel** (Ephraim)."

This was an unmistakable reference to the prophecy given in **Isa.7**. In this passage both **Ephraim** and **Syria** are mentioned as being under the judgment of God, and both are spoken of in terms of a coming future tense. It was as if the Holy Spirit had inspired Isaiah to drop this passage precisely there, that He might create the future link, so that someday it might be discovered as it references the two timelines as being interconnected.

On a purely related side-note, if these two timelines are one and the same, this would be an additional proof that the timeline of Isa.7 has an end time third fulfillment, as the total destruction of Damascus has never occurred in all of recorded history. Damascus today is the oldest surviving Biblical city still in existence, dating all the way back to Gen.14:15 and the time of Abram (even before he was Abraham).

It was at this time that I began a verse by verse examination of the book of Isaiah in search of any other potentially missing portions of this timeline. It would be this quest that would soon bring me to **Isa.21:16 "For this the LORD has spoken to me: within a year, according to the year of a hired man, all the glory of Kedar will fail..."** I was stunned, there it was that word **"within"** again, this time as it would relate to another timeline that would lead to another approaching judgment.

It would be by this passage that I would become fully convinced that what I was looking at was one singular timeline that had been broken up into multiple parts, or stages, in order that it might illuminate various other judgments that would befall other people groups (Moab and Kedar), as they would occur at various times following the judgment of Ephraim.

Equally astonishing was the terminology used in both Isa.16 and Isa.21 referring to "the years of a hired man" and "the year of a hired man". It would be the use of this wording that God would prevent the reader from attempting to apply anything other than a totally literal interpretation for these years, just as the "65 years" of Isa.7 wcre intended to be literal years. I was thoroughly convinced that what I was discovering was a complete and totally accurate prophetic timetable of the last generation leading up to Christ's return.

Here is another interesting side-bar: "Kedar" according to Gen.25:13 is listed among the 12 sons of Ishmael. By this prophecy of Isa.21:16 God may be giving us the actual timeline of the "Ps.83 war" as it falls "within" the countdown of the "fig tree" generation. Likewise, "Moab" is listed within this same prophecy. It could be possible that this timeline as it joins itself to that of Isa.7 would fill in the blanks as to the exact times that we might expect this war, that so many have studied so strenuously to discover. How appropriately placed is God's method of revealing it through the timeline of the rebirth of the nation of Israel as the "sign" that would begin that countdown as well.

In addition to this, "Kedar" is also mentioned in Ps.120:5 as it is related to a land, and or a people which are called "Mesech", which is also the same people group of "Meshech" of the "Ezk.38 war". It would be these two points of fact that would only further cement the issue for me, that these are all one and the same timeline, albeit three separate parts of that timeline.

In any case, it came to me soon after that, that I had seen this revelatory method used once before in a strikingly similar manner in none other than Dan.9 itself. One singular timeline divided into multiple parts, separate, and distinguishable, while remaining continuously one (70 weeks), while at the same time representing separate times of 62, 69, and 70 weeks, as well as clearly referencing different people groups (the Jews, the church, and "the one new man"), that equally would represent different events to occur within that same timeline, and likewise would be sporadically dispersed throughout Scripture through the means of multiple genealogies.

In truth, this method of God should not strike any of us as being anything out of the ordinary. In fact, this is precisely the method that he uses throughout Scripture to divulge all of His revelatory wisdom. Take for example God's very own covenant: God clearly demonstrates His covenant in multiple parts. First, through the Adamic Covenant, then later through the Noaic covenant, afterwards we have the Abrahamic covenant, and soon after that the Levitical covenant, next is the Davidic Covenant, and finally, we have the New Covenant of the "Firstborn" of God (Jesus Himself), with yet one more covenant to remain, and that of "the one new man."

These are not merely singular and solitary covenants as God has designed them and strategically set them in their place down through history, they are much more than that. They are beyond the shadow of a doubt the extensions of one another, forming and bonding into one greater and larger covenant overall.

I was immediately struck by the awe of the unfathomable wisdom of the Holy Spirit as I witnessed the great lengths that He had gone to in order to so ingeniously conceal this information in plain sight. I myself had studied over these same passages many times, before finally seeing the subtle linkage of these timelines, and even then, I only discovered it because He allowed me to see it.

I was invigorated as I meditated on the detail and preciseness of the word of God, but it was clear that the work was not yet finished. I had found three separate and distinct timelines that were most certainly linked together into one, but there was still one year missing. I had only uncovered a three part timeline that would account for 65 years (Isa.7:8), plus 3 more years (Isa.16:14), and then 1 year (Isa.21:16) totaling 69 years, but not 70. The search would have to continue.

It would finally be in **Isa.32:10** that the final piece of the 70th year of the timeline would be added, **"In a year and some days you will be troubled, you complacent women"** (New King

177

James Version). It must be stated right off that this chapter must be read in its entirety that one might see clearly the context in which this statement is given. As one might expect, it speaks of the end time deliverance of Jerusalem and the Jews, and the ushering in of the kingdom of our God, which is precisely what we would imagine it to say within the framework of the 70th and final year of the overall timeline.

It should also be noted that this chapter is an extension of Isaiah chapter 31, and as such it is fully addressed to the modern day nation of Israel and her people of the "end times". In fact, this is in my opinion the timetable for "the time of Jacob's trouble" (Jer.30:1-11).

I would also add that in the entire book of Isaiah there are no additional specifically comparative timelines given than these that I have already disclosed, or at least none that I am aware of.

In short, the "65 years" of Isa.7 is a preliminary timeline for the judgment of the northern kingdom of Ephraim, as it relates to its third fulfillment of the end times. Moreover, the completion of 70 years will see the end time deliverance of Jerusalem and the Jews (Judah) following the time of "Jacob's trouble", shortly after the "Ps.83 war", and the "Ezk.38 war". (For those of you that may not be overly familiar with these two terms of the "Ps.83 war", or the "Ezk.38 war", there will be a further explanation of these prophesied end time events later on in the book, as detailed in the section of "The volatility of the Middle East")

Moving still ahead, let us also not forget that this finding is exactly what we see in the prophecy of **Isa.8:14-15** where God pronounces a future judgment (a third fulfillment of Isa.7) **"To**

both the houses of Israel." In all of history past, since their division into two separate and distinct kingdoms, there has never been one all encompassing judgment on both houses of the northern and southern kingdoms of Israel at the same time.

History tells us that Ephraim suffered its judgment around 722BC, and Judah in 586BC, but never at the same time as this end time prophecy declares. In 722BC Ephraim is judged and Judah is delivered. In 586BC Judah is judged, and Ephraim has already been in captivity for 136 years.

Additionally, the judgment of 70AD (Christ's generation) can in no wise qualify as a total fulfillment of this prophecy, as that judgment would have only pertained to a very small remnant of both houses, where the third fulfillment of Isa.8 clearly states that "both houses" will be judged.

It is about this time that I would choose to bring this particular section of the book to its close. It was of course my awkward attempt to provide and make sense of the former inconsistency that we had encountered in the two previous sections in which we clearly developed our preliminary constructs of the Biblically described "65 years" of Isa., and the "70 years" which we found in Zechariah. Hopefully by this time, if I have done my work well, we have added the much needed further development to our initial framework in which we shall base the remainder of our study.

As persuasive as all of this might seem, many of you may be asking yourselves right about now: "Who is this end time Ephraim that the prophecy speaks of?" For now I can only respond to that question with what is unfortunately a deafening silence. For reasons that I cannot explain at this time, I am not at liberty to divulge the identity of this "latter days" entity called Ephraim. What I can tell you, is that if you have any doubts as to whether or not this end time Ephraim will actually exist in the "last days" of Daniel's "69th week", preceding the coming of Christ, I would recommend that you read Ezek.37:1-28.

Once again, we must not sidestep the process, nor become unfocused of our primary goal and intentions. There is still so much more that we must cover in order to provide the sufficient evidence for what we have already learned. I will however promise you this: by the end of the final chapter of this book, you will for a fact see all of this, so much more clearly than u do now.

THE END TIMES ACCORDING TO ENOCH

A perfect illustration of much of what we have learned to this point is the life of "Enoch" as described in Gen.5:21-32. This portion of scripture is truly amazing when one carefully dissects it through the lens of "duality". As we move forward in our study of its contents let me first just offer you this slight note of caution; some of what I am about to share with you may seem to be a bit confusing, or in some cases even a bit harder to digest. Let me just say that I can certainly appreciate the difficulty that some might encounter over the seemingly abstract manner in which I shall offer my interpretation of these following verses. Nonetheless, I would rather run the risk of your not being in total agreement with my assessments, rather than totally leave out this section altogether, and have never shared its remarkable contents with you at all.

Moving forward, it is my hope that this passage will serve to powerfully substantiate the prophetic process of Biblical duality, while at the same time providing a profound evidence of my earlier interpretations of Daniel 9; the two coming's of Christ; the church age as a whole; the *"Parable of the Fig Tree"*; the final timeline of Isa.7; the gathering together of the saints (mistakenly referred to as the rapture); the seals, trumpets, and bowls of Rev., as well as the final judgment and the millennial kingdom; and all of this in just 12 short verses. As you can see at the onset I have undertaken a very tall order.

To begin with let us take a casual look at the passage of Gen.5:21-32:

(v21) "Enoch lived sixty-five years, and begot Methuselah;

(v22) and Enoch walked with God after he begat Methuselah three hundred years, and begat sons and daughters:

(v23) And all the days of Enoch were three hundred and sixty-five years:

(v24) and Enoch walked with God; and he was not; for God took him.

(v25) And Methuselah lived an hundred eighty-seven years, and begat Lamech.

(v26) And Methuselah lived after he begat Lamech seven hundred eighty-two years, and begat sons and daughters;

(v27) and all the days of Methuselah were nine hundred sixty-nine years: and he died.

(v28) And Lamech lived an hundred eighty-two years, and begat a son;

(v29) and he called his name Noah, saying, 'This one shall comfort us concerning our work and the toil of our hands, because of the ground which the LORD has cursed.'

(v30) And Lamech lived after he begat Noah five hundred ninety-five years, and begat sons and daughters;

(v31) and all the days of Lamech were seven hundred seventy-seven years; and he died.

(v32) And Noah was five hundred years old; and Noah begat Shem, Ham, and Japheth."

At face value this passage of scripture does not exactly scream out to us "revelation knowledge!" On the contrary, it is one of those dreaded genealogies that may seem so tedious and burdensome for us all to read through. In fact, if it screams anything at all to the average reader it might be saying "skip over me, I'm not important!" However, let us not forget one very important fact... this too was inspired by the Holy Spirit, and if we have learned anything by now, we know that one cannot even begin to unravel its underlying mysteries until its author has begun to teach it.

Obviously it's truest heart and soul as it relates to revelatory knowledge is in the actual 10 literal generations that would represent the first leg of Daniel's "70 weeks", in the holy ancestral lineage that would eventually reveal our Lord and Savior Christ Jesus through His two comings, just as we have learned previously in our studies. However, as the nature of "duality" goes, it is fully representative of a great deal more than what the naked eye is capable of detecting on its own.

Our starting point for addressing the extensive dual meaning behind this passage begins with two very essential truths: first, this passage is setting the stage for the buildup to the judgment of the great flood; and secondly, it is primarily addressing the 7th generation from Adam to Enoch preceding that great judgment, as we shall soon see.

By these two points alone it becomes an invaluable pattern for the 7th and final church generation of the "end times" leading up to the final judgment of God (the tribulation period of Rev.); and I believe with great certainty that this was exactly the additional shadowed intention of God's Holy Spirit when He inspired its writing.

Now, let me first say that in my ensuing attempt to explain the depth and profoundness of the hidden wisdom and knowledge that exists within this text I am completely inadequate for the task. Once again this is a clear case of the message being exceedingly greater than my own ability to convey it, so I will apologize a forehand as I will clumsily attempt to point out the shadows and types as they exist, and the rest I will leave to the trust of the True Teacher, who is of course the Holy Spirit.

A) Enoch represents the 7th and final church generation (Rev.3:14-22), as he is the seventh generation from Adam, and we are clearly the seventh church generation from the second Adam (I Cor.15:45-47).

B) A monumental event occurs within the 65th year (Isa.7:8) of Enoch's life, this event is the birth of a son (Isa.7:14) that will eventually act as "a sign" of the coming of the end of God's grace to the world, and the ensuing judgment.

- Methuselah will live a total of 969 years (v27); he will live 187 years at which time he will "begat Lemech" (v25). Afterwards, Lemech would live 182 years and have a son named Noah (v28-29); this would make Methuselah 369 years old at Noah's birth.

- According to Gen.7:11 Noah would be exactly 600 years old at the time of the great flood, this in turn would also make Methuselah exactly 969 years old when the flood waters came. By this elementary math we can easily see that Methuselah died the exact same year of the flood, which is why he is not listed as a passenger on the Ark. What we have here is a perfect illustration of "the fig tree" generation of Matt.24:32-34, "This generation shall not pass, until all these things be fulfilled.

- Likewise, Methuselah's name itself means in the Hebrew language "His death will bring"; this definition not only confirms what I have just stated but just as importantly it confirms that he was "an appointed generation" just as "the fig tree generation" is "appointed". Just as the end of Methuselah's generation would similarly bring both judgment for the world, and deliverance for the children of God (Noah and his family), so also shall the "fig tree generation" preceding Christ's return. The parallels are entirely unmistakable.

- Furthermore, let us not forget that this is exactly what we found in Isa.7, in Isaiah's portrayal of the "Parable of the Fig Tree", and the mention of "65 years", as well as their combined connection to a coming judgment.

C) Noah in this context is a shadow and a type of Jesus Himself. Noah's name in Hebrew means "Rest and comfort" (Heb.4:1-3, 9-11).

- In Gen.5:29 Noah is presented as "This one will comfort us concerning our work and the toil of our hands, because of the ground which the LORD has cursed." By this verse he is a similitude of the One (Jesus), who is "our rest", and who would come and end the "work and toil" of our self-righteous works, and put an end to the "curse" of the law. Furthermore, He shall accomplish this work through the power of His Holy Spirit who is called in John14:16, 26 "the Comforter".

- Additionally, it would be Noah who would build "the ark" that would result in a great deliverance during the time of judgment; even so it is Jesus who sits forever enthroned upon "the ark of the covenant", who forever makes intercession for God's children, acting as their heavenly mediator to deliver them from the eternal judgment which is to come.

D) Equally astonishing is this: if one does the math from Enoch's birth to Noah's birth, it comes to a total of 434 years. This would be calculated through adding the "65 years" of (v21), with the "187 years" of (v25), and lastly with the "182 years" of (v28-29). This is a shadow of Christ's first coming in the 62nd week of Dan.9:26, or (62 x 7 = 434 years).

- Similarly, we find this: according to Gen.5:23-24, "And Enoch walked with God: and he was not, for God took him" Moreover, these verses tell us that Enoch was "365 years" old at the time of this event. By subtracting the 365 years from the 434 years, this would firmly place the time of Enoch's departure unto heaven exactly 69 years before the birth of Noah (Jesus' similitude), and thereby creating a subtle linkage between the number 69 with the actual rapture event itself.

- It is in my opinion, that given the intricacies that we have already observed in this passage, it is quite possible that this is a fleeting glimpse of the 69th week of Dan.9:25, and Christ's second coming, in which the church will be "caught up" to be with the Lord at the conclusion of the 7th church generation (I Thess.4:16-17).

E) In addition to all of this, the term "walked with God" as it is used in reference to Enoch (7th church representative) shadows the counsel of Jesus to the Laodicean church of Rev.3:14-22 to reject the "lukewarm" attitude and to "open the door" to intimacy and relationship with Him preceding His return.

- Not to be lost is the fact that this term: "walked with God" is mentioned twice, this is likewise a prophetic shadow of the "former and latter rain" of Hos.6:3; Joel2:23, 28-29; Acts2:16-21, and Zech.10:1-9, which would be appointed to occur in both the "62nd week", and the "69th week" of Daniel, at the precise time of both of Christ's appearances. I make this assumption based purely on the Biblical fact that one could only achieve this impossible unity and fellowship with God except through the indwelling and filling of the Holy Spirit.

F) Moving on now to Lamech, according to (v31) he lives a total of 777 years, which symbolizes the 7 seals, 7 trumpets, and 7 bowls of Rev.6; 8; 16, signifying the tribulation period, and similarly the triumphant return of Jesus soon afterwards, just as Noah himself would later come down from Mt. Ararat (Gen.8:4) after the judgment had subsided.

- Additionally, as one might expect the name "Lemech" in Hebrew means "despairing", denoting the judgment of God that would serve as the preliminary event leading up to His Son's arrival. It is also instrumental to our understanding that we realize that mathematically he also dies 5 years before the flood which signifies the same space of time between the 65 years and the 70 years of Isaiah's timeline in which the end time judgment will fall, as it relates to us today.

- Mathematically it would look like this: Lamech lives 182 years before the birth of his son Noah. He then would live another 595 years after the birth of Noah totaling 777 years. This would make Noah 595 years old at the time of his father's death, and as we know the flood would come in the 600ᵗʰ year of Noah's life, exactly 5 years later. A truly remarkable likeness to that of Isa.7:8; 16:14; 21:16; 32:10.

- And even yet more precise is the passage of Gen.8:13-14 where we see the conclusion of the flood after one year and 10 days, this would be a perfect illustration for the fulfillment of Isa.32:10 "in a year and some days"; which is also Jer.30:7 "the time of Jacob's trouble", or the 70ᵗʰ year of the Isaiah timeline, as represented by the flood.

- Likewise, the 600 years of Noah's age at the time of the flood may clearly represent the end of 6,000 years (Gen.2:1-4) of man's human government.

G) Immediately following the judgment we see the sons of Noah; Shem, Ham, and Japheth, symbolizing the sons of Abraham: Isaac and Ishmael, as well as the gentile nations that have been brought through the judgment, re-inhabiting the earth after its cleansing of sin during the Millennial Kingdom. In this illustration everything is totally present, modern day Israel, the Arab remnant, and likewise the Church.

H) And let us not forget, as the prophecy of Dan.9 would have it, all of this is revealed to us through the genealogical bloodline of the first Adam, and the second Adam, as it aligns with the "70 weeks", and all to be revealed through the use of scriptural duality (Eccl.1:4-11).

I) And lastly, all of this is strategically placed by God in scripture, as it finds its origins in the 7th generation (7th church generation) of Enoch, while simultaneously placing it within the larger framework of the first 10 generations from Adam to Noah, which would equally serve to spell out the entire Gospel message by use of the Hebrew definitions of each generational name given:

English	Hebrew
Adam	Man (creation)
Seth	Appointed to (Gen.3 "the garden")
Enosh	Mortal (the curse of sin "death")
Kenan	Sorrow (the fall)
Mahalelel	The blessed God (Christ's deity)
Jared	Shall come down (1st coming)
Enoch	Teaching (ministry of the word)
Methuselah	His death will bring (crucifixion/grace)
Lamech	Despairing (judgment)
Noah	Rest or comfort (2nd coming)

It should be needless of me to say at this point that the comparisons and parallels go on and on. In fact, I am quite certain that still lying within this text is a wealth of hidden treasure that is yet to be prophetically unearthed.

For that matter, at this time I did not even choose to expose the 1,335 days of Dan. 12:12, or the appearance of the Antichrist for that matter, which are also hidden within this monumental text; and to that I can only say that I have my reasons.

However, we will stop here with what we have already uncovered, as it would seem to me that we have accomplished our initial purpose in which we had originally set out to do.

For the sake of the question that we were initially attempting to answer coming in to this passage: "How long is the 69th end time generation?", what we have seen is a striking similarity to both the timelines of Dan.9 as well the Isaiah timeline itself, albeit ever so concealed and linked together as two parts of one single timeline as a whole, just as Isaiah's is.

In short, the passage begins with a period of 65 years leading to Methuselah's birth (last generation), and ending with Lemech's death 5 years prior to the flood (tribulation period), after which Methuselah dies in the exact year of the flood, or 5 years later. And through it all it must not be lost that Enoch as the 7th generation is the common denominator that binds it all together.

Again, I must apologize for taking you, the reader, in such an around the bout manner to get to this knowledge, but once again you can clearly see just how intricately the Holy Spirit has hidden this information, as He has reserved it only for the end time generation, and even then, only for those in whom He chooses to reveal it.

As we conclude this section of our study I would wish to leave you with the words of **Hab.2:3 "For the vision is yet for an appointed time, but at the end it shall speak, and not lie, though it tarry, wait for it, because it will surely come, it will not tarry."**

THE WILDERNESS EXAMPLE
(1 COR.10:11)

"Now all these things happened to them as examples; and they were written for our admonition, upon whom the ends of the ages have come."

By this verse Paul is making it absolutely clear that the events of Israel's wilderness experience was fully documented with the subsequent intention of instructing the end time generation. Paul is saying, under no uncertain terms, that we the 7th and final church generation can learn much from their generation. If one takes a closer look you will be sure to find that the parallels are strikingly undeniable once again: there's the coming of a deliverer (Moses/ Jesus); there's also an Antichrist prototype (Pharaoh); there's a final judgment (10 plagues/bowls of Rev.), and a great heavenly deliverance (Red Sea crossing/ "the gathering together" of I Cor.15:51-52), culminating with the Promised Land ("inheritance of the saints"); and these are but a few of the many similitude's and comparisons that exist between their generation and the generation that is to see the fulfillment of the "latter days". As one can easily see this makes for a superb case study as it regards our 7th and final church generation.

Moreover, lying hidden beneath this text, as we shall soon see, is another uniquely constructed generational timeline in which to compare with all that we have learned through our previous research. This passage like the others that we have studied is unmistakably fertile ground for the proper scriptural use of end time duality, as Paul himself so perfectly testifies in I Cor.10:11.

We will now take up this search beginning in the book of Numbers, but first, a little background knowledge might be very useful. In Num.13-14 we read of the detailed account of the children of Israel after the Red Sea crossing, and after the events of Mount Sinai and the Ten Commandments.

By this time Israel has been led by the pillar of fire by night, and the pillar of the cloud by day, as they have traveled along the rugged wilderness route to their much anticipated destination. It at this time that God has brought them at last to the very border of the Promised Land, and positioned them ever so strategically to gain its long awaited possession.

Furthermore, it is at this time that Joshua sends out the twelve spies to spy out the new land and bring back a report to the children of Israel. Shortly after, the spies would then return with a less than favorable report concerning the sizable obstacles that would stand in the way of the new nation from inheriting the land.

Upon receiving the discouraging report, the children of Israel would then make a monumental blunder, they would choose to believe the negative report of the spies over the command and promise of God to "take the land at once". In this the most crucial of all moments, when they should have been swelling with faith, courage, and great anticipation, they have shrunken back in fear, unbelief, and rebellion against God, and as they would soon find out, this would not be without the severest of consequences.

We are now ready to take a look at **Num.14:22-39**. For the purpose of our study we will focus primarily on verses 29 and 34, **(v29) "Your carcasses shall fall in this wilderness; and all that were numbered of you, according to your whole number,**

from twenty years old and upward, which have murmured against me... (v34) After the number of days in which you searched the land, even forty days, each day for a year, shall you bear your iniquities, even forty years, and you shall know my breach of promise."

This very passage has caused many to question whether or not a "Biblical generation" could possibly be associated with a forty year period of time, this however is clearly a mistake. It becomes obvious from the context of this scripture that those that fell under this judgment were already 20 years old and over at the time that the judgment was handed down by God. This would place the youngest of this effected group at a minimum of 60 years of age by the time that the prescribed 40 years would have concluded, and numerous others even older than that. Using this logic it becomes plain to see that the "forty years" is only one part of a larger period of time that would make up this "wilderness generational timeline"; that sounds awfully familiar, does it not? (The Daniel and Isaiah timelines)

However, what can help us in determining the length of this generation is not our being so dependent on our search for who doesn't inherit the land, but more importantly those that do. Consider this: this generation as we know does not see the fulfillment of the crossing over to the Promised Land, thereby leaving it incomplete for our use of substantiating a definitive timeline. Although, those that would enter into the Promised Land at the end of the forty years, these would be our most likely candidates in which to pursue our study. As they would eventually complete the transition to the Promised Land, they would likewise, uniformly fulfill the timeline and see it to its completion as well.

I now turn your attention to **Num.1:2-3**: **"Take you the sum of all the congregation of the children Israel, after their families, by the house of their fathers, with the number of their names, every male by their polls; from twenty years old and upward, all that are able to go forth to war in Israel; you and Aaron shall number them by their armies."**

Here we see the foundational basis for God's initial command to number all of those that were 20 years old and older. He is plainly organizing an army, by ranks, for the ensuing conquest of the land. This in turn would make perfect sense that God would so harshly judge all those that were numbered over twenty years of age, as they were to be the very men that would bear the brunt of the military campaign, and thus clearing the way for the children of Israel to inherit the land, prior to their refusal to do so.

When the children of Israel shrunk back from their obligation to take the land as God had commanded them, it would be of a necessity that the military would be found right off, as the foremost negligent party in its duties. This was in every respect an ancient example of a military mutiny, and so we see the judgment of God being administered to a delinquent and cowardly AWOL army.

Later in **Deut.2:14-18** we read this: **"And the space in which we came from Kadesh-barnea, until we were come over the brook Zered, was thirty and eight years; until all the generation of the men of war were wasted out from among the host, as the LORD swore unto them. For indeed the hand of the LORD was against them, to destroy them from among the host, until they were consumed. So it came to pass, when all the men of war were consumed and dead from among** the people, that the LORD spoke unto me, saying, 'You are to pass over through the Ar, the coast of Moab, this day..."

So now we see more clearly that the 40 year judgment was not to the nation as a whole, but more precisely directed at only those who were of military age at the time that God had passed down His original judgment. Additionally, we should be able to see the fruitlessness of pursuing this avenue of investigation any further. With this understanding firmly seated in our minds let us now turn our sights on those that did enter the Promised Land.

Returning back now to **Num.1** where we found the initial numbering of all of those who were of military age, we shall likewise find our potential subject of research. Beginning in **(v45-50)**, we read in **(v47)**, **"But the Levites after the tribe of their fathers were not numbered among them. (v48) For the LORD had spoken unto Moses, saying, (v49) Only you shall not number the tribe of Levi, neither take the sum of them among the children of Israel; (50) but you shall appoint the Levites over the tabernacle of testimony..."**

In this passage it is plain for all to see, the priesthood was not a part of the census that would later fall into judgment, in fact, they were wholly excluded by Divine order from participating in the actual combat of future military campaigns, theirs was to be a holy order unto the service of their God and His holy tabernacle, only.

By the very nature of their ministries they were to be exempted from the repercussions of God's prohibition for entering into the land, and as a result the priesthood would in fact be among those that would enter the Promised Land.

It is by this knowledge that we shall redirect our central focus solely upon the priesthood of Israel.

In all of my research, I have found that there are only two other potential timelines given in the entire account of the wilderness event that may qualify as possible fragments of "the wilderness generational timeline", and as it should come as no surprise, they are both directly related to this same priesthood.

The first that we shall look at comes from **Num.4:1-3 "and the LORD spoke unto Moses and unto Aaron, saying, 'Take the sum of the sons of Kohath from among the sons of Levi, after their families, by the house of their fathers, from thirty years old and upward..."**

In this entirely different calculation, of an entirely separate and distinct people group from that of the military census, we see a significantly different approach to the numbering process as ordered earlier by God. Rather than the previous census in which the men were numbered from "twenty years of age and upward", here the prescribed method would entail all of those from the age of "thirty years old and upward".

Jumping immediately ahead to our second potential subject of study, we shall see yet another completely separate census from that even of "the sons of Kohath". Look now at **Num.8:24 "This is it that belongs unto the Levites; from twenty and five years old and upward..."**

At a quick glance these two passages would appear to be a contradiction of one another, as one clearly offers a cut off of 30 years of age, while similarly the other provides a precise cut off of 25 years, this is actually very easily explained. These are not the same group, but rather two separate and distinct groups. One group is clearly addressing "the sons of Kohath"

(Num.4:1-3), while the other group is singularly directed at "the Levites" (Num.8:24) in general. Now for the sake of clarification, it should be noted that both are clearly Levites, but both are not clearly Kohathites. If this is a source of confusion for you, a perfect illustration of this in modern terms would be: All native born Texans are clearly Americans, but all Americans are clearly not Texans.

The tribe of Kohath was a specific family of the Levites that were given the very personalized ministry of handling all of the leadership responsibilities of the priesthood in its entirety. It was from this very same ancestral family line that Moses and Aaron themselves would stem from, similarly, every High Priest of Israel would likewise find their origins through this same tribal genealogy.

On the contrary, the Levites as a general priestly tribe as a whole, were subordinates to the Kohathites, given a much different administration by God in regard to their duties and service of the tabernacle. By this understanding we can see that the two distinct cut off ages of 30 years and 25 years are not contradictory at all. In fact, it could be quite possible that because the Kohathites bore a much higher level of responsibility concerning the things of the tabernacle, it would make perfect sense for them to be a little older and more matured as a precondition to their preparation for their priestly duties.

In any case, what we end up with is two distinct families of priests, both entering the Promised Land, one group would be at a minimum of 65 years old (after the 40 year wilderness judgment), while the other group would be a minimum of 70 years old; and once again we see the familiar 5 year segmental divide that we have witnessed in the earlier sections we have previously covered. Here, God in perfect continuity, is once again in His most unique manner, providing an additional insight to the two timelines of 65 and 70 years as they converge to form a singular timeline.

And let it not be lost upon us, our consideration of the elusively disguised manner in which God has once again encased this knowledge out of the sight of the casual reader, while simultaneously placing it in the plain view of all to see. How magnificently and uniquely God.

The final point that I would wish to make in the conclusion of this section is found in Josh.14:6-14. A brief summary of the thirteen chapters of Joshua leading up to this passage details the crossing over the river Jordan, and the conquest of the new land.

Fast forwarding now to **Josh.14:7-10**, where we see Caleb speaking: **"I was forty years old when Moses the servant of the LORD sent me from Kadesh-Barnea to spy out the land..."** And then in **(v10)**, **"And now, behold, the LORD has kept me alive, as He said, these forty five years, ever since the LORD spoke this word to Moses while Israel wandered in the wilderness; and now, here I am this day, eighty-five years old."**

The significance of this passage is powerful when fully understood. This passage marks the final battle recorded in the initial conquest of the Promised Land. According to the information of these two verses the conquest of the Promised Land would have lasted a total of five years. These 5 years have an extreme prophetical significance in the understanding of the overall timeline.

What you have here, is a circling back in the manner of "Scriptural duality" on the part of God in the telling of the events of the last five years of the end time timeline. A foretelling so to speak of the dramatic events that would transpire during this same mysterious period of time that would lead up to the eventual "inheritance of the saints" as spelled out in the book of Revelation. This is precisely why the conquest would begin with the crossing over of the river Jordan and then proceeding on to the amazing details of the historical account of the victory at the city of Jericho.

What God is demonstrating through all of this is the second "outpouring of the Holy Spirit" of the "latter days" (Joel2:28 and Zech.10:1-9), by means of "the latter rain" (crossing the Jordan), even as the "former rain" had been fulfilled by the "Red Sea crossing" (Acts2:14-21) upon a generation that had gone before them; and then the subsequent events of the 7 seals, 7trumpets, and the 7 bowls of Rev., as represented by the city of Jericho's detailed account, that would immediately follow.

Lastly, we see the appointed generation as they arise to the task of the "overcomer" and valiantly inherit the land as God Himself provides the victory. In short, the 5 years of the conquest of Joshua are representative of the prophetic end time 5 year period that would be fulfilled between the 65th and 70 years that would be required to inherit the land, leading to the coming return of our Lord Jesus.

Additionally, by this prophetic shadow of the entering into the Promised Land we are looking at the end time fulfillment of the same 65 and 70 years as it would be fulfilled through both the northern and southern kingdoms of Ephraim and Judah, of Ezk37:16-23 simultaneously, thus we see them represented by two distinct priestly families.

In conclusion, what we find in the wilderness account is another perfect illustration of the end time timeline that we saw in the book of Isaiah, and let us not forget that this is exactly what we found in Gen.5 (Enoch) as well. In the case of Enoch it begins with the 7th church generation (appointed generation), and then a 65 year time period, and then ends with the death of Lemech after 777 years (seals, trumpets, bowls, and fully illustrated by the victory at Jericho), and ends 5 years later with the great flood (judgment), and Noah (which means: "rest") coming down from the mountain high above as a direct correlation to that of Christ's return. And all of this to be extensively drawn through the same method of incremental and segmental divides of multiple timelines as they form into one single and solitary timeline consisting in its completed form of 70, just as with all of our other prophetic examples (Dan.9 included).

The parallels are profoundly precise if studied closely, and under the impeccable toolage of the Holy Spirit of God. These are definitive Scriptural witnesses that must not go ignored. I firmly believe that the primary distinction between those that actually enter the land and those that do not are also fully representative of the Laodicean church of Rev.3:14-22, and a remnant of that church that will enter "His rest".

A CLOSER LOOK AT JESUS' FIRST COMING

Earlier in the book we touched briefly on many of the specifics regarding the two comings of Christ as they would perfectly correlate with the "62 weeks", and the "69 weeks" of Dan.9. We had clearly determined at that time, through the means of much study, that the word "weeks" was a precise representation of a multi-varied collection of Biblical "generations" leading up to the two comings of our Savior and Lord Christ Jesus.

In this section, my primary aim will be to provide you with still yet another timeline that equally pertains to the very same prophecy of Daniel. In this one we shall discover a substantive truth as it concerns God's own use of the word "weeks", and that truth as we shall soon find out, lies in the Hebrew definition of the word "seven", as this is but another way of Biblically defining the word of "weeks". It will also be through this definition that we shall discover another most interesting insight to the next timeline on our list.

Go back with me now to the prophecy of **Dan.9:25**, where it clearly states, **"Know therefore and understand, that from the going forth of the commandment to restore and to build Jerusalem unto the Messiah the Prince shall be seven weeks, and sixty two weeks..."** (69 weeks total).

Earlier on, I briefly covered my reasoning for believing that King Artaxerxes of Persia would have been the one best suited, according to the specifics of this prophecy, to have given this decree. Among the three decrees that would be instituted prior to Christ's 1st coming, only Artaxerxes decree clearly defines the rebuilding of the city and the walls of Jerusalem, as the book of Nehemiah clearly attests to, where the other two decrees of King Cyrus and King Darius seem to be more centralized upon the actual reconstruction of the temple itself.

The Encyclopedia Britannica lists the reign of King Artaxerxes of Persia from 464BC to 424BC. This time frame is considered as being historically accurate by many, if not most Biblical scholars today. Assuming that this dating is correct, let us move now to Neh.2:1 where we read, "And it came to pass in the month of Nisan, in the twentieth year of Artaxerxes the king..." This verse gives us the exact year of Artaxerxes reign in which he fulfills Nehemiah's request to go and rebuild the city of Jerusalem, placing the precise time of his decree in the year of 444BC, according to the dating in which we have just established.

Now, if we do the math of Dan.9:25 we come up with a simple calculation of 69 (weeks) x 7 (1 week) = 483 years, to be fulfilled after the decree of Artaxerxes, "unto the Messiah".

By this most basic of deductions, we shall then continue forward 483 years from our initial computation of 444BC (time of the decree), this would leave us at the exact year of 39AD as the year of the actual crucifixion of Christ (Dan.9:26).

Furthermore, if we then subtract 34 years (Jesus' life span rounded off), moving back in time from the cross, we come to the year of 5AD. It is here that we see the perfect alignment of the date of 5AD with that of the prophecy of Isa.7:8-14. This math places Christ's birth at the exact year of 5AD, and exactly 65 years before the judgment on Judah and Jerusalem of 70AD, as precisely prophesied according to the passage of Isa.7:8-14.

Additionally, it is a perfect illustration as well of Dan.9:27 (Daniels 70th week) where it states: "He shall confirm the covenant with many for one week ("the passion" week), and in the midst of the week (Wednesday crucifixion) He shall cause the sacrifice and oblation to cease..."

As an additional dual fulfillment, it says in **Luke 3:21-23** **"Now Jesus Himself began His ministry at about thirty years of age..."** This too would also serve as a precise multiple fulfillment if we were to consider that He was born in 5AD, therefore, 30 years later would place the year of His baptism (start of His 3 1/2 year ministry) at 35AD, and this too would be exact in representing "the midst of the week", as it would be thoroughly precise in its placement of the "middle" or "midst" of a 70 year countdown that would lead to judgment, concluding in 70AD.

Now some of you may be saying to yourselves right about now... "Wait a minute. This guy is just appointing whatever amount of time is most convenient for him to qualify his own interpretations."

The actual truth of the matter is this: the "weeks" of Daniel are representations of many interchangeable periods of time as they are to represent various illustrations of the God Man Jesus, as well as representations of the Father Himself, and of the Holy Spirit simultaneously, while at the same time fully illustrating His Church, and the Jews as well; and as such, let us not forget that time itself is God's own creation. In order for time to accurately portray such a wide variance of God in all of His revealing's to man, time itself must carry with it the multiple characteristics and patterns of God.

Now consider this: God in His essence is a trinity, and therefore He may be understood in a multiple of ways without ever creating a contradiction. Likewise, his earthly genealogy may at one time represent 7,000 years (Adam to the millennium), while at the same time represent 70 generations, which can also be represented by the inclusion of a singular church age, or a division of 7 church generations comprising of "one week".

Furthermore, the "weeks" can find their meaning in singular years such as the 483 years of Daniel's countdown to His 1st coming. Likewise, it can be a perfect illustration of the 49 days leading to the Holy Spirit, or in another space of time a "week" can carry the obvious meaning of a singular week, or 7 days (as in the week of His crucifixion). And lastly, as we shall see later on in another chapter, a "week" can also refer to a millennium (1,000 years).

As we had discussed earlier in the book, these are all examples of God using the repetitive cycles of time as they exist within the spiritual framework of "duality" in order to utilize a singular prophecy of Scripture to illuminate a vast collection of multiple events as He would desire them to be brought to their fulfillment over a varied set of appointed times.

Now, let us examine the Hebrew definition for the word "seven" (a "week") as we find it in the *Strong's concordance*: (#7651,) "a primary cardinal number; seven (as the sacred full one); also seven times; by extension an indefinite number: - (by) seven [-fold], sevens, times,"

In short, what we find is that the "weeks" of Daniel can be defined in a multiple of ways, and they are all interchangeable at any given time as God Himself sees fit to utilize them in accordance with whatever it is that He wishes to convey at that moment in time in which He wishes to address. Time is His faithful servant, and the Biblical timelines bare the multiple reflections of His character, nature, and many plans and purposes, as it is the true expression of Him, His Son, and His Holy Spirit, given to man.

Furthermore, when God say's **"I am the same yesterday, today, and forever" (Heb.13:8)**, the timeline of **Daniel 9** illustrates this reality perfectly; this is all but a small thing for God. In another passage, when speaking with Moses, He Himself qualifies His own personage with the name **"I Am that I Am" (Ex3:14)**, this is another inflection to the multiplicity of the expansive Biblical expressions of God. In order for time to reflect such an Eternal God within the structured scaffold of time itself, it must be multi-layered and accessible to express a wide variance of times and multiples, over an unlimited period of time, while simultaneously remaining forever consistently one.

The prophecy of Daniel 9 is the personification of this truth, although it clearly represents a singular timeline from Adam to the millennium, it additionally carries a multiple of timelines that represent the fall of the northern kingdom, the fall of the southern kingdom, the first coming of Christ and the judgment of 70AD, the coming of the Holy Spirit, the church age as a whole, or broken down into generations, likewise, the second coming of Christ, as well as the millennium separately and by itself; and it does all of this without ever compromising the integrity of a singular word... "Weeks".

This is the essence of the nature of "Biblical duality" and what makes it work. Time is His obedient servant and creation, just as God Himself has ordained it. God is not a servant of time (as we so often seem to be), God is, as should be expected, the Master of time.

With all of that said, let me now tie all of this in for you as best I can. Let us not have missed the point of this section entirely: once more, what we see here again, in the generation of Jesus' 1st coming, is the fulfillment of another obscurely hidden timeline ingeniously interwoven within the prophecy of Dan.9, as Daniel 9 is simultaneously linked to that of other prophecies, as well as the historical record itself; and accurately portraying a fragmented period of 5 years (5AD), and another one of 65 years (to conclude in 70 AD), and yet once more combining the two into a total of 70 years, as with the book of Isaiah; and Gen.5 (Enoch); and "the wilderness generation"; and unless we forget, all five are similitude's of the "end times" of the book of Revelation, and all five (Jesus' generation included) equally concluding with a great judgment. This would seem to beg to ask if this same 70 year pattern (65 years and 5 years) might reemerge again in this final end time generation.

There is so much more that I could add to what I have already shared, but by this time I should have given you enough to keep you meditating on these things for quite some time. I will, however, just add this: as we continue to find this same repetition re-occurring over and over again, spaced out over the entirety of the historical Biblical record, do we really believe that this exact same theme will not play out once again at the close of all of human history?

Is this logical thinking on our part to ignore this truth, or to assign it as something to be of little importance? Or are the facts so great that we must sit up and take a much more sober approach to the way we see the times in which we now live? Let us not forget that as I am writing these very words, at this very moment, we are coming to the rapid close of the 65th year

(May15[th], 2014) since the nation of Israel was formed in May of 1948, and the *"Parable of the Fig Tree"* was fulfilled (Matt.24). What does this all mean for us as a planet as we find ourselves proceeding into that same dramatic 5 year period between the 65th and the 70th year of these prophecies and historical events? In closing, I can assure you of this much... we won't have to wait long to find out.

THE TRIBULATION PERIOD OF JOB

In the event that there may be some of you that still remain unconvinced of our findings thus far, possibly still unswayed by the multiple points of study I have chosen to highlight, here is another hopefully startling proof to add to the collection. My goal by now should be perfectly obvious, it is to make it as plain to the reader as I know how, when I say, this 70 year timeline that we have been studying is everywhere throughout scripture, and there are no other opposing timelines offered throughout the word of God that I have been able to find, in which for us to draw from.

Our next stop will be in the book of Job. In order for us to properly begin we must first attempt to understand: who does Job represent prophetically? Our purpose for determining the answer to this question is that it will help us extensively in creating a foundational footing in which to examine the contents of this book, within any prophetical significance that it might contain, and that would otherwise go unnoticed.

A good starting place for resolving the solution to this inquiry is found in the definition of Job's name itself, after all, it was Solomon who stated in **Eccl.6:10 "Whatever one is, he has been named already."**

Initially, the name of Job in the Hebrew language means: *Strong's concordance* (#347,340) "Hated; persecuted, be an enemy, to be hostile, as one of an opposite tribe or party." This definition according to the *Strong's Concordance* is extremely revealing. It is emphatically alerting us to the simple truth that Job, at the onset, has an enemy. For that matter, the reality of this truth becomes immediately obvious for anyone that reads the book of Job.

In Job1:6-12; 2:1-7 the book wastes no time in revealing the identity of this hated foe by name, it is Satan himself. Additionally, the name of Satan in Hebrew means: *Strong's concordance* (#7854, 7853) "an opponent; the arch-enemy of good, adversary, withstand, attack, to accuse, resist."

In plain language, by the very definitions of the names of both Job and Satan, these would seem to indicate a predetermined combative encounter that would eventually be inevitable between the two parties, and as u shall soon see, this knowledge will serve us well as we continue on with our research of the underlying premise that clearly exists beneath the casual observations of this book.

It is instrumental to our understanding that we realize that the events that would follow throughout the book of Job, were not spontaneous as the writing might seem to indicate. In this book, Job is highly beloved by God, and is prospering beyond any reasonable earthly expectations as the result of God's favor.

In fact, in **Job 1:3** he is even said to be **"...the greatest of all the people of the East."** This is an all inclusive statement pertaining not just to Job's wealth of spiritual knowledge and wisdom, but also his financial status as well. Job is unquestionably more blessed than any other of his time.

However, as the book continues it takes a very sudden and unexpected turn. Job is plunged into a series of horrific events that seem to befall him without any warning or explanation. At an initial glance we may be tempted to see this episode unfolding as being a shocking occurrence, as well as unfair and inconsistent with the goodness and mercy of God. Unless, we go into this study realizing that this seemingly tragic series of developments is actually a predetermined, and preordained encounter by God Himself. It is by this knowledge that one thing becomes quite certain: God has an immense purpose that is not easily seen or understood at the start of this book, and His purpose is for the good of Job, as well as for the good of every reader of this book, as we shall soon see.

Fast forwarding now through the many manifold sufferings of Job, and we come to the end of the book, where atlas Job is vindicated by God, and recompensed for his faithfulness. Job has been tested, proven, and refined like pure gold after it has come out of the furnace of affliction. He has become in all actuality, the standard for what it means to be an "overcomer" (Rev.2:7, 11, 17, 26; 3:5, 12, 21; 21:7).

In short, God has exemplified His great love of Job by allowing him to go through this suffering, and triumphantly bringing him out on the other side of this enormous adversity, as the greatest of testimonials, exemplifying him as the personification of what it means to be steadfast and faithful in the face of the cruelest of hardships and trials; and all of this to be done for all the world to see.

Now you might ask: How could this all be true? How could a loving God permissively allow this type of grave injustice to be done upon His own beloved Job? I will let the Apostle Paul answer this question in the way that only he can: **Phil.1:29 "For to you it has been granted on behalf of Christ, not only to believe in Him, but also to suffer for His sake, having the same conflict which you saw in me, and now hear is in me."**

And again, we read in **Phil.3:8-10 "...that I may know Him and the power of His resurrection, and the fellowship of His sufferings, being conformed to His death..."**

By these passages we can see more clearly that it was out of God's great love for Job that He "granted" Job the extreme privilege of "suffering for His sake", that he might "know" Christ on the deepest of levels, through "the fellowship of His sufferings", and experience first-hand "the power of His resurrection". Job through all of his trials, would gain most importantly of all, the gift of uniformity and experiential oneness with the persecutions of Christ.

Moreover, Job too would experience a form of the resurrection when he was miraculously brought forth from the impending grave of death and restored double-fold as it states in **Job42:10 "...the LORD gave Job twice as much as he had before."** In short, in its most basic and fundamental form, Job is not merely being taught the gospel of Christ, he is living it first-hand.

This is precisely what the Holy Spirit was indicating when he spoke these words from the mouth of Job in **Job 42:3 "... therefore have I uttered that I understood not; things too wonderful for me, which I knew not."** This would seem to undeniably suggest that through all of what Job had so grievously endured, at its closing moments there was the moment of great epiphany (Job.19:23-27).

Furthermore, Job would be commanded by God to forgive his friends, who had formerly persecuted him through his trials, and to offer sacrifice for them, and to pray for them (Job42:7-9). This additionally is the perfect shadow and type of

Christ offering Himself as the perfect sacrifice for His offenders (you and I), that we might be forgiven of God.

Similarly, it illustrates Christ's prayer on the cross for all of us, where He says... **Luke 23:34 "Father forgive them, for they know not what they do"**, and this too to occur at the closing moments of His great sufferings, just as it was with Job also. And finally, Job say's this in **Job 42:5-6 "I have heard of you by the hearing of the ear, but now my eye sees you..."**

The end of the matter is this: Job is a profound prophetic similitude of Jesus Himself, and not just that, he is perhaps the most extensive record that we have in all of scripture, of the internal sufferings, and hidden mental anguish that Christ endured upon the cross. Many (not all) of the comments of Job throughout the book are the Spirit inspired utterances that God would choose to best replicate the nearness of the torment of His Son's cross. Job's record of agony will forever bear testimony to the agony of Christ's cross in a way no other will ever be able to duplicate.

Moreover, it would be this same stupendously and seemingly inconceivable injustice that was to befall Job that would best be suited to paint the most accurate portrait of the unfathomable unfairness and implausibility, lacking all comprehension, of the sinless Christ suffering on behalf of a sinful and wicked world.

It is in this understanding that we see God's appointed purpose, and unprecedented love for Job. He has granted him the extreme privilege of becoming one with His Son, despite his being born thousands of years earlier before Christ's own earthly life. And unless we forget, it is the marked expression of the totality of His love for us all as well, as He determines to document it for all mankind, and for all future generations, that we too might know Him through our own sufferings, as comparatively seen through the writings and experiences of Job.

Now that we are clearly able to see that Job's suffering is a poignantly defined representation of the suffering of Christ's cross at His first coming, we must logically assume that there should equally be a definitive representation of His second coming as well, as duality would almost certainly require.

We can likewise make the determination with some certainty that the book of Job must be strongly affiliated with that of the prophecy of Dan.9, and Christ's 1st coming, for by the very nature of "Biblical duality" it would almost demand it to be so.

Job through his tribulations illustrates the cross of Daniel's "62nd week", as well as the resurrection from the dead, and also Christ's "appearing", of Daniel's "69th week". Remember, it was only when God appeared to Job in Job 38:1 that Job was able to say in **Job 42:5 "...but now my eye sees you"**.

It would also be this appearing of God that would be the determining factor which would deliver Job from all of his sorrows, and reinstate him to a position of double portion blessing, and removing the curse of the judgment that had befallen him. This is the duality of scripture painting a portrait of both of Christ's comings, and thus we see the obvious reflections of Dan.9.

Which brings me to my next point: Job was said to have received **"twice as much as he had before"** Job 42:10 following his restoration. Upon a closer examination of this fact, we see from **1:3**, and **42:13-16**, that Job's possessions have been perfectly doubled from that of 7,000 sheep to 14,000 sheep, from 3,000 camels to 6,000 camels, from 500 yoke of oxen to 1,000 yoke of oxen, and from 500 female donkeys to 1,000 female donkeys. In every instance, a perfect doubling of all the possessions that had been formerly lost, had now been given back to Job.

However, it is within this same passage in 42:13 where we first seem to come across a mathematical discrepancy: "He had also 7 sons and 3 daughters." This number of his children is not double the number of the children in which he lost, on the contrary, they are exactly the same as scripture records in **1:2**, before his calamities. A doubling of this number would have given Job 14 sons and 6 daughters, as one might expect. It is not until one realizes that Job is the representation of Jesus and His salvation, that this apparent inconsistency is easily resolved.

In **1:5** we read, **"...Job sent and sanctified them, and he would rise early in the morning and offer burnt offerings according to the number of them all"** This is a picture of Christ as our High Priest (Heb.4:14-15), and His heavenly intercessions on our behalf, as well as His "sending" (John16:7) of the Holy Spirit, who is the Spirit of "Sanctification" (II Thess.2:13).

It is by this understanding that we see that God has in fact doubled his children, because the 7 sons and 3 daughters that were no longer alive in the flesh were still alive in the spirit, and with God. This too is a type and shadow of the 2nd coming of Christ (Daniel's "69th week"), as recorded in **I Thess.4:16-17** **"And the dead in Christ shall rise first. Then we who are alive and remain shall be caught up together with them..."**

Moreover, the loss of Job's children, and then the eventual restoration of his additional children, is a clear representation of the *"Parable of the Fig Tree"*, as the parable itself is clearly defined by an "exile", and then followed by a long awaited "return" of God's children. And this as well, is found to be totally contiguous with what we find in Matt.24, Isa.7, as well as in the "69th week" of Dan.9, and in Christ's own generation at His 1st coming ("62nd week" of Dan.9)

Finally, we come to the last item on the list to be doubled, in Job 42:16 it states, "After this Job lived 140 years..." By the use of some basic mathematical skills, this would put the age of Job, prior to the judgment that would be unleashed upon him, at exactly 70 years old. If in truth Job's years were doubled, as was everything at the conclusion of the judgment, than surely the 140 years given to Job at the last, would also have to be a doubling of the 70 years that he had lived prior. And there it is again, a subtle but profound mention of the elusive "70 year" timeline, and it too, as with all the others would transpire beforehand, leading to the great judgment to follow.

Add to all of this, that **Job2:13** states: **"So they sat down with him on the ground 7 days and 7 nights (a week)..."** and what we have is yet another Divine depiction of a "week" (or 7), of the church age that would immediately follow the "62nd week" (Christ's cross) of Daniel, again a precise use of "duality" as it would equally and unmistakably be so neatly planted between the "62nd week", and the "69th week" of Daniel.

Additionally, it may also in some way serve as an obscure fragmentation of Daniels "70 weeks", or 70 x 7, as a vague but yet carefully crafted disguise of the interconnection of the 70 years of the age of Job at the time of the judgment, as it is intertwined with this final week (7) following the judgment. It is also very possible that the wording itself of this passage, as it clearly delineates between the "7 days" and the "7 nights" is in itself a dual reference to the 7 seals and 7 trumpets of the book of Revelation. Again a type of prophetic circling back of the events to conclude the 70 years, as is so commonly found within the framework of "duality". At any rate, there is your timeline, hidden and disguised ever so craftily once more!

It should likewise be noted that there is no meaningful obvious mention of a third 7, as with the book of Rev.(the bowls), that is because Christ bore that final judgment (God's wrath) on the cross for us, in which Job was mimicking through his final week (Christ's own Passion Week) of sufferings. Job as a detailed example of the cross of Jesus is himself the recipient of the bowl judgments (final 7 of Rev.) and the wrath of God, just as Christ was. As it states in **Gal.3:13 "Christ has redeemed us from the curse of the law, being made a curse for us"**.

Furthermore, just as God would so willingly unleash His judgment upon His own Son (on our behalf), thus we see additionally, the preordained purpose of God for the perceived combative encounter which we had detected earlier on in the definitions of the names of both Job and Satan (similitude of Christ and Satan's showdown).

If there is still yet remaining an unanswered question regarding this testimony and witness of Job, it might be that of: "How does this pertain to the other subjects of our study where we clearly found two separate and distinct timelines of 65 and 70 years?" It is of course a sensible question to ask.

My initial response to this inquiry would be that the delineation of the timeline of 65 years is potentially inferred, or implied within the whole of the 70 years, where the 65 is not given, and in fact that is precisely what occurs in so many other passages that clearly indicate the same 70 year timeline, of which I have not yet had the opportunity to share with you.

At the same time, the answer could be as simple as I haven't discovered it as yet. This could be equally the case, as it has taken me several years for the Holy Spirit to teach me what I do know. In either case, the 70 year timeline is more than sufficient, in and of itself, as it represents the fulfillment of the totality of all the other timelines which we have methodically uncovered in all of our earlier subjects of study.

In conclusion, we see the 70 year timeline once more, lying subtly beneath the pages of the book of Job, and once again, the Holy Spirit has methodically and systematically disguised it out of the plain view of the casual reader. And let it not go understated that the theme and timeline of the book of Job remains constant and consistent with that of Dan.9; the book of Isaiah; Gen.5; and the wilderness example; as well as that of the actual events of Christ's generation at His first coming, and there are still yet more examples to come.

As we close this section, my question to you the reader is this: At what point do we begin to actually sit up and take notice, as we must begin to draw the same comparisons of these "end time" parallels to our own "end time generation", as prophesied through the book of Revelation? Just as we now know that the 70 year period was exact and precise at Christ's first coming, do we actually presume to make the seemingly grievous error that the same 70 year time-frame will not hold true again, in this the 69th generation of Daniel?

THE RISE OF THE PROPHETS

In this next section we will hope bring to light one of the most interesting revelations that the Holy Spirit has ever shared with me. Similarly, it would be this same revelation that would seem to bring everything that I had previously learned, in regard to the end time timeline, into an intricately harmonized adherence. And as I would soon find out later, it would equally be the surprising illumination of this truth that would become so especially personal for me on a most individual basis as well, as you will soon see why.

But before we begin, let us just take a very brief survey of the 70 year timeline that we seem to have almost continuously uncovered during the course of our research on this topic:

1) We saw it in the book of Genesis, through the witness of the record of Enoch, beginning with a period of 65 years, only to be precluded with the death of Noah's father Lamech in his 777 year, followed by a final period of 5 years just prior to the flood itself.

2) We saw it as well in the life of Moses, during the wilderness journey, through Numbers and Deuteronomy (the numbering of the Levites and Kohathites), and then concluding with the book of Joshua and the 5 year conquest of the Promised Land.

3) At the same time we found it in the book of Isaiah (a four part timeline), leading to the fall of the northern tribes of Ephraim in 722BC.

4) Additionally, it was in the book of Daniel (9:2; 24-27) where we initially learned of the "70 weeks" time-frame

that has acted as the original launching pad for this entire endeavor.

5) Moreover, we saw it in the prophetic writings of Zechariah as he plainly laid out his "end time" account.

6) Most recently, we just completed our study of Job where we found it, still yet again.

7) And then, we have seen it in the Generation of Christ at His first coming, and the *"Parable of the Fig Tree"*, and all leading up to the events of 70AD.

8) And we must not forget, or fail to mention the interlocking connection of all of these episodes to our most relevant case study, as it pertains to us, the 69th week of Daniel, and the 7th church generation of the book of Revelation itself.

Now all of this is very compelling to be sure, but the true purpose of what I am hoping to get across to the reader at this time, by this very short review, is to add a much broader perspective to what we have learned. If we add to all that we have studied, our recollection of the books of

I Kings, and II Kings, as well as Ezra, Nehemiah (the Artaxerses decree), and Lamentations (duality), which all assisted us greatly as supportive bridge studies for the fulfillments of these aforementioned timelines, what we have is an overwhelming collection of evidence found throughout the expanse of both the Old and New Testaments, that consistently declares the exact same timeline of 70 years, regardless of when or where it occurs.

The only remaining piece of the puzzle, as I can see it, is that we have not yet fully touched upon the O.T. prophets as a whole. We have of course seen the timeline most decisively in both Isaiah and Daniel, but there are still yet another 14 books in the O.T. that bears the names of the prophets who wrote them. In this section we will attempt to uncover their voices as they may relate to the same timeline that we have found seemingly everywhere else.

Additionally, I would ask you also to once more pay very close attention to the ingenious manner in which God the Holy Spirit seems to conceal this timeline, as with all the others that we have come to unveil to this point.

As a point of fact, just let me add this: the nearest that I have been able to come to an explanation for His purpose in doing this (hiding it), is more likely found in **Isa.28:7-13 "... The priest and the prophet** (religious leaders) **have erred, through intoxicating drink** (false doctrine, personal gain, and pride),**...They err in vision, they stumble in judgment** (they themselves are deceived). **Whom will He teach knowledge? And whom will He make to understand the message** (the truth)**? Those just weaned from milk?** (the spiritually immature?) **Those just drawn from the breasts?** (unlearned babes, infants?) **For precept must be upon precept, precept upon precept, line upon line, line upon line, here a little, there a little** (a construction of revelatory knowledge). **For with stammering lips and another tongue** (the true baptism of the Holy Spirit)) **He will speak to this people** (those in err), **to whom He said 'this is the rest with which you may cause the weary to rest,'** (salvation through faith in Jesus), **and, 'This is the refreshing.'** (the indwelling of the Holy Spirit); **Yet they would not hear, but the word of the LORD was to them** (they did not rightfully discern the word), **precept upon precept,**

precept upon precept, line upon line, line upon line, here a little there a little, that they might go and fall backward, and be broken (the just recompense for their neglect of the truth) **and snared and caught."**

This is how "remnants" are formed. Judgment befalls us all, but it is those who hear the message and believe it, and repent, and thereby, they become prepared, through faith, in the God of that same message. And the others, they go about their way as drunken men, full of intoxicating drink, their senses altered, they stagger headlong into the snares of judgment, entirely oblivious to what awaits them (the Laodicean church); and these constants remain steadfast throughout every generation.

This is the "threshing" of the *"tares and the wheat"* of Matt.13. It is the "lukewarm" church of Rev.3 as they are "vomited out" from among those that have "opened the door" and do "supper with the Lord". It is the story of *"the ten virgins"* (Matt.25), and those that have oil and those that do not. It is also the *"Parable of the Sower"* (Matt.13), those in which are depicted by the "wayside", the "stony places", and the "thorns", while others are referenced as "good ground", and "bring forth fruit".

And likewise, it is the "good trees" (Matt.7) that are distinguished from the "bad trees"; and it is the "leaven of the Pharisee's" (Luke 12), that Christ Himself warned us to beware of in the opposition to His own teachings. And finally, it is the **"blind leading the blind" of Luke 6:39, "shall they not both fall into the ditch?"**

In the same passage of **Matt.13:10-15** the disciples asked Jesus **"why do you speak to them in parables?"** Jesus reply was this: **"Because it has been given to you to know the mysteries of the Kingdom of heaven, but to them it has not** been given... therefore I speak to them in parables, because seeing they do not see, and hearing they do not hear, nor do they understand. And in them the prophecy of Isaiah is fulfilled, which says: Hearing you shall hear and not understand, and seeing you shall see and not perceive, for the hearts of this people have grown dull (the Laodicean Church), their ears are hard of hearing, and their eyes they have closed, Lest they should see with their eyes and hear with their ears, Lest they should understand with their hearts and turn, so that I should heal them." And with all of that being said, let us now proceed on to the prophets.

To set the stage, we will begin by taking a quick look at **Isa.1:1 "The vision of Isaiah... in the days of Uzziah, Jotham, Ahaz, and Hezekiah, kings of Judah."**

Now it might surprise you to know, as it did me, that it is in this very first verse of the book of Isaiah where we find the timeline that we are looking for. This verse makes it perfectly clear as to the time of Isaiahs ministry, it would span the reigns of these four listed kings of Judah.

Our next obvious step would be for us to do a simplistic search for the years that each of these four kings might have reigned. One can easily do this by the use of any Biblical encyclopedia, commentary, or even a simple Google search for that matter. Depending on the specific tool or website that you might use, the dates may vary slightly, but the variance will not be so great in any case as to inhibit the actual purpose of our inquiry. As you will see, these kings and their reigns are fairly common historical knowledge, and extensively documented.

Now beginning In the order of their succession: Uzziah reigned from792BC to 740BC, as the first king given in this listing. The last king in the listing is Hezekiah, who reigned from 715BC to 699BC. By this we can safely determine that Isaiah's ministry would have fallen somewhere between 792BC and 699BC.

More specifically, we know from our earlier study of Isa.7:8, that the 65 year timeline in which God gave to Isaiah, was intended for king Ahaz. King Ahaz's reign was from 735BC to 720BC. We also know that the timeline itself was appointed for the northern tribes of Israel (Ephraim), and the time of their fall. As history would record, this fall was fulfilled in 722BC, precisely within the time of the reign of king Ahaz. If we then trace backwards 65 years from the fall of Ephraim in 722 BC, that would bring us to 787BC, which is precisely during the reign of Uzziah, the first king mentioned in our listing.

The point of all of this should hopefully be very clear, the 65 year timeline is extremely accurate to the verse of Isa.1:1, as Isaiah's ministry falls perfectly "within" the 65 year time frame of the judgment of 722BC.

Next, we will look at the prophet Jeremiah. The book of Jeremiah is another crucial case subject in our study of the 70 year timeline, as he was the prophet in which God had assigned the task of delivering the message of the fall to come, of the Southern Kingdom of Judah in 586BC. This fact alone makes Jeremiah a prophetical counterpart to that of the ministry of Isaiah.

What is the significance of that? You might ask. This by itself, is extremely imperative as it relates to the law of "duality". We have seen over and over again, how God repetitiously navigates events to form a type of structural map that should in fact speak loudly to the generation of that day, in which He wishes to address. In every instance that we have seen, when great judgment is looming, God Himself has constructed a very specific framework in which to provide the necessary warning of the events that are surely to follow.

Once again, we have seen it in the time of the flood of Noah's day; additionally, we have seen it preceding the judgment handed down in "the wilderness" experience. Again, we witnessed it in the time of the fall of the Northern Kingdom of Israel of Isaiah's day, and still yet again, in the very generation of Christ's first coming, and the judgment to follow soon after in 70 AD. Furthermore we see it clearly outlined in its most futuristic form through the book of Revelation, and the "end times".

This example here, that we are about to examine, is but another identical representation, in that these events will also pattern themselves after all of its predecessors, conforming in like manner to the prophesied judgment of the Southern Kingdom of Judah, and will in fact yield the same similar signs and impending warnings. It is as a result of this knowledge that as we precede we shall look for these very same similarities.

One can only imagine how ignominiously this all is stretching you to the boundaries of your understanding, I know of course how it sterilized my thought process when it was first divulged. And granted, I could never hope to fully illuminate these truths with the same pristine clarity that the Spirit of God has so graciously offered unto me; and to that I say, rest your minds and see what's next.

Turn now to **Jer.1:2-3** where we read: **"...to whom the word of the LORD came in the days of Josiah... king of Judah, in the thirteenth year of his reign. It also came in the days of**

Jehoiaim, the son of Josiah... until the end of the eleventh year of Zedekiah... until the carrying away of Jerusalem captive..."

Long story short, King Josiah's reign is the beginning of Jeremiah's ministry. Josiah reigned from 640BC to 609BC. The 13th year of Josiah's reign would have been around the year of 627BC, this would mark the year that "the word of the LORD" first came to Jeremiah. Now, bear in mind that the prescribed date for the fall of the Kingdom of Judah is 586BC, which is likewise, the last recorded year of King Zedekiah's reign, and by this information we can place Jeremiah's prejudgment ministry as beginning some 41, or 42 years prior to the fall of the Southern Kingdom.

This dating carries with it two very interesting facts: first, it clearly places the prophet Jeremiah within the allotted 70 year time-frame preceding the judgment. The reason that this is most important is that we have learned that a biblical generation always seems to fall within the parameters of the lifespan of that appointed generation, it does not have a fixed set of years in which to gage it. Therefore we see God faithfully sending out His prophets within the same 70 year time frame (life span) of that generation in which He wishes to address, and to warn. By in large, every prophet that we shall look at will follow this same prerequisite, with only a couple of exclusions to this norm.

Secondly, Jeremiah and Isaiah are ministerial counterparts, one to the Northern Kingdom (Isaiah), and one to the Southern Kingdom (Jeremiah), and both addressing the final generations of their perspective peoples, prior to their being conquered and taken into captivity, and as we shall soon see this is of a great importance. Remember, it was during this nearly identical setting that God initially establishes the 65 year timeline of Isa.7:8, and then cements the fulfillment of this timeline with "the sign" of "the birth of a son" in Isa.7:14, and thus assuring the judgment upon Ephraim.

Here is where it really begins to get interesting, turn now with me to I Kin.13:1-6. But before we dive headlong into this, let me just first say: for the sake of doing my best not to over confuse the issue, I will be very abrupt in supplying the parallels that are unmistakably within this passage.

Additionally, I will not offer the extensive explanations that would most certainly only serve to draw this issue out and make it more tedious than it may already seem. I trust that by now, the mere appearance of the parallels themselves will suffice in clarifying the point in which I hope to make.

In addition to this, I will abbreviate the passages in order to point out only those parts of the verses that express these parallels. It is my sincerest hope that you will read the entirety of the passages on your own, as with every passage that I have offered throughout this book, that I would not be mistaken for tampering with the contents of the Word as a whole.

Now on to **I Kings 13:1-6**, starting in **(v2)** **"...Behold, a child Josiah by name shall be born to the house of David, and on you he shall sacrifice the priests of the high places, who burn incense on you, and mens bones shall be burned on you."**

This prophecy was given to King Jeroboam (930BC-910BC) roughly some 300 years before the actual birth of King Josiah (which was likewise the time of Jeremiah's ministry), and more than 100 years before the prophecies of Isaiah.

What I would hope to point out is the undeniable similarities of this prophecy with that of the Isa.7 prophecy. In both cases a son shall be born, by a specific name in which God Himself would provide, as the prelude to the impending judgment of both houses of Israel, at separate and individual times. And we mustn't forget that this was also perfectly replicated by the birth of Jesus as it pertained to the generation of 70 AD as well.

In **(v4)** we read, **"And it came to pass, when king Jeroboam heard the saying of the man of God... that he put forth his hand... saying "arrest him!"** (rejection of the message, and Christ's arrest, and subsequent crucifixion) **Then his hand, which he stretched out toward him, withered** (1st part of the *"Parable of the Fig Tree"*: as the "withering" symbolizes the captivity, Matt.21:19), **so that he could not pull it back to himself. (v5) "The altar also was split apart, and the ashes poured out from the altar..."** (the end of animal sacrifice, the priesthood, and the destruction of the temple); then in **(v6) "So the man of God entreated the LORD, and the king's hand was restored to him, and became as before** (2nd part of the *"Parable of the Fig Tree"*, the "restoration" of the nation and people of Israel).

Another astonishing parallel exists within the actual birth of King Josiah, as recorded in **II Kin.22:1 "Josiah was eight years old when he became king, and he reigned thirty-one years** (640BC-609) **in Jerusalem"**, this would place his birth year at 648BC. This verse uniquely places the birth of Josiah at exactly 62 years ("62nd week" of Daniel) before the fall of Jerusalem in 586BC.

Furthermore, Josiah's reign would end in his 39th year of age, which would act as a perfect illustration of the year of

39AD, that Christ Himself would be crucified (born in 5AD, and lived 33 1/2 years, totaling to 39AD, precisely as recorded in Isa.7:8-14).

In the final analysis, the prophecies as they reference the ministry of Jeremiah are identical to those of all of its predecessors in the following aspects:

1) A child shall be born (a son)
2) The child is named specifically by God (Josiah), as was the case with Isaiah's son (Mahershalalhashbaz Isa.8:1); and with Jesus Himself (Emmanuel Isa.7:14, and Matt.1:20-23). Additionally, Josiah in Hebrew is spelled "Yoshiyah"; remarkably similar to "Yeshua".
3) A "sign" shall be given pronouncing the end of a priesthood and the defilement of its altar (the end of a priesthood, and the destruction of its temple, equally true to 722BC, 586BC, and 70AD.)
4) A rejection of the message which results in a "withering away", and then a "restoration" (two separate parts of the "*Parable of the Fig Tree*" Matt.21:17-20, and Matt.24:32-34)
5) And lastly, the fulfillment of the judgment that would fall within the same generational lifespan as the others (70 year timeline).

In its rawest form, these preliminary events leading to the judgment of the southern kingdom of Judah in 586BC are all in an identical alignment with the fulfillments of the judgment on the northern tribes of 722BC, and the first coming of Christ and the judgment on Jerusalem of 70AD. A further proof that we should expect the same in this last church generation before the second coming.

After all, we have seen the birth of the son (nation of Israel, Emmanuel); we have seen the fulfillment of the *"Parable of the Fig Tree"* (1948); and lastly, we are currently in the 65th year of the 70 year lifespan of the final church generation (Rev.3). Can we truly imagine that God will not perform the judgment of the book of Revelation, preceding the second coming of Christ, during our lifespan, given all that we have learned?

By now it has become time for us to move on. Now that we have some familiarity with the timelines of the prophets as they relate to the kings that were in power at the time of their ministries, we should be able to move through the remainder of the prophets with much more ease.

Our next example is that of the prophet **Hosea**, starting in **Hos.1:1 "The word of the LORD that came to Hosea... in the days of Uzziah (792-740BC), Jotham, Ahaz, and Hezekiah, kings of Judah, and in the days of Jeroboam II (792-753BC)... king of Israel."**

This passage clearly places the prophet Hosea's ministry as occurring no later than 792BC. This dating situates Hosea precisely within the 70 year window of the fall of the northern kingdom of Israel in 722BC. And still again, we see God Himself using His own 70 year time frame as the appropriate designated time to send out His prophet, and to address the generation that will soon be the focus of His judgment.

Next, we come to the prophet **Amos**, in **1:1, "The words of Amos... which he saw... in the days of Uzziah (792-740BC) king of Judah, and in the days of Jeroboam (II) (792-753)..."** This one verse places Amos' ministry as beginning between the years of 792BC and 753BC. Just like the others, Amos is comfortably within the 70 year generational timeline.

Following this we go to **Micah 1:1 "The word of the LORD that came to Micah... in the days of Jotham** (750-736BC)**, Ahaz** (735-720BC)**, and Hezekiah** (715-699BC)**, kings of Judah..."** In this verse, once more, we see that Micah passes the 70 year litmus test as well.

Alright, by now I am sure that I have done a superb job in boring you to tears, so for the sake of time we will shift gears here. Rather than continuing on through the remainder of the prophets, one by one, here is a quick snapshot of what you will find if you continue on with your own personal examination of those that are still remaining: Jonah, Ezekiel, Obadiah, Habakkuk, Zephaniah, and Nahum, all fall within the specified 70 year time frame, as heralds of the impending judgment that would engulf the generations of their day. This leaves us with only three other prophets of the entire group of 16 that we began with.

In its most fundamental element what we are determining is that by in large God sends His prophets out, more frequently than not, to the very generation of that's prophets day. Granted, that by the use of "duality" their messages never fail to be relevant, as they will undoubtedly continue to repeat themselves over the extended time of history. This is also why their prophecies and warnings speak so authentically to us today.

The three exceptions to the 70 year rule are: Zechariah, Haggai, and Joel. Beginning with Zechariah and Haggai, it must first be taken into account that the ministries of both of these prophets begins after the judgments of both the northern and southern kingdoms. Both the houses of Israel are already in captivity at the time that God calls these two men into His service.

Furthermore, we have already seen in our earlier studies how Zechariah's prophecies were clearly directed at an end time audience. His writings are unmistakably a companion book to those of both Daniel and Revelation, and as such he is most certainly an anomaly in regard to the 70 year timeline.

However, as we uncovered in Zech.1:12, he too injected a very abrupt and precise remark concerning a 70 year time period. Though obviously referring to Judah's current state of captivity at the time, there should also be no question as to the fact that the statement itself seems terribly out of place when weighed against the overall content of the entirety of his writings, as they clearly concern the days that would immediately precede the 2nd coming of the Lord.

Haggai was likewise doing the same as Zechariah. Haggai and Zechariah were companions and counterparts, their ministries ran closely together as we found in Ezra 5:1. Both carried the same ministries, at the same period of time, to the same people. Both were designated to make known the word of the LORD to the returning exiles from captivity. They were to be the instruments that God would use to compel His people to rebuild the temple of God.

In this, they themselves are prophetic shadows of the "two witnesses" of Zech.4, and Rev.11, which would come in the "last days", bearing the holy anointing of oil that would pour down (latter rain) on the generation that God would choose to restore His people, Israel, and His holy capital of Jerusalem, and the House of God (the temple). In short, they are prophetic symbols of God's mercy and restoration of Israel, more so than that of His righteous judgment, and therefore, it is in my opinion, that they are found to be exempted from the 70 year timeline.

That leaves us with only Joel. The book of Joel is one that offers no explanation of its dating, however, we can surmise that from the contents of its message, it too is a ministry directed primarily at God's victorious deliverance of His people. Although the harsh hardships of judgment are clearly mentioned, they are primarily directed at the enemies of Israel, and not the nation of God's people itself. Joel's overall context is that of a loving and merciful God who dramatically returns to thwart His enemies and deliver His people. It is a brief synopsis of the climatic events that will encapsulate "the Day of the LORD". Its message, like Zechariah and Haggai is not directed at the chastisement of a generation of Israel, instead, it is one of strengthening and encouraging His people. It is for this reason that I believe that Joel too is exempt from the 70 year parameter.

And with that, this brings our look at the prophets to a close. So let us now take a moment to hopefully sum up these findings. For me, the main point that I was intending to make is that God is always constantly consistent in all of His ways. It is through this knowledge of Him that it should come as no surprise to us that an empirical theme arises when we look at the ministries of His servants the prophets: Where judgment is imminent, God in His faithfulness sends out His messengers of warning, this goes back to His promise in **Amos 3:7 "Surely the LORD God does nothing, unless He reveals His secret to His servants the prophets. A lion has roared! Who will not fear? The LORD God has spoken! Who can but prophecy?"**

The prophet Jeremiah put it this way: **Jer.28:8-9 "The prophets that have been before me and before you of old prophesied both against many countries, and against great kingdoms, of war, and of evil, and of pestilence. The prophet which prophesies of peace, when the word of the prophet shall come to pass, then shall the prophet be known, that the LORD has truly sent him."**

If we can agree wholeheartedly that this is a mainstay in the plans and purposes of God, than likewise, we cannot ignore that scripture bears out a methodical timing of the sending out of these prophets in the implementation of His generational warnings. Even now, if you are reading this, I ask you... is it possible that this message is being brought forth now, precisely because we are in the 65th year, of the 7th and final church generation?

Jeremiah also said, in **Jer.23:20-22 "...in the latter days you will understand it perfectly."** Let me say once again, I make no claims to be anything, let alone anything that I am not, but as it written **Amos 3:8 "the LORD God has spoken! Who can but prophesy?"**

Before we are able to conclude this section of *"The Rise of the Prophets"*, there is yet another example that we must look at, one so blatantly obvious, and yet mysteriously unperceived by most:

The disciples themselves over the years, have received their fair share of undeserved criticism for their seemingly inability to perceive the time of the return of the Lord, and they too had much too say concerning the coming judgment that would precede it. The message was so thoroughly ingrained in their hearts and minds, obviously due to the ministry of the Holy

233

Spirit, that they wrote about it extensively throughout the New Testament, and no doubt preached it everywhere they went. But the Lord did not come as they had expected... or did He?

Consider this: what they didn't know, we presume, was that the generation that they were writing to, and preaching to, and prophesying to, was marked for judgment in only a few short years (70AD). By this they were entirely consistent with all of the other prophets that had come before them. They had found themselves, unknowingly by them, to be at the close of this fatal 70 year generation (Daniel's 62nd week).

It was for them the equivalent of the "last days". It was the eve of a horrendous Divine "visitation" of the wrath of God, and it was the time of the rapidly approaching "Day of the LORD", all rolled up into one, and the Holy Spirit was brazenly testifying within them, and spilling over into their writings, concerning this revelatory fact.

For that matter, John the Baptist himself stated in **Luke 3:7-17: (v7) "O generation of vipers, who hath warned you to flee from the wrath to come?"** And in **(v9), "And now also the ax is laid unto the root of the trees..."**

In this passage John is plainly warning the generation of his day of the impending disasters that would await them. How interesting that John too uses the analogy of a tree being uprooted as a picture type of God's wrath upon the children of his day. It is almost as if John was prophesying the judgment through the use of terminology that would be emphasized by the similar language of the very same parable that Jesus would speak much later, in Matt.24 ("the fig tree"). In this, John too is a keen example of "the rise of the prophets" as he too administers his warnings to the terminal generation in which he too lived (70 year life span).

By this understanding, it is easy to see that they were not wrong at all, in fact, they were absolutely correct, and forever remain documented in the annuls of Scripture as the New Testament providential proof of the **70 year timeline**, as it resulted in the great destruction of 70AD.

This now brings us to the end of our quest to determine "How long is the end time generation?" I now offer these final thoughts to further add validity to the structure that we have constructed through our study thus far. There are many other similitudes throughout scripture that I may have used to further cement the issue of the theory of the "70 year" premise. In all actuality there is nearly as much that i have elected to leave out of this writing as there are those that I have chosen to use.

Finally, it should be noted that what is predominately most important here is not whether or not this interpretation of the 70 year time-frame is totally and accurately precise, but rather, the greatest importance is that we realize that however much time we have left, the evidence would seem to strongly suggest that the time that we do have is extremely short, which should beg us to ask a question of ourselves with all honesty... am I ready?

At the start of this section I made the remark as to how this revelatory knowledge would prove to be so intensely personal for me on a most individual basis, well that is all borne out through the many sleepless nights, and thousands of hours of study that have formulated together to become what is now my life. I cannot help but to say, that one could not even possibly begin to imagine the Holy Hand that has rested so firmly upon me, and most lovingly, and yet forcefully, determining that this message should be learned, and taught, and shared, and shared now. For me it is more than clear as to why. We are within the 70 year window, and God is so faithfully sending out all of His to lay hold, their hands upon the shofar. I say again... are u ready?

CHAPTER FOUR

"BEHOLD THE FIG TREE, AND
ALL THE TREES" (LUKE 21:29)

The passage of Luke 21:29-32 is yet another rendition of the *"Parable of the Fig Tree"*, as it is the joint companion to the text's of Matt.24:32-34, and Mark 13:28-30. In this version there is an obvious addition to the text that does not present itself in its two sister passages of Matthew and Mark, the variance being in the statement... "and all the trees". Considering that we have learned that the "fig tree" is a clear reference to the nation of Israel itself, than one can easily surmise that the phrase of "all the trees" is a representation of all the other existing nations that will be set in their place at the time that the nation of Israel returns to its land. By this slight inclusion to the parable we are told not only to watch Israel, but to also examine the nations of the world as a whole, as they too will present a prophetical Biblical alignment as the time of the end would draw near.

In this next chapter we will explore the world as it exists around us today. If it is true that we are living in the generation that will see the coming of the Lord, than the world around us should reveal itself to be in an emerging configuration with the "end time" prophecies of scripture. We should be able to gage our approach to the nearness of the time of Christ's return by taking a detailed look at some of the prophecies that are uniquely marked for "the last days". With this goal in mind, we will examine closely the political, economic, and religious climate of our planet today, and measure these findings against the carefully crafted pictorial of the days leading up to the Lord's return, as documented by scripture.

In fairness I must first say, there is so much material here to cover, that I will have to be very strict and conservative with the time allotted to each individual topic, and as a possible result of this "hit and run" tactic there may be many things concerning these subjects that may go unfortunately unmentioned. My overall purpose of course is to cover as many of these subjects of study as I can, while purposefully streamlining the time in which we will devote to each one of them on their own individual basis. It is not to give a detailed "play by play" narration, but rather to provide a vast scope of events as they poignantly relate to our world today, allowing us the unique opportunity to observe them from the distinct vantage point of centrality as a whole.

TRAVEL AND TECHNOLOGY

To begin this study I have chosen a verse out of the final chapter of the book of Daniel which I feel is quite remarkable, and may be one of the most exemplary prophecies in all of end time prophecy. In the light of what we have come to know in regard to the monumental instruction of Dan.9, this selected verse should carry with it an additional weightiness, as it is profoundly and specifically aimed at Daniel's "69th week".

Dan.12:4 "But you, oh Daniel, shut up the words, and seal the book, even to the time of the end: many shall run to and fro, and knowledge shall be increased."

In this verse we see three exceptionally important statements given to its reader: the first, would be that it offers a very explicit time-frame for the prophecy spoken. Daniel is told to **"shut up the words, and seal the book, even to the time of the end."** These words unmistakably mark this prophecy for the 7th and final church generation of Daniel's "69th week", and for no other.

One only has to read the three verses that precede it, of Daniel 12:1-3, and what you will find is this prophecy is indisputably linked to the "great tribulation" of Matt.24:21-22, the "resurrection of the dead" of I Thess.4:13-17, and the "bodily glorification" of the saints, as it is found in I Cor.15:50-55, and all of this to take place at the "coming of the Lord". Adding just a further proof that this prophecy is not directed at any other generation, other than the generation of "the time of the end".

Now let us read **Dan.12:1-3 "And at that time shall Michael stand up, the great prince which standeth for the children of thy people** (the Jews, as well as the Church)**; and there shall**

be a time of trouble (Jacob's trouble), **such as never was since there was a nation even to that same time** (great tribulation); **and at that time thy people shall be delivered** (coming of the Lord), **everyone that shall be found written in the book** (the saints, both Jew and Gentile). **And many of them that sleep in the dust of the earth shall awake** (resurrection of the dead), **some to everlasting life, and some to shame and everlasting contempt. And they that be wise** (ten virgins of Matt.25) **shall shine as the brightness of the firmament** (bodily glorification); **and they that turn many to righteousness as the stars for ever and ever** (eternal life)."

Returning back now to (v4), what we see in the next two statements of Dan.12:4 is God giving two panoramic worldwide signals, or sign-post, that should exude the world over... "End time now!" An unmistakable pronouncement that Christ's return approaches.

First, He states that "many shall run to and fro". This word "run" in Hebrew has only one implied meaning: it means "to travel; a mariner; to row"; and not just to travel, but to travel globally. It should additionally be noted that at the time of Daniel's writing of this prophecy, sea travel would have been the only means in which one could possibly travel large expanses of territory on any type of a global scale. Camels were sufficient of course, for more intermediate journeys, but there is no implied reference to camels in our definition of the word "run"; there is however, the definite mention of "mariner", and to "row". By this God is telling us that when we see a vast explosion of global travel, as never before experienced in all of the recorded history of man, then we are to open our eyes and realize that we are in "the time of the end".

I can easily assure you, that there is no one that can deny, or would dispute that we have passed that sign-post, with the utmost of certainty. Similarly, measuring this prophecy against the timeline of 1948 (the rebirth of the Nation of Israel (the starting line for the final generation), which is also the fulfillment of the *"Parable of the Fig Tree"* of Matt.24, we see a most obvious and unprecedented eruption of global travel as never before realized in all of our past history.

Now here is a mathematical equation for you: if there are 10 centuries to a millennium, and man has been in existence for approximately six millenniums, as the Bible would seem to strongly suggest, than man is roughly 60 centuries old, give or take. When one then takes into account that for more than 58 of those centuries, conservatively speaking, man has forever in the past been relegated to a life of horse back and candlelight. Through this reflection we should be able to see much more extensively just how phenomenally this prophecy has uniquely sprung into fulfillment. And not just that, but seemingly all at once when weighed against the whole of man's time on earth, and most expressly within this very last and abbreviated moment of time in which we find ourselves alive today.

In order to further expound upon this point we must first read the rest of the verse of Daniel 12:4, which states, "and knowledge shall be increased." This second sign-post goes hand in hand with the first, and likewise, it so perfectly illustrates the times in which we live today, with an extremely surgical like precision that only God could have foretold.

In short, our advances in technology have forged a new horizon in which the otherwise impossible, or even unthinkable, has become commonplace in our world today. Consider this:

today it would be almost redundant or mundane to think about sending a man to the moon; not in this, our age of the mars rover, the space shuttle, or the multiple super telescopes that are currently exploring and traversing the vastness of our entire galaxy as we speak.

Today we pick up a magazine and see a picture of some far off celestial body, literally astronomical light years away from our own planet, and we think to ourselves…"wow, isn't that pretty", and then we yawn and throw the magazine to the side, and never realizing that this is a definitive fulfillment of Daniel's end time prophecy.

Furthermore, we can pick up our phone and Google any place within the scope of mans arena of knowledge, and it suddenly becomes just a fingertip away. We can literally penetrate any knowledge that man has ever accrued and documented by the simple touch of a phone. We can in a moment transcend the limitless boundaries of space and time with the utmost of simplicity, at the instant that we desire to satisfy a mere whim. The global communications network that we take for granted each and every day is foundationally but another fulfillment of Dan.12:4.

Needless to say, it would be senseless for me to go any further with this point. There is no one, in any speck on this globe which cannot attest to the innumerable ways in which these two statements (sign-posts) have become so thoroughly true, in just this past generation. Science, medicine, education, global governance, economics, finance, travel, communications, and even religion, you name it, it is all the creation and advancement, as we know it today, of the fulfillment of this singular Bible prophecy.

And yet, even for those of us that may know this prophecy well, many of us live our lives completely oblivious to the implications of what all of this means. God intended for these two signs to be so enormously momentous as to be impossible for anyone to miss, let alone ignore, and that they would imperatively draw our attention to the realization of the preceding statement within that same passage of Dan.12:4, where it says, "…the time of the end".

And last, but certainly not least, it is a clear indication that the very fact that I am able to share all of this with you now is a resounding reminder of the fact that the book has been opened and is no longer sealed. And with that said, we must move on.

THE RETURN OF THE NATION OF ISRAEL

This next segment quite assuredly should have been listed first among the "end time" prophetical comparisons among those which we shall cover in this chapter. It is only because we have previously expounded upon it in such great detail in the earlier portions of this book that it falls to the place of second mention; but make no mistake, as it pertains to the matter of its overall importance, this is emphatically the master sign of all signs for depicting our final generational status.

As I have previously stated on multiple occasions, it was on May 15th, 1948 that Israel was "restored" as a nation after more than nearly 19 centuries, following the exile of 70AD, and this is of course as numerously stated the fulfillment of "the *"Parable of the Fig Tree"*.

As we know it would be Jesus Himself that would give the clarion call concerning this prophecy in **Matt.24:32-34 "Surely I say to you, this generation will not pass, until all of these things be fulfilled."**

It is vitally important to understand that to ignore this prophecy is to ignore the One who offered it to us. We can try to confuse, or to dispel its meaning in order to avoid the obvious discomfort that it may create among some who would choose to delay His coming, but all that I would say to them would be: "good luck with that." The Apostle Paul stated it this way in Rom.3:4 "...let God be true, but every man a liar"

In truth, it is quite a pickle to be in, to hope to wish this warning away, and I would not recommend that any attempt to do so. If it seems to come at a time of significant inconvenience, or personal disruption to one's own life, my suggestion most plainly put, is to "get over it". And likewise, if it unapologetically slaps you harshly in the face, then let it be known, that's exactly what it is intended to do; and for that matter, you may consider yourself blessed, as there are many throughout the world today that do not know, nor will ever know the significance of this imperative truth. Now you may run from it if you must, but trust me when I tell you, you cannot run fast enough, or far enough to evade it.

As a sharp contrast to all of these undesirable responses, my advice to all is to take it in as the great gift that it is. Embrace it, and hold it close as something precious and invaluable. Your Savior comes, and He has chosen you to be an intricate part of His welcoming committee. You have been hand chosen by the Master of us all, to be a partaker of the greatest event in all of human history. You have been artfully selected, not just to read about His Triumphant Entry (Matt.21), but to participate in it. Rise up now and give glory to the King of Glory; and while you're at it, get to the business of handing out some invitations as well. Don't go alone, bring as many with you as you can. Make it your life's work, however much time we have remaining, to be become a skillful wedding planner.

JERUSALEM 1967

This next section is actually a continuance of the last section, as common sense would dictate that Israel could never gain possession of Jerusalem until it was first restored as a nation, and its people had returned to the land of Israel themselves. However, the true significance behind this prophecy is in the extreme importance that the city of Jerusalem would play in both the first and second comings of Christ, as was foretold by God in Daniel 9.

In **Dan.9:25** we read this, **"Know therefore and understand, that from the going forth of the commandment to restore and to build Jerusalem unto the Messiah the Prince shall be seven weeks, and sixty-two weeks; the street shall be built again, and the wall, even in troublous times."**

We have seen through our previous studies, how this verse in particularly clearly announces the coming of the "Messiah" in both the 62nd and 69th generations of man. It should be additionally noted, that as it was true at His first coming, so likewise, it will be true at His second coming; and this is structured behind the basic spiritual principle of "duality" as we have also learned.

In regard to Jesus' first coming, we saw how this timeline of Dan.9 was precise to the exact timing of His first "visitation" to man; similarly, it would be foolish to think that it will not be equally as accurate upon His soon return. By this knowledge we should be able to plainly see just how instrumental the city of Jerusalem is to His second coming, which in turn places a special emphasis on the events of 1967, which resulted in the "Six Day War", and inevitably would bring to pass the prophetic fulfillment of the re-constitution of the whole of Jerusalem as it fell firmly into the grasp of Israeli control for the first time in nearly 2,000 years.

Continuing on now to the following verses of **Dan.9:26-27** we read, **(v26) "...and the people of the prince** (the Antichrist) **that shall come shall destroy the city and the sanctuary; and the end thereof shall be with a flood** (Rev.12:15), **and unto the end of the war desolations are determined. (v27) And he shall confirm the covenant with many for one week; and in the midst of the week** (3 ½ years) **he shall cause the sacrifice and the oblation to cease** (II Thess.2:4-5), **and for the overspreading of abominations** (Matt.24:15) **he shall make it desolate, even until the consummation, and that determined shall be poured upon** (Rev.16:1 The Bowls) **the desolate."**

Easily one can see how these final two verses of Daniel are clearly relating to the "end times" return of Jesus at His second coming. Moreover, they provide a distinct connection between His eminent return, and the existence at that time of a re-emerged city of Jerusalem, as it would pertain to the Jews.

To start with I would like to bring to your attention the two separate uses of the term "the prince". In the first use of the word "Prince" of Dan.9:25 it is clearly capitalized as it references Jesus "the Prince of Peace" (Isa.9:6). However, in its second use in (v26) it is clearly not capitalized, as it references Satan and the Antichrist, who is the **"the prince of the power of the air" (Eph.2:2).**

As expected, this prophecy concerning Satan and his destruction of the city of Jerusalem was initially fulfilled in 70 AD (The Romans) after Jesus' first coming. What we are looking at now is the duality of scripture as it pertains to the 69th generation of Daniel, just before Christ's second coming.

Additionally, in this passage we read, **"...and the people of the prince that shall come shall destroy the city and the sanctuary; and the end thereof shall be with a flood..."**

As an absolutely perfect comparison we likewise read in **Rev.12:15 "So the serpent spewed water out of his mouth like a flood, that he might cause her** (the Jews) **to be carried away by the flood."** These passages are obviously synonymous. Here Satan is coming against the Jews in "the end" with **"a flood"**, just as Dan.9:26 so clearly states.

In **Rev.17:15** we read what that flood consists of, **"The waters which you saw, where the harlot sits, are peoples, multitudes, nations, and tongues..."** By this Biblical symbolism as interpreted by the Lord Himself, we can plainly see that Satan through the use of his Antichrist, will give the command "out of his mouth", to the nations, and they will rise up against the city of Jerusalem and the Jews, in "the end."

Next, we read "unto the end of the war (Armageddon) desolations are determined." This is the fulfillment of the words of Christ in **Matt.24:15** where He stated, **"When you see the abomination of desolation, spoken of by Daniel the prophet, stand in the holy place..."** This speaks of the Antichrist's end time intrusion into the city of Jerusalem following its takeover, and seating himself in the temple as god himself (II Thess.2:4-5).

Next, in this Dan.9 passage we read, **Dan. 9:27 "...he shall confirm the covenant with many for one week; and in the midst of the week he shall cause the sacrifice and the oblation to cease..."** This speaks of the means in which he will

248

begin his conquest of Jerusalem, and eventually the world. He will initially deceive Israel into believing that he is an ally, concerned with the peace and security of Israel. He will even broker a covenant between Israel and "many" for what might possibly be a period of 7 years, but it will be in "the midst" of this covenant (3 ½ years) that he will betray Israel's trust.

At this time he will "cause the sacrifice and oblation to cease…" This again, speaks of a temple that will exist in Jerusalem, or a "sanctuary" as Dan.9:26 puts it, that would be used at that time by the Jews to offer "sacrifice and oblation" to God. It is important to note, that the word "oblation" in Hebrew means: "to bestow; a donation; tribute; a sacrificial offering (usually bloodless and voluntary); gift; present".

In short, he will not only cause the sacrificial animal sacrifices to stop in Israel, but he may additionally command a prohibition against all prayer to God as a whole, on a worldwide planetary basis. This is the direct fulfillment of **II Thess.2:4 "… the son of perdition, who opposes and exalts himself above all that is called God or that is worshiped, so that he sits as God in the temple of God, showing himself that he is God."**

And lastly, we read in the final portion of **Dan.9:27 "…and that determined shall be poured out upon the desolate."** This marks the culmination of these "end time" events with the "pouring out" of "the bowls" of Rev.16:1 and "the wrath of God". Consider the terminology used in this passage: the "seals" are broken; the "trumpets" are blown; but only the bowls are "poured out". This is God's final retribution upon the earth, the Antichrist, and all of those who would choose to follow him.

Alright, we have laid all the groundwork for what I have actually intended to share with you. As imperative as all of this information is for all of us to know, as we head speedily into this period of time and the fulfillment of this passage, let me draw your attention back to the fact that what we are actually looking for is how does this information manifest itself today, in our generation?

The most consequential point of this Dan.9 passage is of course that the people of Israel would have to return to a newly restored land of Israel for this end time prophecy to be fulfilled. As we have stated on multiple occasions, Israel had not been in the land for nearly 19 centuries, from 70AD until 1948, thereby making this prophecy impossible to fulfill until our current generation. Check one.

Secondly, the city of Jerusalem would have to be in the firm control of the Israelis in order for this prophecy to be even further fulfilled. This was not the case until the "Six Day War" of 1967.

Although most of the city of Jerusalem had been in the possession of Israel since 1948, eastern Jerusalem and the temple mount was not, this land portion remained under the control of the Jordanians. It was not until the military campaign of "the Six Day War" on June 7th, that Israelis paratroopers poured into east Jerusalem and for the first time in 2,000 years the temple mount, the wall, and East Jerusalem itself would experience its re-unification, as it fell to the control of the nation of Israel. This of course was an essential part of the Daniel prophecy, considering that the prophecy states that there will be a newly re-built temple. It goes without saying, you can't have the temple without the temple mount. Check two.

Next, there must be "a covenant" made between Israel and "many". This term "covenant" we must remember, is not one involving God. It is a covenant between Israel and many, therefore it speaks of an earthly treaty among men.

At this moment, as I am writing this, our Secretary of the State (John Kerry) is feverishly engaged in dialog with both the Israelis and the Palestinians, seeking to bring about a long awaited treaty between the two. Make no mistake, a treaty between Israel and the Palestinians would equally involve the interests of all of Israel's neighbors, who continually site on the worlds stage, their opposition to the way Israel has allegedly mistreated the Palestinians. The whole of the Middle East has aggressively used this issue as a means to provoke violence and hatred of the Jews among their Arab populations. In turn, the United States and others, have seen this "peace process" as involving a great deal more than merely a treaty between the two nations, but rather a treaty that would encompass the many nations that are aligned with the Palestinians.

The true significance of all of this, is not so much as to how, or when will this treaty actually be set in its place, but in the very fact that as we look at the time in which we live today we can easily see the obvious calls, from all parties, for such a treaty as Daniel emphatically tells us will come. Check three.

Moving still ahead, we turn our attention to the statements regarding "the temple" itself, or as Daniel would call it "the sanctuary". Today it is a well known fact that all of the planning, designs, and preparations for this new temple have been completed. The religious leadership of the nation of Israel has been fully aware that the temple must be in place before the coming of their long awaited Messiah. Even now as we speak, all of the vessels and utensils have been replicated to their precise Biblical specifications as given by Moses through the Torah.

The altar, the candlestick, and all of the other temple furniture has also been completed. The curtains and its hangings have all been finished, and for that matter they have even recreated the Arc of the Covenant itself; and it is all accessible for easy viewing by a simple Google search of the web-site entitled "Jerusalem Temple Institute".

In addition to all of this, the architectural plans have been drawn for some time now; and add to that, stored away in warehouses are the prefabricated constructions of temple walls ready to be assembled at a moment's notice.

And lastly, but certainly not least, a Levitical priesthood has been selected by rigorous DNA testing to ensure that its members are genuinely of the ancient tribe of Levi as prescribed by Mosaic law, and have undergone an extensive training in the Levitical law of animal sacrifice, and are ready and prepared to take their place in the temple as soon as it is constructed. This too can be easily confirmed by a Google search of the "reformation of the Sanhedrin Priesthood". Check four.

Simply put, everything is falling precisely into place as one might expect in order for this "end time" prophecy of Daniel 9 to be fully fulfilled. Furthermore, don't be surprised if when this treaty is finally enacted, whenever that might occur, it might somehow involve the actual setting up of this temple, as Israel will be deceived into believing that it has finally attained the much desired peace it has been longing for.

It may even be used as a bargaining chip by the negotiators of the treaty to further enlist the cooperation of Israel. It could equally include some type of a parceling out of the temple mount, a joint sharing arrangement of sorts that would provide access to both the Jews and the Muslims to the holy ground. After all, this would be a reasonably expected concession on the part of the Muslims considering that Israel may have by that time relinquished their sovereignty over parts of Jerusalem, along with other land grants, in order to attain the rights of its construction.

In any case, the moment the treaty is set in its place the way will be paved for the construction of the new temple, at which time the animal sacrifices will begin shortly after, and of course we know what comes after that. The unmistakable and clearly undeniable fact is this: there is an obvious certainty that the prophecy of Daniel 9 is definitively in its formational process at this specific time of the prophesied "69th generation", in which we live today.

Finally, I leave you with this: **Zech.12:2-3 "I will make Jerusalem a cup** (God's wrath) **of trembling to all the surrounding peoples... and it will happen in that day, that I will make Jerusalem, a burdensome stone for all people, all that burden themselves with it shall be cut in pieces, though all the people of the earth be gathered together against it."**

THE GLOBAL COMMUNITY

Our next subject, is today perhaps one of the most widely known prophecies among both believers and unbelievers alike. Over recent years the object of this prophecy has taken on a variety of depicted names, however, the name in which it is most commonly referred to, and known as today, would probably have to be called "the New World Order".

Initially it should be stated that the prophecies themselves concerning the actual "end time" institutions of this clearly "end time" system can appear to be very illusive at times, when attempting to nail down its specific participants by name, as there seemingly appears to be many ambiguous qualities and statements involving its Biblical descriptions, and actual identity. Although, there is one thing concerning this prophesied entity that seems to be fairly obvious, and widely accepted by everyone who reads it closely, it would seem to unmistakably constitute a widespread unification of nations on a global scale.

For a brief overview of the prophesied alignment of this global governmental construct, for those of you who may have not as yet had the opportunity to be introduced, it is best exemplified by the passages of Rev.13:1-18, and chapters 17-18 of Rev. as well. Additionally, because it is likewise called "Mystery Babylon" within these passages, it can also be studied from its much earlier origins found in Gen.11:1-9.

Once again, the greatest importance of this prophecy, as it pertains to the needs of our particular study, is that it is undeniably referring to the final "latter days" generation of Dan.9, and Matt.24, and as such we must look at it, not just as it appears to us today, but more so from the elevated vantage point of its overall development and growth process since 1948, which as we know was the start of this last generation. By this approach we can not only recognize its emergence, but we can also gain an understanding of the speed and advancement of its formational process.

Since World War II ended in 1945 the gradual construction of this global concept has gone into a full blown implementation. The world's think-tanks have theorized among themselves that war has three basic and root causes: political disagreement; economic need; and religious enmity. These intellectual giants have surmised that a perfect world without war would require the unification of these three most elementary and foundational ideological struggles.

It was precisely this thinking that brought about the birth of the United Nations (185 nations) in 1945, immediately after the war; likewise, in the exact same year the Arab League (22 nations) was formed. And then again we saw it only a few short years later, with the construction of the European Union (28 nations today) in 1951. Add to that, in 1963 the formation of the African Union (53 nations) was fully set in its place. And what we see by all of this is the actual birthing process of the prophesied "end time" entity of the book of Revelation.

This was all done in an attempt to jump start the process of building a singular one world governmental super agency, by beginning with the political aspect first, of the three pronged architecture that would eventually be needed. Since this initial step was taken they have moved forward with lightning like speed in forging one alliance after another, in order to shrink down the vast numbers of moving parts of a world that had been previously separated and divided through its geographical borders, and individual national sovereignties.

Since then, they have equally wasted no time in moving ahead with the economic unification of the planet, or phase two of their carefully crafted master plan. The IMF (International Monetary Fund) and the World Bank were implemented, and are today two of the most powerful and influential financial organizations in the world. Additionally, we have seen clearly, the rise of many economic alliances such as the WTO (World Trade Organization/ consisting of 117 nations), APEC, OPEC, ASEAN, NAFTA, and the BRICK nations, not to leave out the EU itself which today has developed its own unified currency. In short, the entire world today speaks of global finance as the master engine that runs, and oversees the entirety of our economies on the individualistic national level.

Even the judicial aspect of this pervasive systematic amalgamation has not been left out. We have seen the rise of the World Court, or the ICJ (International Court of Justice) be fully implemented, and unabashedly exercising its international global rights as our planets highest judiciary overseer. In recent years several cases of "crimes against humanity" have been held, and have gained great international attention in the world's media's. This court additionally comes complete with all of the authority of international warrants and extradition powers, it is in fact already behaving as a type of a one world international Supreme Court system.

Add to all of this the vast communications network of the WWW (World Wide Web) that has torn down many of the ethnic and geographical barriers that had formerly existed between peoples since the fall of Babylon itself in Gen.11, this too is dramatically serving to initiate, and to indoctrinate the inhabitants of this planet on a worldwide scale as never before, with the subtle intention of gaining its widespread acceptance of its global Frankenstein.

And that brings us to the last and final obstacle of the complete and thorough implementation, or at least the foundational framework of this global societal community, and that obstacle being the very resistant and stubborn obstacle of religion.

Even the religious boundaries that in the past may have seemed so impenetrable are currently being broken down with break-neck speed, with the popular rise of the "politically correct", and "religious tolerance" agenda. For the first time in the world's history it has been deemed "a hate crime" to speak out against anything that does not meet the approval of the congestive whole. The societal norm has joined itself most willingly with this "all inclusive" doctrinal super theology. Even scores of churches have freely embraced this most detrimental policy that suggests that we all serve the same God, and that there are many pathways to Him. It is primarily for this reason that Christianity is being denigrated throughout the world as an "exclusive" and "medieval" ideology.

Add to that, the formation of The world Council of religious Leaders; World Council of Churches; Council for a Parliament of the World's Religions; and the Unity and Diversity World Council - World inter-faith Network, which all operate within the strict guidelines as set down through the United Nations. These organizations operate in lockstep, meeting annually to hold conferences and build alliances on the premise that we should all come together in the support of the many things, that they say, we all have in common. Religious world leaders (the Pope included) of every faith (Christianity, Judaism, Islam, Buddhism, etc.) gather themselves together under the guise of dialog, and to create policies that they have every intention of implementing as they move forward.

And if all of this is not convincing enough, every mainstream religious faith is currently in a state of expectancy of the coming of Jesus, the 5th Buddha, the 12th Imam (Mahdi), or the Messiah (the Jews), opening the floodgate for the possibility of one man emerging on the global scene, and seating himself as all of the above.

Now here is the sum total of it all: this is uniquely the brain-child of a planet that finds itself nearing the close of the 7th and final church generation of Daniel's "69th week". For all that has obviously transpired to bring us to this level of a one world political, economic, and religious system, how much easier it would be to take that final step into an all out finalization of this project, with something as simple as the occurrence of one major catastrophic event. Whether it be by war, economic collapse, natural disasters, or something else, we are on the precipice of seeing **Rev.13** being fully fulfilled.

Lest we forget, it was the flood that brought to pass the construction of the first Babylon. How soon before God once more looks down and says, **Gen11:6-7 "Indeed the people are one, and they have one language, and this is what they begin to do, nothing that they propose to do will be withheld from them. Come, let Us go down..."**

As a final thought, imagine if you will the construction of a puzzle. Like any complicated board puzzle, one starts with the tedious work of adding one singular piece to the other. At the start, the process seems to be a daunting task, as one mulls over the enormity of the seemingly vast numbers of its separately individual pieces. It is precisely at this point that it becomes readily apparent that as a matter of efficiency and expediency, it can be especially helpful to engage the process with a multi-level approach. By isolating the puzzles own commonalities through departmentalizing of its many pieces, greens go with green, brown with brown, blue with blue, and so on, one puzzle becomes multiple smaller puzzles, considerably easier to construct than the overall puzzle as a whole. Individually these smaller puzzles grow and thereby over time provide the desired opportunity for each one to take on its own prescribed positioning in the larger scheme of its assembly. And finally as they grow, at some point in the process it becomes as simple as taking the brown, the blue, and the green puzzles, and just connecting them all together. And what you end up with is a fully operational "New world Order". This is exactly where we find ourselves today.

THE LAND SHALL VOMIT YOU OUT
(CLIMATE CHANGE)

We begin this section with **Lev.18:24-30 "Defile not yourselves in any of these things: for in all these things the nations are defiled which I cast out before you; and the land is defiled; therefore I do visit the iniquity thereof upon it, and the land itself vomits out her inhabitants. You shall therefore keep my statutes, and my judgments, and shall not commit any of these abominations; neither any of your nation, nor any stranger that sojourns among you. For all these abominations have the men of the land done, which were before you, and the land is defiled; that the land does not spew you out also, when you defile it, as it spued out the nations that were before you..."**

By the simple application of a casual reading of this passage one might easily skim over its contents and gain little in the way of true understanding of what God is saying here. Plainly said, God is warning the nation of Israel that its non-compliance with the laws and instructions of God will be manifested over time, by a dreadful response of the land itself, and its environment; carrying with it immense consequences.

This is also unmistakably and eerily reminiscent of God's words to the church of Laodicea in Rev.3:16, where God clearly states, "I will spue thee out of my mouth." In this what we are seeing is God's patience running out on a people, or church, that has become "defiled", and as a result has entered into the prescribed judgment, executed by the land itself.

It is not accidental that there exists this mysterious bond between the behavioral patterns of man and the compulsory response of the earth itself. After all, man was in fact created out of the earth (Gen.2:7), thereby binding him in the physical sense to the whole of the earth.

Furthermore, adding to that the seat of authority ("dominion") in which God had clearly placed in the hands of man over the entirety of His earthly creation back in Gen.1:26, and it becomes considerably more understandable as to how the earth might mimic the behavioral patterns of man. If man is obedient to God, then he will remain blessed by God, and thus the land as well remains blessed, and at peace. However, if man becomes corrupted, defiled, violent, and immoral, than the land will respond in like fashion. Consider the passage of Gen.3:17 where God clearly curses the land in the stead of an actual curse administered directly upon Adam.

In short, this is what the climatologists cannot tell you. The scientific world today is spending great resources in determining the possible causes for the drastic changes we are now experiencing in our climate patterns. Each year we see more and more record highs and lows being shattered. The storm patterns of the past are increasingly becoming more unpredictable, turbulent and violent. Nothing seems to be of any actual pattern at all. The entire world is experiencing this massive assault from its own environment, mass flooding, hurricanes, tsunami's, wildfires, typhoons, tornadoes, earthquakes, volcanic eruptions, deadly heat, and blistering cold, all have become the new norm.

If the earth is the natural barometer of man's sin, then one can easily surmise that by the very appearance of the dramatic changes that the earth is experiencing today in its drastic weather patterns, and chaotic climate issues, what we are truly witnessing is the echoes of the rumblings of a Divine planetary judgment. Which is exactly what Christ foretold in the Book of Revelation, and precisely what one should expect in the close of the 7th and final church generation.

LEVITICUS 26

Next, we will turn our attention to Lev.26, in this chapter God is instructing Moses to teach the children of Israel of the corresponding multiple blessings that would shower the nation of Israel (v1-13), provided of course that they remained faithful in their obedience to the covenant of God while in the land of God's promise. If they obeyed His statutes and commandments, and hearkened diligently to His voice, they could most assuredly expect to see this listing of blessings manifested abundantly throughout every aspect of the land, and its people.

However, as a sharp and sobering contrast, if they refused to obey, and rejected the word of God and His covenant, God also provided a detailed listing of the many curses (v14-39), or retribution, that would surely come upon the people. Upon a closer examination of this listing one thing becomes most obvious, this series of orderly judgments becomes increasingly more and more severe if the nation persists in its disobedience. Each failure on the part of the people to properly respond to the existing judgments, and repent of their evil before God, would in turn bring about an additional judgment, one harsher, and exceedingly more severe than the one before it.

Eventually the culmination of these judgments would result in the catastrophic end of that nation and people, as seen in (v31-39) "I will lay your cities waste and bring your sanctuaries to desolation... I will bring the land to desolation..."

These are unmistakably the words of Dan.9:26-27. Just as the listing would indicate, the end of an unrepentant nation would be finalized with "desolation". In fact, these

263

verses in Lev.26 are clearly linked to Isa.7, Dan.9, and Matt.24 ("abomination of desolation"), and therefore I have chosen this passage specifically for this purpose; because it is presented in such an orderly and synchronized manner, it is in its essence a timetable of judgment.

As just mentioned, in the earlier stages of the retribution for their sin, the judgments seem to be a bit lesser, and more confined in their overall scope. However, as the sin persists, so do the judgments become more extreme and widespread throughout the nation, as they are additionally compounded one upon the other. In my opinion, this then would make this passage a type of a measuring rod of which we may be able to gage our own progression into the same possibility of an impending national judgment.

If this is the last and final generation before the coming of Christ, and if this generation is on a set course to meet its conclusion with "a time of trouble" (Matt.24:21; Dan.12:1) as never before seen by the likes of man (Revelation), and if we are currently in the 65th year of this appointed 69th generation (Dan.9), than we should clearly see within the listing of these judgments not only their existence on a pervasive national level, but by this we should also be able to gage the nearness of the "desolation" of which Daniel speaks of, by the level of the judgments already enacted upon us.

Lest we forget, we have seen this progression played out before with shocking precision in the past, which should make the reliability of this measuring rod an uncontested and invaluable tool.

We have studied the fall of the northern kingdom of Ephraim (10 tribes) in 722BC. We have equally seen the same with the Southern Kingdom of Judah in 586BC. And lastly, we have seen the demise of the city of Jerusalem, its people, and the temple in 70AD. These are all case studies that if studied in an in-depth manner, prove beyond a shadow of a doubt that this same exact listing of judgments was meticulously carried out in each instance, making this Leviticus pattern of judgment a highly accurate measuring instrument to say the least.

Let's begin by taking a look at this chapter beginning with **Lev.26:14-16 "But if you do not obey Me, and do not observe all these commandments, and if you despise my statutes, or if your soul abhors my judgments, so that you do not perform all my commandments, but break my covenant, I also will do this to you; I will even appoint terror over you..."**

This verse represents the first judgment that God would **"appoint"** over His people if they continued in their unfaithfulness to His covenant, in this case the first judgment is simply called **"terror"**. To further amplify the meaning of this word "terror" we will have to go to the Hebrew language, and to do this we will once again use a *Strong's Concordance.*

Initially, we find the word "terror" appears some 29 times throughout Scripture, but only in its use in Lev.26:16 does it reserve a definition that is not incorporated in the other 28 uses of this same word. This definition is the only one of its type in the entirety of the word of God, as it references this particular word, this forces us to see that this use of "terror" is not of the normal variety, but rather as something intentionally isolated and unusual by its rare and in-ordinary definition.

In the Hebrew this word appears as the word "behalah" (Strongs #928, 927, and 926). Now at the risk of being labeled a religious bigot, and throwing all caution to the wind, I would just point out the obvious presence of the primary root word "alah" (Strong's #423, 422, 421). This word "alah" in the Hebrew denotes "an imprecation: curse, cursing, oath, to adjure, i.e. (usually in a bad sense); through the idea of invocation." In short, it depicts an invoking of God to perform an oath of judgment, or evil upon another, on the behalf of the person offering up the prayer: it is an imprecatory prayer.

Returning to the word "behalah" itself, we find this definition: "panic, destruction, trouble, to terrify, to tremble inwardly, i.e. (fig.) be or make suddenly alarmed or agitated, to hasten anxiously, be (make) affrighted, (afraid, amazed, dismayed, rash), thrust out, vex."

In the final analysis of this first judgment, this word "terror" signifies much more than just "fear" itself. My only question is: "Do we see anything in our world today that resembles the implementation of this first judgment?" If we say no, than how do we access the remarkable likeness of the "War on Terror", or "Terrorism", as a national and global threat? Or the many radical extremists that now perpetrate this hatred and violence, who have risen up to use the invocation of their god (Allah) to invoke his wrath and vengeance upon their sworn enemies, through the distilling of their destruction on a planetary scale? Is this just a phenomenon of our times, or are we seeing the first judgment of Lev.26 being fully implemented just as God had warned?

Moving forward to the next judgment on the list we find in **Lev.26:17 "And I will set my face against you, and you shall be slain before your enemies: they that hate you shall reign over you; and you shall flee when none pursues you."**

At the close of 1945 America would experience the heights of its greatest military victory in WW II, since then however, in this 69th and final generation, we have experienced one military blunder after another, just as **(v17)** would plainly declare.

Beginning with the Korean War, in which we were forced to settle for a split of the Korean peninsula, and then Vietnam, where we were not able to secure even that. Then there was the debacle that occurred in both Beirut, and in Somalia. Afterwards there came the war in Iraq, and more recently the war in Afghanistan, added to the decade's long "war on drugs", and the ever looming "war on terror", and it becomes quite obvious that a shift has taken place in this generation.

Victories would appear to becoming more scarce as this generation continues to fester in its sin and rebellion against God. Although we boast of our military prowess we clearly seem to be rapidly losing ground against our militaristic foes. The tide has most certainly changed, just as Lev.26 would so aptly forecast for the nation that would turn away from God.

Next, we move to **Lev.26:19-20 "And I will break the pride of your power; and I will make your heaven as Iron, and your earth as brass. And your strength shall be spent in vain: for your land shall not yield her increase, neither shall the trees of the land yield their fruit."**

These verses describe a nation that has prided itself upon its own wealth and prosperity. It is a nation that has presumably lacked nothing and has become arrogant as a result of its great abundance and societal ease. It has forgotten from whom all of its blessings flow. These are the words of God to a nation that will see a great economic free-fall, its days of plenty have ended.

Many have presumed that America today is witnessing an unprecedented catastrophic decline. If one could only take off the deceptive glasses of "American exceptionalism", it would reveal a nation that is clearly experiencing a plummeting of its social and economic status, and not just on a national level but globally. A nation that only a few short decades ago was the world's leading "lender nation" has now become the world's greatest "debtor nation", even to the extent that it has completely mortgaged its own future.

God is quoted as saying in **Deut.28:43-44 "The alien who is among you shall rise higher and higher above you, and you shall come down lower and lower. He shall lend to you, but you shall not lend to him; he shall be the head, and you shall be the tail."**

America today has accumulated a national debt that is far beyond its ability to repay it, it is for all intensive purposes financially bankrupt. The days of her national wealth are over, all that remains now is for the gavel to fall.

Additionally, these verses of Lev.26:19-20 depict something much more ominous than merely a nation's economic decline (earthly natural application), this passage when understood within the framework of "duality" is a perfect depiction of a nation who has lost its ability to call upon God in prayer (spiritual application). The stench of its pride and arrogance has risen to the nostrils of God, and as with all kingdoms that have come before us, **"Pride goes before destruction, and a haughty spirit before a fall"** (Prov.16:18).

This is for all intensive purposes a nation and people that have fallen out of the favor of God as the result of its reprobate condition. It is the spiritual law of **Matt.16:19** being enacted upon a Godless nation: **"...and whatsoever things thou shalt bind on earth shall be bound in heaven: and whatsoever things thou shalt loose on earth shall be loosed in heaven."**

It is here that we will end our brief comparisons of Lev.26. The remainder of this passage (v21-39) consists of great famine (black horse), pestilence (pale horse), destruction of high places, images, and idols (religious element/white horse); and lastly warfare (red horse), that will lead to the final "desolation" of that nation. It should be easy to see why the comparison ends here, these are the "four horseman" of Revelation.

In closing, we have seen how the preceding verses of this passage of Leviticus share a powerfully marked resemblance to the America in which we live today in this 69th generation of Daniel. There is a clear and precise order of judgment given, consisting of "terror", then military might being broken, then economic decline, leading to an eventual collapse, and finally, a nation that cannot, nor will not pray (spiritual collapse). Even down to the precise order of the judgments we see an identical replication to that in which we are witnessing today in our once great nation of America.

Where the similarity ends is at the emergence of the "four horseman". It is by this understanding that we should clearly see that we are at the doorstep of the "seals" of Revelation, which is precisely where we would expect to be, considering that we are currently in the 65th year of this final generation, preceding the coming of Christ.

A NATIONS REJECTION OF GOD

At this time we shall briefly touch upon one of the most fearful of all the preludes to judgment that I could think of. In all of my studies and research there has always been this one singular element that has stood out prominently amidst all the others. The people, places, and times may all vary, but one thing consistently remains the same: when man rejects his God, his God eventually will reject him also.

In the Lev.26 passage that we have just looked at, the predominate precursor to the listed judgments could not have been made more clear; the nation that has rejected God's "commandments, statutes, judgments, and covenant" is equally guilty of the all encompassing rejection of God Himself, and thereby fully warrants the full weight and measure of these same judgments. Similarly, the gravest of all the consequences that a nation could heap upon itself is the absolute rejection of God of that nation.

When God in return rejects man as the just response to his hardened heart, He simply turns His back, He hides His face, and He dismisses His hand. And when that happens, man is left to his own devises, not to mention that Satan and his dark forces equally become emboldened and unrestrained. It will assuredly be soon after that judgment and calamity will be the end result.

I liken it to a great battle of tug of war. Two forces jointly opposing one another, one pulls intensely on the one side, while the other pulls vigorously on the other side. The rope, wound tightly, strained and unbending between them bears the load of the pressure of this back and forth struggle. A painful balance ensues as both sides maintain their persistence and will to overcome the other. When finally, at the last, one side releases the rope, sending the other side flailing and wheeling violently backwards; it is in this moment that one realizes that the hard fought victory is no victory at all, but rather it becomes a shameful violent embarrassment that is not without its wounds. If man persists in his defiance of God, it is only a matter of time before God turns loose of the rope. It then becomes little to do with God unleashing His own judgment upon man, for man is more than quite capable in doing this all by himself.

In every case throughout scripture leading to judgment the circumstances remain indelibly the same: man defies God; man rejects God; God then departs from man; and man falls into judgment. In fact, this process is so certain and absolute, that this is precisely the process that was utilized upon our own Savior Himself while He suffered on the cross.

In ways that we with our finite minds cannot fully understand, nor even begin to grasp, Christ through His own personal choice relinquishes His eternally unbreakable bond with the Father in-order to become one with our sinful rejection of God, and thus He becomes accursed on our behalf. Although He Himself had at no time rejected the father, He had become so completely one with us, and our evil nature, who had undoubtedly rejected God, that through this joint union with us, and our guilt and shame of rejection, that then would have resulted in God the Father departing from Him upon the cross, and thus we find the words of **Ps.22:1 "...why have you forsaken me."**

Jesus as "the Word" of God (John 1:1) knew full well that His aligning Himself so intimately with us, and with our guilt, upon the cross, would without fail result in God's departing from Him. It was this inevitable departure of God's presence that Christ anguished over in the garden of Gethsemane. For Jesus the departure of God's presence was far more the frightening eventuality than even the actual sufferings of the cross itself. If only this generation would learn from the events of the garden of that night. When God departs, Satan will come, and when Satan comes, judgment will prevail, and the entire world will know the horrific and just execution of the curses of Lev.26, as they play out through the book of Revelation.

At this moment I could supply numerous examples from Genesis to Revelation where this bedrock conclusion would be thoroughly substantiated, but for the sake of time here are but a few to read at your own leisure: Jer.6:6-8; Jer.7:23-29; Job.13:20-21; Ps.30:7; Ps.51:11; I Sam.15:23; Deut.23:14;Judg.16:20; Ezek.20:25, Ezek.23:18; Hos.9:11-12; Luke 20:17-18.

Instead, I would rather spend the remainder of this time examining the spiraling condition of this 69th generation. Does this generation meet the litmus test of a generation bound and determined to reject God, and in turn receive its just reward?

Let me just say at the onset, for those of you that may be younger in age, you enter this brief discussion at a clear disadvantage, as you have very little to draw from in the way of generational comparisons. You may have been born and raised in this generation of the superiority of man's reason and human logic. You have been wowed by the accelerating genius of this generation's inventiveness and ever growing intellect. You have only known that which is "politically correct", and have been sublimely indoctrinated into this so called "age of tolerance". It all seems quite impressive, but when it is weighed against all that we have lost it proves to be an illusion of advancement and progression.

All that one has to do is to look backwards in time to the earlier days of this same generation, and what you will find is the cost that we have paid to gain what we now have. To exalt man to this current lofty state we have in turn debased our God. For our culture and society to reach higher for more, for self, we have likewise chosen to diminish God and His supremacy in our lives, and in our thinking.

In order to lay hold of the "big bang theory" we have had to relinquish our faith in the Creator. In order to resolve the question of the "evolution" of man, we have had to reject the Biblical truth that we are made in "His image and likeness." And to maintain our own brilliance we have had to dispose of the mere concept of God and relegate Him to the place of a delusional fairy tale, as outdated and antiquated fodder.

This of course over time has resulted in the political and judicial policies of the separation of church and state, the banishment of school prayer, gay marriage and gay rights, legalized abortion, legalized cannabis use, the revising of American history text books that minimize the influence that faith had on our founding forefathers, and the newly constructed laws that relegate the Christian Biblical perspective spoken publicly as tantamount to "hate speech" and much, much more besides.

In principle we have elevated the government of man above the merciful hand of God. In short, we are witnessing the desecration of all things holy, pure, and moral, as God has ordained them. We are by in large legislating sin and the whole world is watching us simmer in our own hypocrisy.

Furthermore we have become a Biblically illiterate society, knowing more about Justin Beber than we actually do of God. We are rearing up a generation of young youths who know little if anything about God. We have become a people unrestrained as all moral boundaries have continued to be removed and replaced by man's statutes that appeal to his own sensory and fleshly lusts.

Paul in his letter to Timothy put it this way: **II Tim.3:1-7 "But know this, that in the last days perilous times shall come. For men shall be lovers of their own selves, covetous, boasters, proud, blasphemers, disobedient to parents, unthankful, unholy, without natural affection, trucebreakers, false accusers, incontinent, fierce, despisers of those that are good; having a form of godliness, but denying the power thereof,.... ever learning, and never able to come to the knowledge of the truth."**

In **Isa.5:20** we read, **"Woe to those who call evil good, and good evil; who put darkness for light, and light for darkness; who put bitter for sweet, and sweet for bitter."**

And these are but the smallest of samplings that I have chosen to make the case. There is not enough time to go into the details of our broken and anemic political system, with all of its lies, treacheries, greed and corruption. It's abandonment of the public trust as it sells it legislative privileges to the highest bidder.

Isa.1:23 say's this: **"Your princes are rebellious, and companions of thieves: everyone loves gifts, and follows**

after rewards; they judge not the fatherless, neither does the cause of the widow come unto them."

Adding to all of this, our nation's imperialistic foreign policies that make no qualms about the sacrificing of the lives of our young men and women in order to further advance its hidden agendas. And if all of that is not enough, then consider this: government sponsored torture and its black sites, illegal surveillance techniques, the drone war policies, unsustainable debt crises, subversion of the constitution, and legalized corporate bribery, not to mention the political back stabbing and the continuous inability to legislate. **Isa.3:4** put it this way: **"I will make children to be their princes, and babes shall rule over them."**

Furthermore, time will not permit me to speak in an in-depth manner of the class warfare that even now is building to its feverish pitch as a result of the greed, larceny, and manipulation of our banking system and Wall Street elites. While they enjoy the benefits of government sponsored tax payer bailouts, the working class diminishes to new all time generational lows. The middle class shrinks, the 401K's disappear, the housing crises forces many out of their homes, and many are reduced to government assistance. And those that are unmistakably most to blame are still heading our financial system as we know it today. Add to all of that our Federal Reserve debacle, and our trade laws that reward corporate outsourcing, and on and on it goes. These are all but the tip of the iceberg, and we ourselves are fully ensconced on the Titanic.

In **Isa.10:1-4** God sums it up this way: **"Woe unto them that decree unrighteous decrees, and that write grievousness which they have prescribed; to turn aside the needy from** judgment, and to take away the right from the poor of my people, that widows may be their prey, and that they may rob the fatherless! And what will you do in the day of visitation, and in the desolation which shall come from far? To whom will you flee for help? And where will you leave your glory? Without me they shall bow down under the prisoners, and they shall fall under the slain."

Now there may be some of you who have noticed that I have only given a national view of the wickedness and evils as they present themselves here in America alone. What about the rest of the world you might ask? For me that is simple enough to reply to: in this generation of global finances, and interdependent political structures, as well as communications networks, it should come as no surprise that as America rapidly degenerates so goes the rest of the world.

We have seen the economic catastrophe of 2008. We have seen the carnage that our militaristic policies have inflicted on many innocents throughout the Middle East. And we are now seeing the unprecedented contributions of our national immorality being shipped and sold abroad through our gross consumerism, our Babylonian harlot we call a movie industry, our idolatrous worship of celebrity, our billion dollar pornography industry, and our insatiable lust for bigger, better, and more. As we continue to fall even deeper into our own immoral abyss we drag the rest of the world in with us, and all the time our enemies are awaiting to pounce. These are all but the low hanging fruit on the branch of the tree that is our rejection of God.

Now, this is not to say that we are altogether responsible for the state of the condition in which we find this planet spiraling downward. What I am saying, is we have given up our moral responsibility to stave off the evil, and to maintain any sense of moral boundaries. We have in fact abandoned our post as a Christian culture and society, and have become altogether AWOL in our duties. Now, surely these are just the simple observations of one lone man, however, I leave it up to you to decide for yourself. The question remains: Have we as a people, in this last and 69th generation, rejected God? My answer is yes, and if I am right, it will not be long before God lets loose of the rope.

THE VOLITILITY OF THE MIDDLE EAST

In the previous sections leading up to this one, it cannot go ignored that we are continually finding stark similarities between the prophecies of the "last days", and the world in which we live today. Additionally, we have witnessed some very distinct parallels between our generation and those generations of the past that had neglected the stern fore-warnings of God, and eventually themselves descended into the prescribed judgments as foretold by the prophets. It would seem that if one were to take an honest and unbiased survey of the times in which we find ourselves, one could easily draw the conclusion that everything seems to be forming into a perfect alignment, as one might expect, for the 7th and final church generation, as well as for the "69th week" of Daniel.

As it appears, the evidence would suggest that we may even be on the threshold of the riding of the "four horseman", and the opening of the "seven seals" of the book of Revelation. According to these findings, it would also logically make sense that we should additionally find a Middle East that strongly resembles the prophecies that have been given, as it has been appointed that this would be the region of the world that would see the calamitous end of the battle of "Armageddon". In this section we will take a closer look at some of those prophecies, and allow our world today to reveal to us the extent of the nearness of these events as well.

We will begin our look into this geopolitical region of the world beginning with the passage that uniquely specifies the location of the final battle of Revelation. Turn now with me to **Rev.16:12** where we read, **"Then the sixth angel poured** out his bowl on the great river Euphrates and its water was dried up, so that the way of the kings from the east might be prepared."

In this passage the "Euphrates River" is unmistakably named. Furthermore, the context of this passage undeniably addresses the "the bowls" of God's judgment, clearly placing these events at the conclusion of the book of Revelation's "seals", "trumpets", and then the "bowls", as they are listed in their descending order.

Likewise, we are told that the "kings of the east" are preparing their pathway to the battle, and place of "Armageddon", found specifically mentioned by name (only four short verses later) in (v16), "And he gathered them together into a place called in the Hebrew tongue Armageddon." For the sake of the purpose of our study, logic would seem to dictate that our next step forward would be to determine where exactly is the Euphrates River located?

By the use of a simple on-line Google search we can precisely identify the river of Euphrates as being located in the definitive region of the Middle East. More specifically, the river at its northern tip begins at the southern border of the nation of Turkey, it then comes down on a southeast trajectory through the nation of Syria, and into Iraq, at which time it continues on a south-easterly course to the southwest border region of Iran, and eventually ending up in the Persian Gulf.

According to Rev.16:12-16, it is this particular region of the world where armies will amass for the last and final battle, so infamously known as the battle of "Armageddon". Moreover, these armies are stated as crossing over this same river and into the geographical territory of the nation of Israel itself. By these findings alone we should easily see that this is a geographical location of extreme importance, which should gain the utmost of our attention when looking for Biblical comparisons of the "last days", and our world today.

It should not be of any stretch of the imagination to assume that if we are in the 65th year of the 69th generation of Daniel that we should be able to see some formational resemblance between this region and the prophesied course of events as Bible prophecy has laid them out for us.

As merely a point of interest, it was in 1990 that the construction of the Ataturk Damn was completed in Turkey. This damn was the grand project of the Turkish government in their attempt to harness the mighty headwaters of the Euphrates river basin. The stated purpose for this project would be to provide irrigation and hydroelectric power to south eastern Turkey, however, the damn has equally become responsible for supplying a large part of both Syria's and Iraq's water supply today.

Concern over these water rights in the region arose to a critical mass when Turkey closed off the Euphrates for three weeks in January of 1990. Additionally, there were reports made by those that had witnessed the event, that the riverbed itself had so drastically dried up that it had become possible for a man to walk across the river to the other side (Rev.16:12 "...and its water was dried up"). This can all be verified on the web-site entitled "The Turkish Gap Project and Bible Prophecy", or "the Ataturk Damn" itself.

In another prophecy found in Ps.83:1-8 we are given an actual listing of the enemies of God, or the nations that would rise up against God's people in the land of Israel. This prophecy is widely accepted and taught as an "end time" event by many, if not most Bible prophecy scholars today.

In **(v4)** we read: **"They have said, 'Come and let us cut them off from being a nation, that the name of Israel may be remembered no more."** This is a definitive explanation of the plan and purpose of this end time **"confederacy" (Ps.83:5)**: they have joined themselves unto one cause, and that cause is to exterminate the Jews.

This particular prophecy is clearly different from any other that we have seen. In the earlier historical conquests of the Assyrians, the Babylonians, and the Romans, it was never the stated aim of these invading forces to eliminate the children of Israel to the point of extinction, this prophecy however, states the set goal clearly as one of genocide. For the kingdoms of the past, conquest was always a matter of power, land possession, spoil, and indentured servitude of the captives, in this prophecy the driving force behind this "confederacy" is clearly no less than the rawest emotions of hatred and annihilation of the Jewish people altogether.

Additionally it should be noted, that the empires of the past were all under one supreme leadership or authority. The Assyrian Empire was headed by King Sennacherib, the Babylonian Empire was headed by King Nebuchadnezzar, and the Roman Empire was headed by the Caesar Titus in 70AD. By contrast, this Ps.83 prophecy is an alignment of several nations coming together to form a "confederacy" of nations (v5), this in turn makes it unlike any of the previous historical conquests that have befallen the nation of Israel in its most painful past.

Add to that the words of the prophecy: "cut them off from being a nation", and "That the name of Israel be remembered no more", and what you have is a clear declaration of the existence of a singular nation called Israel. This terminology was not the case, and did not apply to any of the preceding military campaigns of the past, thereby making this prophecy unique unto itself. The wording of this prophecy could have never been historically accurate until the actual formation of the nation of Israel in 1948, and the beginning of Daniels 69th generation.

It should equally be mentioned that the Prime Minister of Israel (Benjamin Netanyahu) has been continuously warning the world that the not so hidden agenda of the enemies of Israel, are to annihilate, and exterminate the people of the nation of Israel today; unfortunately though, no one seems to be listening. In fact, one of the primary stumbling blocks of the peace negotiations as they exist today between Israel and her neighbors, is that Israel's neighbors refuse to publicly acknowledge Israel's right to exist as a sovereign nation, eerily reminiscent of this same end time prophecy.

Moreover, in **Ps.83:6-8** an actual listing of the names of the parties engaged in this "confederacy" is given: **"The tents of Edom, and the Ishmaelites, Moab and the Hagrites, Gebal, Ammon, and Amalek; Philistia with the inhabitants of Tyre; Assyria also has joined with them; they have helped the children of Lot."**

Upon an initial reading of this listing one might come away with little more than a definite state of confusion, as these names given are the ancient Biblical names of various people groups dating back to the earliest writings of Scripture. For that matter, one would need to do an ample amount of genealogical study in order to determine the true identities of these people groups as they exist today. For those of you that may be so inclined, a perfect starting place for your research would be Gen.10:1-32, but for the sake of our study, time will not permit us to go into a lengthy research process.

Rather than bore you to tears with the yawning details of each individual name given, I will simply cut to the chase and say: what you see here in this listing are the ancient Biblical names of the modern day nations of Turkey; the UAE; Qatar; Bahrain (and the rest of that area); Saudi Arabia; Lebanon; Jordan; and the Palestinians, among others.

This is an astounding prophecy in that it clearly defines many of the participants as they would be situated in "the time of the end", on the actual border regions of the modern day nation of Israel, just as we see them located today. Along with that, there is the unmistakable mention of the fueling of ancient hatreds that still exist.

It also must be stated as well, that the formation of these various people groups, in their surrounding neighboring nations of Israel, was a creation of the existing colonial powers that were in place following WW II. The entire region was drawn up and re-mapped to form these prophetic nations at the precise start of Daniels 69th generation.

The final proof that I will add, is that which should seem the most obvious: with the rise of the "Arab spring", today it would appear to be a relatively simple matter to see how this "confederacy" of nations might somehow be formed in the future. There is in fact one all encompassing and pervasive thread that binds them all together, and that thread is their shared religion of Islam. Islam acts not only as the cord that intuitively binds them, and makes this confederacy extremely likely at some point in the near future, but additionally it serves the greater purpose as to why they would hate Israel enough to desire to destroy her entirely.

In the final analysis, once again, what we see is the world around us today remarkably aligning itself with the prophecies of the "last days", just as we would expect them to in this late hour of Daniels 69th generation.

In our next prophecy found in Ezk.38:1-13, we find a very similar listing to that of the Ps.83 prophecy. In this passage the circumstances are relatively the same: a group of nations have formed a military alliance and have purposed themselves to go up against the nation of Israel. However, unlike Ps.83 this passage unmistakably clarifies these events as occurring precisely "in the latter years" in (v8).

Furthermore, it indirectly makes mention of the 69th generation of Daniel in the same verse: **Ezk.38:8 "You will come against the land of those brought back from the sword and gathered from many people on the mountains of Israel, which had long been desolate** (since 70AD) **; they were brought out of the nations (1948)... to stretch out your hand against the waste places that are again inhabited, and against a people gathered from the nations, who have acquired livestock and goods, who dwell in the midst of the land."** This is plainly a reference to the fulfillment of the parable of the **"fig tree"** as told by Jesus in **Matt.24**, and thereby aligning itself with the 69th generation of Daniel.

In a closer examination of this alliance we find an entirely different grouping of nations from that of Ps.83. In Ezk.38:2-6 we find the following names: "Gog, Magog, Meshech, Tubal, Persia, Ethiopia, Libya, Gomer, and Togarmah."

Once again, we are not able at this time to go into any elaborate study of the ancient historical origins of these names, but for the sake of time I will now share with you the conclusions of many, if not most Biblical scholars, as pertaining to the identity of these nations as we know them today.

It is widely accepted that the modern day nations that these names represent are: Russia, and its eastern European cohorts; Iran and Iraq; Ethiopia; Yemen; Somalia; Libya; among others. In short, what we are looking at is an alliance of Russia with fundamentalist Islamic nations, throughout the sphere of control of the nation of Iran, and northern and eastern Africa. This of course becomes extremely pertinent when we realize once more, that this is an additional detailed listing of the precise enemies that have emboldened themselves against the modern day nation of Israel in our present day world, as it exists today.

Without mincing words, one only has to look at the political landscape of today to see that Russia has taken the clear stance of choosing to align itself as a big brother and sponsor to the aforementioned nations, either by direct or indirect means. Most recently we have seen Russia's support of Iran, and its right to engage in nuclear technologies. Additionally, we have seen Russia in its full support of the cruel dictatorship of the governmental regime of Syria, in the midst of the devastating violence and bloodshed that is occurring there at this moment. And finally, we are witnessing the rise of Russia's hidden agenda for the annexation of land through political and militaristic power grabs in the besieged nation of the Ukraine, through its covert activities in the eastern region of Crimea.

Furthermore, by the very alliances that Russia has embarked upon in regard to both Iran and Syria, it has indirectly forged its support of those nations that are becoming increasingly more radicalized throughout northern and east Africa, as many of them, if not all receive much of their financial support, training, and weaponry through Iran, who is today the world's leading sponsor of terror. In short, what we find in Ezk.38 is a substantial illustration of the region as we see it shaping up today, alongside with the prophesied regional alliances, just as the prophets had foretold them.

For me the sum of the matter is this: in Ps.83 we are witnessing the foretelling of a confederacy of nations that in their combined nature represents the alignment of Sunni nations (moderates); while in Ezk.38 we are given the nations that have come under the umbrella of Shiite Nations (fundamentalists); this in turn might explain why we see separate and distinct military campaigns as opposed to just one. This would likewise help to explain the timelines to judgment given in Isa.16 and Isa.21 involving both "Moab" and "Kadar" (pg 107).

This is truly a remarkable finding, in that these prophecies were written thousands of years ago. God is plainly giving us a glimpse into the generation of the "fig tree" of Daniel's 69th generation as it relates to Islam, and the two separate and distinct divisions of the Shiite's and Sunni's as they would form coalitions in preparation for the events that would inevitably occur in "the latter days."

On a larger scale, they represent the satellite nations of the east verses west ideological strategy of proxy wars. It is through this lens that we can see the lines that are being drawn as the principle power players position themselves for the ever looming events of Rev.16:12-16. It should also go without saying that there is a great deal more that we could share on this topic, but as always we must move on as there is so much more that we have still yet to uncover.

Next, we will look at two prophecies concerning two specific nations of this region that are inconspicuously missing from Ps.83 and Ezk.38, as they too relate to the world in which we see around us today.

First, we will turn our attention to **Isa.19:1-14** where we find God's own prophetical overview of the end time nation of "Egypt", beginning with **(v2) "And I will set the Egyptians against the Egyptians: and they shall fight everyone against his brother, and every one against his neighbor; city against city..."**

In this verse God clearly depicts the nation of Egypt as violently imploding upon itself in the "last days". A great bloodshed through an internal civil war will bring the nation of Egypt to its knees, and eventually a national repentance unto God (v16-25); but until then, this horrific foretelling of violence will leave Egypt in a complete and utter state of chaos and disorder. Additionally, she will find herself in the midst of a great economic collapse as a result of this momentous turmoil, and it is in my opinion for these reasons that we do not find Egypt mentioned among either party of **Ps.83** or **Ezek.38**.

As this passage continues, we read in **(v4) "And the Egyptians will I give over into the hand of a cruel lord; and a fierce king shall rule over them..."** Then in **(v11-14) "Surely the princes of Zoan are fools, the counsel of the wise counselors of pharaoh is become brutish... The LORD has mingled a perverse spirit in the midst thereof: and they have** caused Egypt to err in every work thereof, as a drunken man staggereth in his vomit."

By these verses it would appear that the nation of Egypt would in turn fall under the rule of a ruthless dictator, perhaps as a result of the aforementioned civil strife; or perhaps the civil strife is the result of this man's coming to power, and it is the end result of their opposition to his governance. In either case, the nation of Egypt is seen as it shall exist under great paralyzing violence and oppression domestically in the near future.

Once again, we must measure this prophecy under the guidelines of the reality that exists in our current generation of today, and not just that, but since we are in the 65th year of the prophesied generation, surely we should see the beginnings of this prophetic warning unfolding and taking shape.

Today Egypt is still very much embroiled in the aftermath of the so called "Arab Spring". For those that may not be familiar with this term, or the events that have taken place to date, here is but a brief analysis as given in a very rudimentary fashion.

The former President of Egypt (Hosni Mubarak) was eventually pressured into relinquishing his presidential post in 2010, after more than 30 years of uninterrupted rule the Egyptian people rose up in a united outcry for his resignation. Amid massive public protests that numbered in the hundreds of thousands Mubarak was ousted and forced out of power, and his decade's long dictatorial reign was ended.

Many months afterwards the Egyptian people would participate in their first ever free national democratic elections, which in turn would result in the election of its new President Mohamed Morsi, under the Muslim Brotherhood Party.

In this case it would only be a matter of a year and some months later that this too would prove to be an unacceptable outcome in the eyes of many Egyptian citizens. Public protests would once more arise and lay hold of the political landscape of Egypt. At its conclusion the Egyptian military itself would seize the reins of power by the public arrest and jailing of the nations former president Morsi, and in addition to this, the Muslim Brotherhood party as a whole has been ostracized and outlawed by the same military machine that is now currently in power. Since then many of its leaders have been hunted down, arrested, and imprisoned as well. More recently, it was just a week ago, at the time of this writing, that more than 500 formerly known leaders of the Muslim Brotherhood Party were put on trial and sentenced to their deaths, solely for their affiliation with the Islamic party.

As things stand today the military remains in power amid an ever growing unrest among the loyal followers of the Muslim Brotherhood as they await the trial of their former President Morsi.

Of course these events are considerably more complex than I admittedly have knowledge of, but one thing is certain: Egypt is currently poised to erupt into a hotbed of civil disobedience and internal bloodshed just as the prophecy declares that it will. We may very well be witnessing the eve of the prophecy of Isa.19 as we inch ever closer to the waning years of this 69th generation of Daniel.

The next prophecy we will look at is found in Isa.17, precariously located in the same proximity of the Egyptian prophecy of Isa.19, I might add. Likewise, it should not go unmentioned that both of these prophecies of Egypt and Syria are equally located precisely within the "end time" four part timeline (70 years) of Isa.7; 16; 21; 32, lending even further credence to the perception that these are all inter-related and precisionally crafted and laid to spell out the events of the Middle East as they are soon to unfold in the "last days".

On another note, what we could be looking at through the isolated coverage of these two prescribed judgments of both Egypt and Syria is a personalized pictorial of the two nations that may soon rise to the leadership roles of these two warring factions of the Sunni and Shiite, and thereby elevating them to the unenviable position of being deserving of an even greater judgment than that of their conspiratorial cohorts.

Returning now to the prophecy of **Isa.17:1-14**, this is by all accounts an ominous one in that it predicts the total destruction of the city of Damascus. In **(v1)** we read this: **"The burden of Damascus. Behold, Damascus is taken away from being a city, and it shall be a ruinous heap."** And finally in **(v14) "And behold at eveningtide trouble; and before the morning he is not."**

This passage is surely a terrifying one in that it plainly reveals a devastating destruction that is sure to come upon the capital city of Syria in a matter of only a few short hours. This is an end to an entire city of several million people within the shortest imaginable span of time, over the course of only a single night. Furthermore, this cannot be mistaken as the result of any type of conventional warfare as this would not seem at all plausible given the precise wording of the passage.

Today at this moment, Syria may be undergoing the bloodiest atrocities of any known location on the face of this planet. Since 2010-11 the nation of Syria has been engaged in a three-way tug of war (civil war) competing for power between its current dictatorial regime, and that of the split opposition of the FSA (Free Syrian Army) and the ever growing emergence of religious extremists. The fighting on all sides has been ruthless and shows no signs of relenting. It is estimated that more than 150,000 Syrians have been killed over the past 3 years of bloodshed, and the count is ever growing each day.

At the present its cities have been laid to ruin, and equally if not more so disheartening, it has tragically produced a worldwide refugee crises that numbers in the millions. There has even been the highly publicized limited use of Chemical weapons upon its civilian population which has created an even greater urgency on the part of the world to somehow save the vestiges of the people of Syria, and all the while the world stands idly by and watches the carnage as it plays out.\

Simply put, Syria is in a grave state of cataclysm and time is running out, as the world continues to sit by and do nothing. My question, however, is this: How long will it be before the events of Isa.17 are fatalistically carried out?

In summary, this is a brief snapshot of the Middle East as it exists today. For all the sins and degradation's of the entire world as a whole, it could easily be argued that this prophesied region of "the latter days" is the most dangerous and most volatile region in all the earth, at this precise moment in time, and exactly as one might expect it to be, if in fact we are rapidly nearing the culmination of Daniel's 69th generation, as it precedes the soon coming return of Christ Jesus.

THE MYSTERY OF LAWLESSNESS

For our next prophetical look at the events of which we might expect of the "end time" Biblical generation, we will begin with a subtle prophecy that has gained very little attention, except of course among those who stringently study the prophetic passages on a regular basis:

I Thess.2:1-8 (v1) "Now, brethren, concerning the coming of our Lord Jesus Christ and our gathering together to Him... (v3) for that Day will not come unless the falling away comes first, and the man of sin is revealed, the son of perdition; (V4) who opposes and exalts himself above all that is called God, or that is worshiped; so that he sits as God in the temple of God, showing himself that he is God... (V6) And now you know what is restraining, that he may be revealed in his own time. (7) For the mystery of lawlessness is already at work; only He who now restrains, will do so until He is taken out of the way. (8) And then the lawless one will be revealed, whom the Lord will consume with the breath of His mouth and destroy with the brightness of His coming. (9) The coming of the lawless one is according to the working of Satan..."

The first thing that I would hope to bring to your attention in regard to this passage is found in the opening verse: (v1) "...concerning the coming of our Lord Jesus Christ". Paul is unmistakably and plainly telling the Church that the events of this passage, as he will outline them, will closely precede the coming return of our Great Savior Jesus. In short, what Paul is attempting to do through this instruction to the church of Thessalonica is to provide a simplified ABC approach in answer to their earlier inquiry involving "...the coming of our Lord Jesus Christ".

In (v3), the first event in which Paul mention's is regarding an instrumental sign-post of sorts, that he uniquely labels himself as "the falling away". In an effort of my own to maintain a strict and orderly explanation of these individual "pillar events", we will cover this particular forerunner of Christ's return in the next section as it shall find itself to be most exclusively applicable to the church only.

Next, Paul lists the second event to transpire before "the coming of our Lord", this event he calls "the man of sin is revealed". In (v4) he describes the actual circumstances surrounding this defining stage event that would optimize the "revealing" of this "man of sin" to the world as a whole, and thereby would decisively divulge the true identity of this man to all the inhabitants of the earth that would have knowledge of this prophecy. In Paul's amplification of the arrival of this man he clearly singles him out as the one who will "sit as God in the temple of God, showing himself that he is god".

This is truly extraordinary in that we had covered earlier in our study how the nation of Israel today has completed all the preparations to rebuild this selfsame "...temple of God". According to this prophecy once the temple is rebuilt, a time will come in which a man will enter that same temple and seat himself within it, and proclaim himself to be God; this according to Paul's instruction will be "the man of sin." The very fact that all things are prepared today for the construction of this temple should alert us to the nearness of the revealing of this man of sin, and likewise the soon return of Christ. This is precisely the type of alignment we should expect for the generation that would soon see the return of our Lord.

Moving on to (v7-9) we see Paul further expounding on this term "the man of sin", in these verses he mentions "the mystery of lawlessness" as it is "already at work" in the world, although he states it is currently being "restrained". Immediately after these statements he further relates this "mystery of lawlessness" as being directly linked and associated with this "man of sin", that he now calls "the lawless one".

A rudimentary analogy of this explanation by Paul would be the equivalent of saying that "a carpenter does carpentry". The term "carpenter" suggests a title of who one is, he is a "carpenter", it likewise represents what he does, he does "carpentry".

Similarly, "the mystery of lawlessness" is what the "the lawless one" does. The reason this distinction is so monumentally important is that Paul is clearly saying to us today that we will be able to see "what he does" before we are ever actually able to see him directly. My purpose is quite simple for pointing this out, it is to raise the question: do we in this 69th generation of Daniel see "the mystery of lawlessness" at work in our world today?

First we must determine what does this word "lawlessness" actually mean? *Webster's Dictionary* defines "lawlessness" as: "not regulated by or based on law; not restrained or controlled by law; unruly; illegal." In the Hebrew language we find this definition: "anomos: - lawless, not subject to (the Jewish) law; (by implication a Gentile), or wicked: without law, transgressor, unlawful."

By these definitions we might easily say that this "mystery of lawlessness" has been with us from the very beginning, even from the initial incursion of sin into this world through Adam until now, and we would be correct in saying so. However, we are leaving out one invaluable piece of this message concerning this "mystery", Paul states in **I Thess. (v6-7) "you know what is restraining... He who now restrains, will do so until He is taken out of the way."**

By this statement alone we can conclude that as we approach the arrival of this "man of sin" leading to the "coming of Christ", that the "mystery of lawlessness" as we should be able to see it will become increasingly more and more "unrestrained", and this is precisely what I would argue is occurring all over the globe today in an unprecedented manner.

As we are progressing forward in this 69th generation of Daniel, in this ever waning generation of the "fig tree", we are continuously witnessing as never before, a global unrest of the people and nations of this entire earth. Anyone even remotely familiar with international affairs as they are occurring today can tell you that the various populations of this planet are uprising against their national governments on an unparalleled scale.

If these governments represent the customary "rule of law" as we have known it, than what we may be seeing is the rejection of that law on a global scale. Rioting and civil unrest have become the pervasive norm, and there is virtually no corner on the planet earth where these mob actions and rebellious uprisings are not presenting themselves today.

Now it must be said that mine is not to determine if these uprisings are warranted or not, or if they are long overdue, or if they are unjust and illegal, mine is only to announce that they are currently with us in a most uncommon and unfamiliar fashion, and to bring to the forefront that the "mystery of lawlessness" is rearing its ugly head as never before, in an increasingly "unrestrained" manner exactly as Paul had prophesied that it would.

Consider what Paul writes in **(V4) "...who opposes and exalts himself above all that is called God,"** In this verse Paul himself is providing a Spirit inspired definition of this "mystery of lawlessness". This "lawlessness" is a spirit of opposition and self-exaltation, it is a spirit that despises authority, and it is a usurper of authority. Additionally, it is a spirit of pride and all out rebellion, and make no mistake, it is in fact the spirit of the Antichrist. The prefix "anti" itself contains within it the clear meaning of "instead of", as a form of "replacement". It is likewise the very same spirit that seduced Eve in the garden and usurped Man's dominion in **Gen.3:5 "For God doth know that in the day ye eat thereof, then your eyes shall be opened, and ye shall be as gods..."**

In **Rom.13:1** it states: **"Let every soul be subject unto the higher powers. For there is no power but of God: the powers that be are ordained of God."** Jesus Himself was the prime and exemplary example of this, at no time did Jesus ever "oppose or exalt Himself" over the ruling Roman power structure of His day.

Satan on the other hand exemplifies the flip-side of this spirit in Isa.14:12-16, it is the spirit of "I will" as opposed to **Matt.26:39 "not as I will, but as thou wilt"**. And unless we forget, it is also the driving spirit behind the Islamic militants of today, just as it was the selfsame spirit that drove the Sadducees and the Pharisees of Christ's day.

More precisely, on every continent, and in every corner of the world, governments are under siege by their own constituents. Many governments have already fallen, and many more are fighting for their very lives to remain in power. The populations are gathering, marching, protesting, rioting, and fighting back as never before.

We can look at the riotous bloodshed that has occurred most recently throughout the Middle East, including Tunisia, Egypt, Iraq, Libya, Syria, Turkey, Bahrain, and others. Add to that the sporadic upheaval of Greece, London, Spain, Italy, Ukraine, Venezuela, Thailand, and the Philippines; and this does not include the even larger growing list of those nations that are currently undergoing the assault of rebel forces that have determined to undermine and over throw their governments throughout the continents of Europe, Asia, Africa, and Central and South America. These forces are actively at work in many nations as we speak.

In summary, what we are witnessing is the chaotic results of this "mystery of lawlessness" as it springs into an ever growing unrestrained frenzy worldwide. It is posturing itself on a global scale as it makes ready the path of the "revealing" of "the man of sin", who is "the lawless one."

In fact, it may be this very same political confusion, religious zealotry, rebellion, disorder, and civil unrest, which may soon someday set the stage for the forming of a one world government, and thus paving the way for the Antichrist. In any case the "mystery of lawlessness" is evidently hard at work in this the "69th generation" of Daniel, and by this we know that the return of Christ is sooner than we might think.

THE FALLING AWAY

We have just completed a brief look at one of the two major "signs" that Paul had given to the church of Thessalonica pertaining to "the coming of our Lord", and by it we have learned of the prophesied event of an all encompassing worldwide backlash of the inhabitants of the earth against all established governance, authority, and judicial law. It was this first sign that Paul himself so profoundly entitled "the mystery of lawlessness".

In this next section we shall attempt to explore the second "sign" of equal importance which Paul so aptly discloses in the same passage of II Thess.2:1-9 as "the falling away". As I stated earlier this particular sign is predominately addressed to the church as a whole, likewise, it must not go unnoticed that as this most significant of prophesies is aimed with great precision at the church in its most general sense, it is also clearly and undeniably honed in at the 7th and final church generation of the Laodiceans of the book of Revelation.

Return with me now to **I Thess.2:1-8 (v1) "Now, brethren, concerning the coming of our Lord Jesus Christ and our gathering together to Him... (v3) for that Day will not come unless the falling away comes first, and the man of sin is revealed,"**

If one reads (v3) slowly and carefully it is not difficult to see that "the falling away" precedes the "the coming of our Lord Jesus Christ", just as the "mystery of lawlessness" will also be detected beforehand, and additionally both of these two signs leading up to the curtain call of the Antichrist. According to this passage we should be able to identify the sure fingerprints of this so called "falling away" as we advance ever closer to the eminent return of our great King Jesus.

In reaching for a *Strongs Hebrew and Greek Concordance* once more, we find that the prescribed definitions for the word "falling", and the word "away", both carry the exact same definition: the Greek word "apostasia" (#646). If this word "apostasia" looks familiar to you it is because this is where we get our common English word "apostasy". The Greek definition reads this way: "defection from truth; forsake; divorce: - writing of divorcement". As an enlargement to this meaning the Webster's English Dictionary adds this to the word "apostasy":- "to revolt, renunciation of a religious faith; abandonment of a previous loyalty; defection."

By Paul's use of the words "falling" and "away", both carrying the same identical meaning of the Greek word "apostasia", what Paul would seem to be doing here is adding a double emphasis to this statement which in the Greek would read "apostasia apostasia". One may conclude from this that Paul is emphasizing an extreme and wide spread "apostasy" to occur. This would not constitute an isolated defection of the church but rather one that would be pervasive throughout the church by in large.

It appears to me that looking back at what we've discovered concerning "the mystery of lawlessness", this "falling away" is but another ramification of the selfsame spirit. In our earlier examination of the workings of this spirit we have seen how it is creating a chaotic upheaval against governance, law, and order", and this occurring a midst an unsaved world. Likewise, this same spirit is attacking the Church of Christ in an identical manner. Where the world without knowledge of God directs its revolt at the earthly governing powers that it can so carnally identify, the presumed church aims its attack at its self, and the truth of the Word of God, and thereby knowingly or unknowingly creating an enmity between themselves and God Himself. The end result is a church that has similarly taken the same destructive stance as that of the rest of the unsaved world by turning its back on the governance, law, and authority of God Himself.

In this process the church becomes more divisive and contentious amid denominational lines previously drawn, due largely in part to its rejection of truth, and misinterpretation (intentional or otherwise) of Biblical foundational principles. It is during this process that true scriptural doctrine is thrown by the wayside as lies and deceptions lay hold of many congregations and their pulpits.

What we have here is those who are without the church preparing the way for the Antichrist by means of "the mystery of lawlessness", through political and governmental revolt, this primes the way for a one world economic and political leader to arise on the scene, while simultaneously the church itself is actively engaged in the indiscernible preparations for the way of "the false prophet" of Rev.13:11-15.

By the means of its own gross immoralities, backbiting, bickering, lack of the indwelling presence of the Holy Spirit, and all rejection of any revelatory knowledge or true doctrine, every ailment of the church today as a whole is actually just another shrewdly and carefully crafted manifestation of the "mystery of lawlessness." In short, the world rejects its own earthly authorities, while similarly the church itself rejects the very heavenly authority of God. In both cases a chasm is opened, a void left unfilled, uniquely positioning both the saved and unsaved to fall prey to leadership and guidance of two satanic impostors.

In the remainder of this section of our study I will draw upon the prophetic scriptures and allow them to best explain the state of the church that will usher in the coming of our Lord, and this to be done in an attempt to draw out of the darkness the elusive deceptions that accompany "the falling away". As we begin I would just like to quote an old saying for those of you that may be currently feeling your temperature rising: "If the shoe fits wear it."

In II Tim.3:1-9 **"But know this, that in the last days perilous times will come; for men will be lovers of themselves, lovers of money, boasters, proud, blasphemers, disobedient to parents, unthankful, unholy, unloving, unforgiving, slanderers, without self-control, brutal, despisers of good, traitors, headstrong, haughty, lovers of pleasure rather than lovers of God, having a form of godliness but denying its power....always learning and never able to come to the knowledge of the truth....so do these also resist the truth, men of corrupt minds, disapproved concerning the faith..."**

This is a clear depiction of an end time church that is a mirage, a virtual optical illusion. In our earlier study of Christ's letter to the church of Laodicea (Rev.3:14-21), which similarly is a direct representation of the spiritual state of the end time church, we see Jesus rebuking this same church for its lack of true faith and intimacy with Himself. A church by all outward appearances, but entirely disconnected from a true and living faith in Christ Jesus. A church more heavily invested in religious activity, traditions, and ritual, than with an actual true relationship with God based on a personal and individual faith in Christ. It is this church that is completely devoid of the presence and power of the Holy Spirit, and thereby it is dying if not already dead. Moreover, this a church that is highly diluted and self-deceived, lacking any remnants of true godly sorrow or repentance as it relates to their sins.

While bearing all of this in mind it should not be difficult at all for anyone who has an observant eye, as it pertains to the state and welfare of our current day church, how similar and exact these various representations are in fact manifesting themselves throughout our present day church bodies and congregations.

Next we shall take a look at **I Tim.4:1-2 "Now the Spirit expressly says that in the latter times some will depart from the faith, giving heed to deceiving spirits and doctrines of demons, speaking lies in hypocrisy, having their own conscience seared with a hot iron..."**

In this passage what we see is an infectious disease that shall infiltrate the church in the "latter times" through the means of a corruption of the otherwise holy and pure doctrine of the Gospel as handed down through the centuries first from Christ Jesus, and then through His disciples and their Holy inspired writings.

In **II Tim.4:3-4** we read this: **"For the time will come when they will not endure sound doctrine, but according to their own desires, because they have itching ears, they will heap up for themselves teachers; and they will turn their ears away from the truth, and be turned aside to fables."**

What we are unmistakably seeing today throughout our churches is an unprecedented rise in the misleading doctrines of tolerance and inter-faith teaching. The church has by in large became so inundated with the culture of the day, and the prescribed norms as the world would institute them, that they have made the grievous error of compromising the truth of Christ for the sake of presenting itself as a "seeker friendly" church. Within this intended premise the church has stepped away from all forms of doctrine that might otherwise be construed by others as inflammatory or offensive.

In this age of mega-churches the primary importance of pure Scriptural doctrine has shifted to that of one which is best described as the "feel good" doctrine. Under this instruction the true message of Christ and His salvation is of a secondary importance, more instrumental to this damnable approach is the permeating theme of self. In this gospel, which is no gospel at all, the teaching of sin is expressly prohibited. Far be it for the church of Christ to speak of anything that would be of such an offensive and inconvenient nature for those that would fill its pews. No, in this new and revised approach it is the love of God, and His mercy and temperance that best delights the listeners and solidifies the almighty church attendance, and equally thereby maintaining its extensive coffers.

Other such controversial and taboo subjects include homosexuality, abortion, and even hell itself, and this "people pleasing" gospel does not stop there, it has the audacity to extend its drivel even to the very core of Christianity, as it nervously shutters at the preaching that Jesus is the Son of God and thereby there is no other way but through faith in His shed blood to reach the Father. How dare the church so blatantly and intolerantly create an exclusion to all other faiths that may so vehemently attest that their god, and their prophets, and their books, are likewise adequately sufficient. I say this of course facetiously and with immense disdain for any church that would attempt to set my Savior on par with that of any other false religion and their deceptions. God forgive us!

Simply put, what we are experiencing is the moral decay of this societal generation as it pours its way into our houses of worship. Paul's admonition as he gives it in **Rom.12:2** "**... be not conformed to this world, but be transformed by the renewing of your mind**" has gone largely ignored by today's 21st century church.

Paul voiced his warning this way to the Corinth church in **II Cor.11:2-4 "For I am jealous over you with godly jealousy: for I have espoused you to one husband that I may present you as a chaste virgin to Christ. But I fear, lest by any means, as the serpent beguiled Eve through his subtility, so your minds should be corrupted from the simplicity that is in Christ. For if he that cometh preacheth another Jesus, whom we have not preached, or if ye receive another spirit, which ye have not received, or another gospel, which ye have not accepted, ye might well bear with him."**

Today many of our so called institutions of Biblical higher learning are actively engaging in these very same practices that Paul so vehemently warns us of, even as going so far as to contest the actual presence and power of the Holy Spirit Himself. For these, the workings of the Holy Spirit, along with His gifts and callings are strictly a mute point as they would argue that all of this has been done away with since the passing of the generation of the Apostles. They are in fact by their hideous lies and hypocrisy are creating a lifeless and spiritless church of misguided converts.

In Paul's letter to the church of Galatia he writes: **Gal.1:6-9 "I marvel that ye are so soon removed from Him that called you into the grace of Christ unto another gospel: Which is not another; but there be some that trouble you, and would pervert the gospel of Christ. But though we, or an angel from heaven, preach any other gospel unto you than that which we have preached unto you, let him be accursed."**

Moreover, in this generation of the television evangelist we give witness to an entirely separate and equally disdaining practice of thievery and mass manipulations. In this debauchery the gospel is sold on the open market as merchandise. It has become the common practice of many (not all) to attach a price to the desired blessing of the masses. In this hell spawned corruption everything is marketable from handkerchiefs to holy oil. Many of these unnamed churches today come equipped with their own extensive catalogs listing every item and article that would best assist the foolish and weak among us to purchase for their own spiritual enrichment. God help us.

This is precisely what Christ encountered at His first coming when He stampeded His way through the temple of God with whip in hand violently cleansing it of the influx of every type of nefarious character.

In **Matt.21:12-13** it reads this way: **"And Jesus went into the temple of God, and cast out all them that sold and bought in the temple, and overthrew the tables of the moneychangers, and the seats of them that sold doves, And said unto them, 'It is written, My house shall be called the house of prayer; but ye have made it a den of thieves."**

Once again what we are seeing is a clear cut case of Biblical duality in action. As it was at the time of Christ's first coming, so we are witnessing the events as they unfold today in this 69th generation in preparation for its ominous repeat performance.

In **Tit.1:10-16** "**For there are many unruly and vain talkers and deceivers, specially they of the circumcision: whose mouths must be stopped, who subvert whole houses, teaching things which they ought not, for filthy lucre's sake... Unto the pure all things are pure: but unto them that are defiled and unbelieving is nothing pure; but even their mind and conscience is defiled. They profess that they know God; but in works they deny Him, being abominable, and disobedient, and unto every good work reprobate.**"

The epistle of **I Pet.2:1-3** puts it this way: "**But there were false prophets also among the people, even as there shall be false teachers among you, who privily shall bring in damnable heresies, even denying the Lord that bought them... And many shall follow their pernicious ways; by reason of whom the way of truth shall be evil spoken of. And through covetousness shall they with feigned words make merchandise of you...**"

As we near to the close of this section of our study I would just like to focus our attention on one final ill of the church, which in my opinion may be as harmful as any of the other aforementioned grievances listed. In this perhaps the most fatal neglect, we find our modern day church once again following in a synchronized lockstep with that of its ancient forerunners of the Old Testament.

Throughout the historical record of the Bible there has always remained a steadfast constant that is undeniably present among the children of Israel: despite the various attempts and multiple methods of God to warn His people of the impending dangers of judgment they remained in a terminal state of ease, complacency, and denial. This was due in large part because of their leadership who although they professed to know God, and His word, were proven time and time again to be firmly ensconced in a malignant spirit of slumber. The prophet and priest alike were found to be more than oblivious to the rapidly approaching destruction's that were so hurriedly racing toward them. And as the result there was no watchman upon the wall to warn the people and lead them to safety. Today's church is no different.

In **Jer.6:13-15 "Because from the least of them even to the greatest of them, everyone is given to covetousness; and from the prophet even to the priest, everyone deals falsely. They have also healed the hurt of my people slightly, saying 'Peace, peace!' When there is no peace. Where they ashamed when they had committed abomination? No! They were not at all ashamed; nor did they know how to blush. Therefore they shall fall among those who fall; at the time I punish them."**

These are the words of God to the prophet Jeremiah at the very same time that the Babylonian Empire was set to inflict its ruthless carnage upon the inhabitants of the southern kingdom of Judah. And this was by no means the exception but rather the customary norm as Scripture would go on to record. The same would hold true with the fall of the northern kingdom of Israel at the hands of the Assyrian Empire, and again with the Jews just prior to their being ravaged by the Romans.

We have seen it all before dating as far back as to the flood of Noah, men perilously asleep at the time when their lives hung most precariously in the balance, and unless we forget

Christ Himself warned that as it was in the days of the flood so it would be preceding His return (Matt.24:38-39). Why should we think that our 69th generation of Daniel should be any different? The prophecies plainly tell us that we are assuredly marked for a repeat performance.

Here are but a few examples: **Ezek.13:1-16 "Son of man, prophesy against the prophets of Israel who prophesy, and say to those who prophesy out of their own heart, hear the word of the LORD! .... Woe to the foolish prophets, who follow their own spirit and have seen nothing! .... Because you have spoken nonsense and envisioned lies, therefore I am indeed against you. ... Because they have seduced my people, saying, Peace! when there is no peace ....Thus will I accomplish my wrath on the wall and on those who have plastered it with untempered mortar** (false doctrine), **and I will say to you, The wall is no more, nor those who plastered it, that is the prophets of Israel who prophesy concerning Jerusalem, and who see visions of peace for her, when there is no peace, says the Lord God."**

In **Jer.28:8-9** we read this: **"The prophets who have been before me and before you of old prophesied against many countries and great kingdoms of war, and disaster and pestilence. As for the prophet who prophesies of peace, when the word of the prophet comes to pass, the prophet will be known as one whom the LORD has truly sent."**

Mic.2:11 "If a man should walk in a false spirit and speak a lie, saying, I will prophesy to you of wine and drink, even he would be the prattler of this people."

Mic.3:5-8 "Thus says the LORD concerning the prophets, who make my people stray; who chant "Peace", while they

chew with their teeth, but who prepare war against him who puts nothing into their mouths; Therefore you shall have night without vision; and you shall have darkness without divination; the sun shall go down on the prophets, and the day shall be dark for them. So the seers shall be ashamed, and the diviners abashed; indeed they shall all cover their lips; for there is no answer from God."

Zech.10:1-2 "Ask the LORD for rain in the time of the latter rain, the LORD will make flashing clouds; He will give them showers of rain, grass in the field for everyone. For the idols speak delusion; the diviners envision lies, and tell false dreams, they comfort in vain, therefore the people wend their way like sheep; they are in trouble because there is no shepherd."

Deut.29:19 " And so it may not happen, when he hears the words of this curse, that he blesses himself in his heart, saying, I shall have peace, even though I follow the dictates of my own heart - as though the drunkard could be included with the sober."

And finally in I Thess.5:3 "For when they say, "Peace and safety!" then sudden destruction comes upon them, as labor pains upon a pregnant women. And they shall not escape."

There are many other examples and passages that I could site to further illuminate this point, but hopefully my point is well made by these few that I have chosen. The shocking truth is this: that despite the many proofs that I have attempted to share with you, the reader, in this book, concerning the nearness of the coming of our Lord, and subsequently the harsh and difficult times that lie directly ahead of us, there remains a deafening hush and ignorant silence throughout the body of

Christ by in large. At a time where we find ourselves immersed in the waning stages of this the 69th generation of Daniel, where are the trumpet blowers? Where are our shepherds readying the people, alerting them, and warning them to prepare?

I will tell you where they are, they are off preaching the gospel of health, wealth, and prosperity. In turn they are appeasing the masses with their eloquent oratories, and light shows, and auditorium concerts, and stage props. They are on the ever growing circuit of the motivational speaking tour, and the carnival act and sideshows of the so called healing ministries.

Throw in to the mix the ever popular divine deliverance that awaits us in the fictitious rapture, and they are sending us off, all their congregants to ride euphorically home and get comfortably nestled within our beds feeling thoroughly satisfied and entertained. As a truth, they are out spreading abroad the milktose message of "Peace and safety", that's where they are. God help us all!

And even with all of this said, there still remains a plethora of Bible passages that continuously spell out the vast duplication's of our church today as it replicates every evil of its ancient predecessors. The point that I would hope to make should be perfectly clear, and that is that the church as we see it today in this foreboding 69th generation of Daniel is strategically positioned itself to experience firsthand the very "falling away" or "apostasia apostasia" of which Paul speaks of so plainly in II Thess.2:1-9.

Time will not even permit me to touch upon the extensive and overly pervasive doctrinal teachings of the so called "mother church" of the world which boasts that its role-call numbers at more than a billion congregants. Spreading its lies, deceptions, and hypocrisy across the globe in an unprecedented fashion. And yet none of this should be of any real surprise to any of us, it was prophesied and openly declared to be the state of affairs as we would approach the glorious coming of our great God and Savior Christ Jesus. I conclude this section by asking a simple question: What further must God do in order to convey to us His warnings?

THE NUMBER OF THE BEAST

In this next section we will once again take an abbreviated look at a very familiar prophecy, and perhaps the most familiar of all. Today there is hardly a believer or non believer alike who has not heard something concerning this end time prophecy of **Rev.13:16-18**: **"And he caused all, both small and great, rich and poor, free and bond, to receive a mark in their right hand, or in their foreheads; and that no man might buy or sell, except he that had the mark, or the name of the beast, or the number of his name. Here is wisdom. Let him that has understanding count the number of the beast: for it is the number of a man; and his number is 666."**

Getting straight to the point, the crux of the matter as I see it is this: there can be little doubt that the fulfillment of this specific prophecy has never in all of human history past, ever been even remotely possible to fulfill, that is until now, in this generation in which we find ourselves today. If we are that generation that will see the coming of our Lord, than for a certainty we should see the plausibility of this prophecy as it could be carried out in our lifetime.

In my opinion there should be little room for debate as to rather or not we find ourselves smack dab in the middle of the technological advances that would be necessary to implement such a mass distribution of this number on such a prophesied global scale.

Let me just remind you that today there is an ever growing field of science called bio-metric science. The very definition of the name itself of this science translates as such: bio: "body", and metric: "numbers". This is a technology that has literally exploded over the past couple of decades, and more recently has been extensively implemented with a wide variety of uses throughout the everyday world in which we live. Additionally, I would whole heartedly suggest that everyone reading this material do a personal internet research on your own, of the term "bio-metrics", as it has in fact yielded many applications that are currently relevant to our daily lives.

This particular field of science has been responsible for such recent technological advances as voice recognition; facial identification; fingerprint scanning; retinal iris scans; pupil identification; and signature analysis, as well as certain DNA technologies; and these just to name a few.

Adding to all of this technology we cannot forget the associated sciences that have interconnected with one another offering us the 21st century mainstays of our already cashless society: such as the microchip, bar code, data processing technologies, global internet communication networks (through the implementation of the WWW), data storage, and global economic trade inter-dependence, interwoven banking and financial systems, our electronic monitoring and public digital cameras, and our current satellite GPS tracking and surveillance systems, and what you have beyond any shadow of a doubt is a fully existing planetary system that is more than capable of implementing the final stage of tagging, numbering, and tracking the entirety of the total inhabitants of the earth. All the foundational structures have been securely set in their place and are more than capable of becoming fully operational within our lifetime; this could not have been said of any other generation before us.

The 69th Generation

Once again we find ourselves exactly where we might expect the 69th generation of Daniel to be, a global culture and society that has become fully welcoming, and openly excepting of these same prophesied technologies.

314

WEAPONS OF MASS DESTRUCTION

This next section is one that I am completely unequipped to address. It is truly an ominous prophecy which may make many people extremely uncomfortable, and I myself am included. Nonetheless, it is without a doubt an end time prophecy, and it is spelled out for us with a perfect clarity that its content and explanation should be simple to understand.

Furthermore, it provides a perfect testimonial to the 69th generation of Daniel as perhaps few other prophecies do, as this particular prophecy could have never met its fulfillment until the generation would come in which its fulfillment had been appointed. As a final disclaimer I feel the need to say that it brings me no pleasure to set this prophecy in its rightful place of the forefront of our understanding, but for certain it has been written and spoken by our Creator and Father, and as such it is altogether true.

Beginning in **Rev.6:8 "And I looked, and behold a pale horse; and his name that sat on him was Death, and Hell followed with him. And power was given unto them over the fourth part of the earth, to kill with sword, and with hunger, and with death, and with the beasts of the earth."** This passage represents the clear repercussions of the "opening of the fourth seal".

In a completely separate and distinct event, we move ahead now to **Rev.9:15-18 "And the four angels were loosed, which were prepared for an hour, and a day, and a month, and a year, for to slay the third part of men. And the number of the army of the horsemen were two hundred thousand thousand (200,000,000); and I heard the number of them. And thus I saw** the horses in the vision, and them that sat on them, having breastplates of fire, and of jacinth, and brimstone, and the heads of the horses were as the heads of lions; and out of their mouths issued fire and smoke and brimstone. By these three was the third part of men killed, by the fire, and by the smoke, and by the brimstone, which issued out of their mouths."

In an unmistakable manner these prophecies use an assortment of various types of symbols to depict a massive military confrontation unlike the world has ever witnessed before. The statements which I have underlined in the texts are the clear pronouncements of the unprecedented fatalities that will result from this warfare. Beyond the obvious significance of this horrific warning there are two points within these passages that I believe clearly marks their fulfillment for our generation today, and no other generation before us.

The first point that I would hope to make is that of the formation of the plainly stated 200 million man army, let us now consider this within logical terms. It was not until the turn of the century around the year of 1800 that the earth's population for the first time surpassed the one billion inhabitants mark. Rationally speaking, even at that mathematical total it would have meant that one out of every five people on the earth would have had to be a part of that military buildup in order to fulfill that staggering 200 million man amount at that time. This of course does not take into account the elderly, the women, or the children as well, that would have been included in that first one billion total. The simple truth is this: the math just doesn't even come close to adding up. From a completely rational standpoint this prophecy could have never been fulfilled at any time preceding the 19ᵗʰ century.

However, from the time of the year of 1800 we entered in an exponential growth spurt in our global population that today finds those numbers well over the 7 billion mark. This reduces the earlier fraction from 1 out of every 5 people on earth to one out every 35 people on the earth in order to sustain such a force, clearly a much more sensible and attainable possibility. For the first time in the history of Mankind, the prophesied amount of a 200 Million man army is fully within the realm of reality when one measures the military capabilities of all the nations of the earth. No other generation before ours could have made such a chilling boast.

Add to that the shocking statements of "over the forth part of the earth", "to slay the third part of men", and lastly "the third part of men killed". These are unmistakably numbers so vast that they cannot be accurately numbered. The carnage is so pervasive and widespread that it can only be represented by a fraction of the whole. In this we find the second point that uniquely qualifies our generation today as that generation in which this prophecy may finally be able to be fulfilled.

History tells us plainly that at the close of WW I the total number of the dead was tallied somewhere in the vicinity of 8 million people. Likewise, at the end of WW II the numbers were estimated upwards toward 52 million people. These numbers as staggering as they are to imagine do not come close to the prophesied totals of this Revelation passage. Using a simple mathematical deduction of "one third" of 7 billion, we are talking about a fatality total that would extend into some

2 billion people, this would be the mathematical equivalent of WW II x 40.

Add to this, that both the book of Daniel and Revelation projects the time-frame of this incomprehensible destruction to take place within the very short period of 3 ½ years, and it is plain to see that we are not talking about merely a conventional war. Jesus in His foretelling of these events in **Matt.24:22** said this: **"For then shall be great tribulation, such as was not since the beginning of the world to this time, no, nor ever shall be. And except those days should be shortened, there should no flesh be saved..."**

It is undeniable that this type of foreseen destruction could have never been possible in any other generation before ours today. We all have learned in school how the close of WW II in 1945 ended with the horrendous invention, and its use of the nuclear bomb, almost identically aligning itself with the start of Daniel's 69th generation in 1948.

Today the weapons of mass destruction are more than capable of amassing these devastating prophesied totals, and easily within the allotted 3½ year time frame. And it is yet once more highly conceivable that what we are witnessing is a perfectly chilling alignment of these end time prophecies of Revelation with that of the current generation in which we now live.

THIS GOSPEL OF THE KINGDOM SHALL BE PREACHED IN ALL THE WORLD (MATT.24:14)

By now I am sure that you must be growing tired of hearing me say this, but this prophecy too, as the others that we have previously covered, is incontestably a prophecy that could only speak to this generation in which we live today. I am reminded of the very first prophecy that we examined at the beginning of this chapter: **Dan.12:4 "...many shall run to and fro, and knowledge shall be increased."** It is this very same explosion of travel and technology that has clearly paved the way for **Matt 24:14 "this gospel of the kingdom to be preached in all the world."**

Today's technological advances have mainstreamed the Gospel to the farthest reaches of the earth. Going back only a short span of fifty years ago, our exploration of space laid the groundwork for the satellite and global telecommunications, and later on, the Worldwide Web. It would be these advancements that would soon give rise to the first ever 24 hour Christian Broadcasting Networks that are literally blanketing the planet today with the good news of the Gospel of Christ Jesus, let alone, the innumerable websites and online ministries that have cropped up among every nation, tribe, tongue, and people.

Add to that the convenience and accessibility of global travel has blown open the doors of the missionary field as never before. Today many evangelists and missionaries are able to leap frog from one nation to the next in their quest to share the Gospel with the whole of the world.

319

Furthermore, today our knowledge of the various cultures and languages of the world permit us to translate and to distribute the Gospel into any language known to man.

Ministries are being birthed, new church constructions are being built, Bible instructional courses being taught, medical centers bringing healing, emergency food relief centers feeding the hungry, are all being accomplished today with a speed and rapidity that would have been unimaginable only one short generation ago.

As true as all of this is, it is not to say that the work that remains to be done is not immense. It must be stated plainly that for all that has been done, there remains so much more to do. In truth, it is for this very reason that I was compelled to write this book, it is the smallest of contributions to the otherwise enormous task of advancing the kingdom of the Gospel. I myself have no doubt that as the nearness of the return of our Lord approaches, the work of Christ's church will go forward with an ever increasing urgency and unbridled commitment. It is for certain that we have only begun to see what God has in store for this 69th generation of Daniel. We have yet to witness the ministry of the "two witnesses" of Rev.11 and Zech.4, or that of the "144,000" of Rev.7, and the evangelism of the nation of Israel of Rom.11, and unless we forget the "latter rain" of Joel 2.

For a certainty there can be no doubt that we as "the body of Christ" have only begun to see the truest form of the fulfillment of this prophecy, but as with all of the earlier prophesies we have looked at, this generation is surgically positioned to usher in the coming of our King, as no other generation before it.

FOUR BLOOD RED MOONS

Luke 21:25-28 "And there will be signs in the sun, in the moon, and in the stars; and on the earth distress of nations, with perplexity; the sea and the waves roaring; mens hearts failing them for fear, and for looking after those things which are coming on the earth: for the powers of heaven shall be shaken. And then shall they see the Son of man coming in a cloud with power and great glory. And when these things begin to come to pass, then look up, and lift up your heads; for your redemption draws near."

These are the words of our Savior spoken to His disciples in response to their question in **Matt.24:3 "...when will these things be? And what sign will there be when these things are about to take place?"**

Likewise in **Joel 2:31** we read, **"The sun shall be turned into darkness and the moon into blood, before the coming of the great and awesome day of the LORD."**

In these two passages of Scripture what we find are definitive warnings that prior to the coming of our Lord Jesus there will be celestial signs that will act as heralds of the coming event. The sun and the moon are specifically mentioned in both of these passages and cannot go unnoticed. Even as at the first coming of Christ, where there was the celestial appearance of "His star" (Matt.2:2), so also at His second coming there shall be additional "signs" in the heavens.

In **Gen 1:14** God says this: **"And God said, Let there be lights in the firmament of the heavens to divide the day from the night; and let them be for signs..."** God in this passage is clearly defining one of the purposes for the sun and the moon, and that is to act as some sort of a divine heavenly billboard as He chooses to provide His celestial signs for the whole of humanity to observe at certain given times throughout history.

In the earlier two passages of Luke 21 and Joel 2 God is prophesying that before the return of Christ these heavenly signs will show themselves and speak loudly to the inhabitants of the earth announcing the impending time of Jesus' future arrival.

According to NASA and their official online website, beginning in April 2014, there will be the first occurrence of four total lunar eclipses, the following three will occur over the succession of a 18 month period. The second will be in Oct. of 2014, the third in April of 2015, and the last and fourth one to occur in Oct. 2015. Directly dispersed in the midst of the 2nd and 3rd lunar events there will additionally be a complete solar eclipse. The importance of these successive events cannot go unnoticed. What we are inevitably experiencing are celestial signs in both the moon and the sun just as the prophets and Christ Himself had prophesied.

Even more dramatic than that is the fact that all of the lunar events are precisely timed to take place on the exact days of the Jewish high holy days as prescribed by God through Moses in Lev. 23. Two shall fall exactly on the day of Passover, while the other two shall fall precisely on the feast of Tabernacles, further evidence that these heavenly signs are under the strict command and control of the One who had made them back in Gen.1.

To further and more clearly illustrate the events as they will occur, here is an extremely abbreviated and unscientific explanation of what these lunar eclipses will engender along with their causes. In short what we can expect is an astrological alignment which would set the earth in the direct path between the moon and the sun. Or in other words the sun will be directly in front of the earth on one side, while the moon will be directly on the back side of the globe, presenting the earth smack dab in the middle between the two on a perfect straight line alignment.

As the rays of the suns light cascades and filters around the earth and extends behind the earth and reaches the moon it will give off the ghastly illumination as if the moon had turned to the bright red color of blood just as the prophet Joel had foretold that it would.

This phenomenon of four successive lunar eclipses, more commonly known as a "tetrad" is extremely rare, so rare in fact that it has only occurred 3 times in the past 500 years, once in 1492, once again in 1948, and then lastly in 1967. At the time of this writing, we are less than 2 months away from a fourth occurrence. Bearing all of this in mind, let us now pause just long enough to take a very brief look at what transpired over the course of history as the former three occurrences had given their rise.

Simply put, the significance of these up and coming solar and lunar events cannot be overstated. One only has to examine the previous three times the "tetrad" has emerged on the scene in order to come to the conclusion that they are in some mysterious way linked to the most recent and most monumental historical events in modern Jewish history.

In 1492 the ominous precursors appeared as forerunners to two very historic and monumental events. First, as all of human history in unison records, the discovery of the western world by way of the voyage and discovery of Christopher Columbus, and secondly, to occur at the identical time that the Jews of Spain were experiencing the most ruthless and terrible persecution and expulsion at the hands of King Ferdinand and queen Isabella of Spain. As we now know today it would eventually be this new found land of the western hemisphere that would result in the much needed and long awaited safe-haven that the Jews had so grievously desired since the diaspora of 586B.C.

Again in 1948 these heavenly harbingers would once again announce the finality of a time of horrendous Jewish persecution by means of the Holocaust of WW II, and subsequently the founding and reconstitution of the newly formed nation that we know today as the modern day nation of Israel.

Finally, in its last and most recent observance in the year of 1967 it would remarkably coincide with the "six day war" that despite the certain anticipation of the complete and utter defeat of the Jewish nation still in its mere infancy, would inevitably at its decisive conclusion result in the annexation of the Jewish spiritual capital city of Jerusalem. For the first time since the traumatic and devastating exile at the hands of the Babylonian Empire in 586BC, some 25 centuries earlier, the Jews would once more regain the complete autonomy of its most ancient spiritual capital city of Jerusalem.

In each case there would seem to be one grand overlying theme that appears to be obviously prevalent in each occurrence of the "tetrad", and that is of the suffering and severity of an extensively traumatic set of "birth pains", culminating with a climactic birth itself. The Spanish persecution and expulsion gives rise to the birth of the America's, where the Holocaust of WW II gives birth to the nation of Israel, and lastly, the "Six Day War" gives birth to the Jewish acquirement of its long awaited lost capital city of Jerusalem.

What does all of this mean for us today who are about to witness the "tetrad" once more? Jesus prophesied of "the time of the end" as being like a woman in "labor pains" (Matt.24:8). Once again what we are about to witness is **Rev.12:2 "And she being with child cried, travailing in birth, and pained to be delivered."**

In **I Thess.5:3** Paul states it this way: **"For when they shall say, Peace and safety; then sudden destruction cometh upon them, as travail upon a woman with child; and they shall not escape."**

And again in **Isa.13:8:13: (v8) "And they shall be afraid: pangs and sorrows shall take hold of them; they shall in pain as woman that travaileth... (v10) For the stars of heaven and the constellations thereof shall not give their light: the sun shall be darkened in his going forth, and the moon shall not cause her light to shine."** (notice the location of this prophecy as it falls within the guidelines of the four part timeline of Isaiah)

And no less astonishing, these "tetrad" events are scheduled to begin no less than 30 days from the very close of the prophesied 65th year of this 69th terminal generation of Daniel, which is uniquely positioned at the exact time that we have observed God's prior delineation's between the 65th and 70th years as shown previously throughout our study.

Furthermore, it should equally be noted that as these four blood red moon events run their full course over the allotted 18 month period and come to the fullness of their expiration, there will be left a very coincidental 3 and 1/2 years remaining in order to bring to the complete fulfillment the prophesied 70 years of the "fig tree" generation, which by the way is the exact amount of time that the tribulation period of the book of Revelation has been prophesied to last. Is this a further proof that we are at the doorstep of the climatic close of this generation, and the eve of the imminent return of the Son of God? As I have clearly said before, we will not have to wait long to find out.

A BRIEF SUMMARY

In this chapter we have looked at a wide array of topics as they relate to the world in which we live today. It goes without saying, that for as many end time prophecies as we have touched upon there are many more that have gone without mention during the course of this study. It was never the intention of this writing to be an all encompassing compilation of the rich vastness of the prophetical scriptures, but rather a noteworthy attempt to construct a stable footing for the general premise of this book. That premise has been clear from the start, Jesus Himself promised us that He would one day return for His church, and that we as His church were not only to believe on this truth, but to wait for it with the Spirit of faith and expectancy.

Additionally I have proposed that Christ has not withheld the knowledge of His return, as many others would suggest, but to the contrary He has uniquely and more than adequately spelled it out for us with the greatest of detail through the instrument of His Holy Word. Likewise, I have hoped to provide the scriptural proof that would sufficiently give evidence to this astounding claim. And finally, I have attempted to instill within this message the true sense of the extreme urgency that such conclusions would so justly warrant considering the findings in which we have uncovered.

Under the most favorable conditions this writing should serve as a testimonial to the faithfulness of God and the inerrancy of the Holy Scriptures, and in many cases a clarion call, a blowing of the trumpet, and the sounding of the alarm that time is short. It should also be stated that at no time during the preparation of this book has it been my intention to ascribe a fixed absolute time for the fulfillment of Christ's return. I have said early on in the writing of this text that I am not positioning myself as a "date setter", this is not my purpose; but make no mistake, I am fully dedicated to the task of making it painfully obvious that the time is extremely short, even to the point of being "at the door". The real issue that is at stake here is not whether we have 5 years, or 7years, or longer, but rather it should be a question of whether or not we are ready now.

About this time, the full gravity of the seriousness of this message should be settling in. Perhaps the chair that you may be sitting in has become a bit less comfortable, or maybe you find yourself inexplicably reverting back in the thoughts of your mind to the discomforting truths that you can no longer deny. Ask yourself if you can lay the book down upon the night stand beside your bed and stand up and walk away while leaving the message there until you choose to return, or does the message go with you? Has the profoundness of this truth somehow struck a hidden cord within your heart that cannot be so easily laid aside? And what does all of this mean for you and for me?

I am reminded of the words of King Solomon who likewise pondered and meditated over difficult and serious questions… **"For in much wisdom is much grief, and he who increases knowledge increases sorrow" (Eccl.1:18).** The personification of this truth was Jesus Himself, as stated in **Isa.53:3 "He is despised and rejected of men; a man of sorrows, and acquainted with grief…"** It's almost comical when you consider the adages that our culture seems to employ of "ignorance is bliss" and "what you don't know won't hurt you".

The fact is that if this message has resulted in an unsettling effect upon your psyche than it has successfully accomplished exactly what it was intended to do. One can imagine the Apostle John who penned the book of Revelation, who stated in **Rev.10:10 "And I took the little book out of the angel's hand, and ate it up; and it was in my mouth sweet as honey; and as soon as I had eaten it, my belly was bitter."** The reality is that the message is precisely intended to interrupt one's state of ease, just as it did with me at the first. Today I more closely identify with the words of **Hab.2:2 "And the LORD answered me, and said, write the vision, and make it plain upon tables, that he may run that readeth it."** This too is my hope for you.

I would close this portion of the chapter now with the words of our Lord out of **John 16:21-22 "A woman, when she is in labor, has sorrow because her hour has come; but as soon as she has given birth to the child, she no longer remembers the anguish, for joy that a human being has been born into the world. Therefore you now have sorrow, but I will see you again and your heart will rejoice, and your joy no one will take from you."**

DANIEL'S 70TH WEEK

And finally, at last, we have come to the place in our study where it should be about the time for us to dot the i's and cross our t's, so to speak. In this our final section of the book, we shall examine the last puzzle piece of our study of Daniels "70 weeks". Turn now with me back to Daniel 9.

Dan.9:24 "Seventy weeks are determined upon your people and upon your holy city, to finish the transgression, and to make an end of sins, and to make reconciliation for iniquity, and to bring in everlasting righteousness, and to seal up the vision and prophecy, and to anoint the most Holy."

These are the words that shall exemplify the conclusion of Daniel's 70th week. They are also words of great encouragement when we realize that the return of Christ is not the end, but only the end of the 69th generation. Another generation has been prophesied afterwards, and in regard to this generation much also has been written in the word of God.

In this section we shall briefly examine this generation as the Bible reveals it so poignantly. This is the generation of hope, and peace, and rest. It is the time of triumph and rebirth, restoration and healing, and it is the time of the Kingdom of God on earth.

For the sake of this study it will not be my overall intent to present a detailed portrait of this 1,000 year generation as some might expect. On the contrary, the goal of this commentary will be primarily focused on the delicate task of proving that this "70th week" of Daniel does in fact represent an additional and final generation of 1,000 years as the Bible records it in the waning chapters of the book of Revelation, as well as within the other prophetical writings.

The purpose for this approach as opposed to the more common approach is simple, if the first "69 weeks" of Dan.9 are clear representations of the genealogical record of the Son of God, as I have attempted to prove scripturally, then to maintain this same consistent approach as we explore Daniel's 70th week would be absolutely necessary. To broaden the view and understanding of the otherwise known "Millennial Kingdom", to that of the closing construction of the ancestral lineage of Jesus the Christ, should permit us to see even more clearly the weighty truth that we have uncovered through our study of the preceding 69 generations.

Even as there was a clearly defined distinction between the "62 weeks" (1st coming) of Daniel, and the "7 weeks" (2nd coming) that would follow, there is also the same distinction made in reference to the "70th week" ("New Jerusalem, coming down" Rev.21:2). My hope is that by maintaining this same course of research it will provide a much needed exclamation point at the conclusion of our study.

Here is where I believe many students of the Word of God make a very common mistake in the way that they perceive the Millennial Kingdom, they put so much focus on the end result that they tend to miss a great deal in regard to the "regeneration" process that occurs over this 1,000 year time-frame.

In **Matt.19:28** we find these words of Jesus: **"Verily I say unto you, that you which have followed me, in the regeneration when the Son of man shall sit in the throne of His glory, you also shall sit upon twelve thrones, judging the twelve tribes**

Israel." Here Jesus is alluding to the kingdom of God, using the very unusual terminology of **"the regeneration."**

This word "regeneration" in the original *Strongs Hebrew and Greek Concordance (3824,3825,1078)* carries this definition: "(spiritual) rebirth (the state or the act), spiritual renovation; Messianic restoration; (through the idea of oscillatory repetition); anew, i.e. (of place) back, (of time) once more, furthermore or on the other hand: - again; nativity; nature: - generation, natural; a generation; by implication an age (the period or the persons): - nation, time."

By this definition alone we can see more clearly how the "Millennial Kingdom" fits perfectly within the construct of Daniel's "70 weeks". Likewise, we should gain a deeper understanding of how Dan.9:24 cannot be completely fulfilled until the 1,000 year Millennial Kingdom is completed.

The reason that this conclusion is so important, is as I stated earlier, if Christ's return at the end of Daniel's 69th generation would simultaneously fulfill Daniel's "70th week", then there would be no need for the distinction that is clearly given in the prophecy. In turn, it would likewise bring into question whether or not the interpretation of "generations" throughout the prophecy was an accurate one.

However, what we find is exactly what we would expect to find, a perfect harmony and substantiation of the generational interpretation as Daniel recorded it. Not only is this significant for the obvious sake of scriptural integrity, and consistency, but it additionally solidifies the time-frames as we have uncovered them found within the prophecy; in essence one reaffirms the other, and does certainly complicate the attempt of others to dispel its truth.

Now, let's look more closely at the prophecy of **Dan.9:24** **"Seventy weeks are determined upon your people and upon your holy city, to finish the transgression, and to make an end of sins, and to make reconciliation for iniquity, and to bring in everlasting righteousness, and to seal up the vision and prophecy, and to anoint the most Holy."**

The first point I would like to make is in regard to the very subtle mention of "your people", as God is clearly addressing the entirety of all 70 generations under this singular term. There is no distinction given whatsoever to that of Israel, and or of the Church. As we have discovered they are in the eyes of God one singular ancestral line, and thus, He refers to them as such. What a revolutionary idea, to dispense with the "them and us" mentality. This is extremely more profound than we as "the body of Christ" seem to realize. In the Millennium we are all Israel.

Now let me make this perfectly clear, this is not my attempt to promote the abomination that is "replacement theology", which I fervently hate, but rather to define the oneness and unity in which God has called us all to, both Jews and Gentiles alike, as God Himself see's us. I ask you now, if the "Anointing" draws any strength from unity at all, than is it any wonder that we as the church today operate only on the fringes of this great Anointing, as we continue to draw lines between us and our brothers.

Just as the Anointing became more and more undiscernible amidst the Church's being so cunningly severed from its Hebraic roots, following the passing of the Apostolic first church generation, so likewise the "latter rain" of the end times will be primarily empowered by the Holy Spirit's reunification of the nation of Israel and the Church (Rom.11), as it was intended at its nativity. If the woman cannot be severed from the man that she has obviously been created out of him, then neither should the Church be separated from that of its natural Hebraic origins as well. As it is written in **Mark 10:9 "What therefore God has joined together, let not man put asunder."**

Even as the ancestral line began with one man, so also the process of regeneration cannot be complete until the Church and the Jews constitute the transformation into "one new man" (Eph.2:14-16). If we are to wonder why today we perceive so little of the power of the Holy Spirit, should we not realize that this lack of His Presence, and manifestations, is the direct result of our lack of disunity with the modern day people of Israel, let alone ourselves?

We cannot even discern the simplicity of Scripture because we are so busy creating divisional lines within our own theological interpretations, always careful to maintain the immovable barrier between Israel and the Church. Make no mistake about it, this is deception. There is no them and us, there is only all of us. Wow! I won't lie; that felt good. Let's move on.

"Seventy weeks are determined upon your people and upon your holy city..." In this portion of Dan.9:24 we see the words "...and upon your holy city", this is a curious statement if you think about it. At the start it makes perfect sense that the "70 weeks" should apply to the "people", as we have learned that this is a reference to the "family tree" of Daniel's "people", but according to the rest of this statement the "70 weeks" have an additional application that deals exclusively with Jerusalem.

Anyone that is casually familiar with the scriptures would know that the city of Jerusalem has a vast and extensive Biblical history as it relates to the children of Israel, so much in fact, that for the sake of our abbreviated study I will not even begin to attempt to unravel that ball of yarn. What I would like to point out however, is that Jerusalem has plainly been an extraordinarily significant part of the plans and purposes of God as He has dealt with His people from the beginning, which is exactly what this prophecy uniquely testifies to. By the simplicity in which this prophetic statement is given it is clear that at the onset of God's creation of Adam (1st generation/ 1st week) the decision to give the land of Israel, and the city of Jerusalem, to the Messianic ancestral lineage (Jesus) had already been "determined".

In many churches and Bible studies the world over Christians are taught the history of Jerusalem and its prophetic significance in relation to the Jews, and they are absolutely correct in their correlation of the two, but this prophecy goes far beyond most of that instruction. This is a clear declaration of the angel of Gabriel proclaiming (Dan.9:21) the message of God to Daniel that Jerusalem was as much a part of the prophetical plan as was the children of Israel themselves.

The genealogy of Daniel's "70 weeks" would not only represent the formation of the children of God that would make up the loyal servants and subjects of the Kingdom of God, but additionally, the "70 weeks" would represent the historical evolutionary process of "the throne" of that same kingdom. This is precisely why Satan goes to such great lengths to possess the city himself, he has essentially a two part strategy, first to assault the people of the kingdom, and secondly to annex the very throne of the kingdom. Sadly enough it would seem that Satan knows more of the significance of this prophecy than many of our politicians, and national leaders, as well as many of the so called "Christians" of today who in their blinded ignorance of the scriptures are so readily transposed to dividing the city of Jerusalem and arrogantly offering it to the enemies of God.

Through the understanding of Dan.9:24 we can easily see that this position taken by many is tantamount to a direct defiance of both God and His Word, not to mention it forges a definite alliance with the plans and purposes of Satan's own end time strategy.

Bearing all of this in mind, this should also further add an extreme weightiness to the prophetic event that the whole world witnessed in 1967 during the "6 day war", when the nation of Israel regained the full possession of the city of Jerusalem for the first time in nearly 2,500 years. In short, the prophecy states emphatically that as Daniel's "70th week" concludes, not only will the ancestral bloodline of the Messiah be completed, but additionally the capital city of the kingdom of God will also meet its prophesied completion.

This in turn brings us to **Rev.21:2-3** where we read: **"And I John saw the holy city, new Jerusalem, coming down from God out of heaven, prepared as a bride adorned for her husband. And I heard a great voice out of heaven saying, behold, the tabernacle of God is with men, and He will dwell with them, and they shall be His people, and God Himself shall be with them, and be their God."**

This prophecy as seen and recorded by John fulfills three unshakable truths as presented in Dan.9:24. The first fulfillment is the obvious mention of Jerusalem as "the holy city" (the exact terminology used in Dan.9) as it comes downs from heaven in all of its pristine splendor and glory.

The second fulfillment is that of John's mentioning of "and they shall be His people", also a synonymous statement to that of Dan.9 when Gabriel refers to them as "your people" as he delivers the message to Daniel.

And finally, the third and undeniably the most powerful of the three fulfillments is found when John writes "...and He will dwell with them", and again when he says, "...and God Himself shall be with them". This is unmistakably a "third coming" at the conclusion of Daniel's "70th week", just as the prophecy would state it, this time it is the Father Himself who comes. How ludicrous it would be of us to actually imagine that the prophecy of Daniel would specifically give attention to the two comings of Christ, as well as of the coming of the Holy Spirit, but in its final culmination leave out the majestic coming of the Father Himself. Once more we see that nothing is lacking or missing in the prophetic timeline of Dan.9.

We must also recognize that this passage, and these fulfillments as John saw them, and appropriately recorded them, will all transpire after the 1,000 years of the Millennial Reign are concluded. Thereby leaving us to rightfully conclude that our interpretation of Daniel's "70 weeks" as 70 generations is entirely accurate.

Through this understanding we can clearly see that the "70th week" is in fact a 70th generation. Just as the "62nd week" and the "69th week" of Daniel were both completed with the 1st and 2nd comings of Jesus, so also the "70th week" is completed with the coming of the Father. For all that could be said about this, at this moment I will have to refrain for the sake of continuing on with additional proofs in support of this 70ᵗʰ generation.

Next we will look at the portion of **Dan.9:24** as it pertains to the statements of **"to finish the transgression, and to make an end of sins, and to make reconciliation for iniquity, and to bring in everlasting righteousness"**. Again, these statements would seem to be very self-explanatory as they are given, that is until we realize that the clear instruction of the Bible testifies to something quite different as it proceeds to describe the prophetic events to occur within the 1,000 year period of the millennial Kingdom.

For instance, to start let's look at **Isa.65:17-22 "For behold, I create a new heavens and a new earth; and the former shall not be remembered or come to mind. But be glad and rejoice forever in what I create; for behold, I create Jerusalem as a rejoicing, and her people a joy. I will rejoice in Jerusalem, and joy in my people; the voice of weeping shall no longer be heard in her, nor the voice of crying. No more shall an infant from there live but a few days, nor an old man who has not fulfilled his days; for the child shall die one hundred years old, but the sinner being one hundred years old shall be accursed... for as the days of a tree, so shall be the days of my people."**

This passage clearly speaks of the Millennial Kingdom as it references the creation of "...a new heavens and a new earth" (where in Rev.21:1 that creative process has been completed). Furthermore, these verses address a return to the lengthy life spans that man had previously enjoyed before the events of the flood.

Also, within this passage there exists a very curious statement which is: "...but the sinner being one hundred years old shall be accursed". Now, I can assure you that I have researched both words "sinner" and "accursed" in the original Hebrew language and have found them to represent exactly what they say. I myself can come to no other conclusion than to believe that this passage is clearly indicating that even during the time of the reconstruction process of the Millennial Kingdom, there will exist some who the Bible records as "sinners", and they will be "accursed". At the same time I have to deduce from this, that in some type of elementary form in which I admittedly do not fully understand, sin has not been completely eradicated, neither has death been totally defeated, or for that matter, neither has the curse completely been abolished and done away with, and all of this during the transformative process of the Millennial Reign.

Now it must be stated that these people that are noted in this passage have not yet received their "glorified bodies" as spoken of in I Cor.15:35-58. In the opinion of many (which I agree), the Scriptures describe a people group that will, by the mercy and grace of God, come through the great tribulation period alive. These people are a completely separate group of individuals that will not be representative of those that will be known as the "the body of Christ" (those that have received their salvation and glorified bodies prior to the Millennium, at Christ's second coming).

A further evidence of this fact is the chapters of Ezk.40-48 where the Bible clearly describes the construction of a Millennial temple in which sacrifices will be offered by a fully functional priesthood on behalf of the people, and this all to transpire during the millennial kingdom as well.

In **Ezk.42:13-14** we read this **"... the holy chambers where the priests who approach the LORD shall eat the most holy offerings. There they shall lay the most holy offerings – the grain offering, the sin offering, and the trespass offering – for the place is holy. When the priests enter them, they shall not go out of the holy chamber into the outer court; but there they shall leave their garments in which they minister, for they are holy. They shall put on other garments; then they may approach that which is for the people."** A further evidence that sin has not been eradicated during this time of the 1,000 millennial kingdom.

With all of this being said, let me return to my original purpose for stating all of this, which is to make the point that the 1,000 years of the Millennial Kingdom is in fact a generational process that must be carried out to its completion before the prophecy of Daniels "70th week" (Dan.9:24) can be entirely fulfilled. Once more I will remind you that if our "generational" interpretation of Dan.9 is correct as I assert, then it cannot be fully consistent without the existence of one final "70th generation". However, what the Bible plainly reveals is precisely the occurrence of such a generation to follow the conclusion of Daniel's "69th week", and the return of Christ. Additionally this lends to the "dotting of the i's and the crossing of the t's" as it brings a congruity and a strict adhesiveness to the whole of the findings of our study.

Let us also not forget that at the conclusion of this "70th generation" there will likewise occur the "loosing of Satan for a short time" which will result in a final rebellion against

God, and "a final war". There will also be the events of the "second resurrection of the dead and the second death" culminating with the "white throne judgment". These are all fully documented in Rev.20:1-15 and are plainly stated no less than 6 times, to take place at the end of the 1,000 years, a further proof that this 1,000 years is a generational process of reconstruction leading up to the time that Dan.9:24 will be utterly accomplished.

Finally, we will look at the remaining portion of Dan.9:24 "... to bring in everlasting righteousness, and to seal up the vision and prophecy, and to anoint the most Holy." Resolving the issue of these statements for me is quite easy when considered through the simplicity of the lens of logic. Simply enough, there can be no "everlasting righteousness" until sin, death, and the curse, are entirely done away with. For that matter there can be no "everlasting" (which is only another way of saying "eternal"), until the monitoring of time itself has passed away, which cannot be the case until the 1,000 years of the millennium have expired.

Similarly there can be no "sealing up of vision and prophecy" until that which has already been seen by visions, and already declared by prophecies have fully run their course. As so much has been seen through visions by the prophets of old regarding the Millennial Kingdom, this must all come to its full conclusion before that which has been recorded has met its final end.

And lastly, when the "anointing of the most Holy" is to take place according to Dan.9:24, interestingly it is marked by its own placement in the verse as being the last and final event to occur at the absolute end of Daniel's 70th week (or 70th generation). By its most unique positioning at the optimum stage of finality of the prophetic timeline, this statement in very subtle undertones heralds the launching of the onset into eternity. If this is the ceremonial royal coronation consisting of the public anointing of Jesus Christ as the Eternal King (which I believe it is since there is no temple to anoint at the end of the Millennium), than is it any wonder that I cannot find any other passage in all of Scripture that adequately describes this event. It is as if to say, "Here is all the glimpse you will need of the future eternity, Jesus is, and will be your King."

In summary, what we have disclosed is that there is absolutely no part of Dan. 9:24 that can, or will be fulfilled until the prophesied 1,000 year millennium has run its course, and is entirely brought to its conclusion. Likewise, the "70 weeks" of Daniel then cannot be finalized until the millennial process has concluded. In short, this finding is perfectly contiguous with all of the preceding interpretation as it relates to the 70 generational theory.

As a final note, I offer this: the 1,000 years of the Millennial Kingdom additionally fulfills the Scriptural requirement of "duality". As Adam is representative of the 1st generation of the Messianic lineage, so also the Millennial Kingdom is representative of the 70th and final generation of Dan.9. The eerily reminiscent missing of the 70 years as it relates to Adam (Adam dies at 930 years of age) could be disguised revelation of how the 1,000 years is transitioned into by the use of a 70 year period. They would be co-joined because Daniel's 70th week would have already been fulfilled for the saints of God at the end of the 70 years of the 69th generation, at Christ's second coming.

AN ORDERLY REVIEW

At last we have come to the place where it might serve us well to take a final pause, in light of the expansive territory that we have covered to this point. It is extremely important for us to remain focused on the bigger picture as it has unfolded before us over our research of several extremely elusive topics.

We began our study asking the most significant of all questions "when will Jesus return? Upon a closer observation of this quest, that question quickly turned in to one of "can we know when Jesus will return? We learned early on in the process that this was much more than just a likely proposition, but when thoroughly questioned the evidence presented a sound affirmation, of not just the possibility of its disclosure, but the actuality of the affirmation, as well as the responsibility to know the time of this forth coming "visitation".

We have seen clearly how timelines and the use of them are, and have always been a pervasive technique and method employed by our God throughout Scripture. As a further confirmation of this truth we uncovered such a timeline in Daniel chapter 9, at which time we set forth on a new expedition to reveal its obscure terminology as it pertained to the mysterious word of "weeks".

It would not be soon after that through the use of various recorded Biblical genealogies that we would discover its hidden meaning of ancestral "generations", but not just that of the nation of Israel, but exceedingly more importantly, to be that of the "Messiah Himself", enveloping within its contents the actual multiple times of "visitation" of the perfect Man Christ Jesus.

As we extended our search in our attempt to carry through this Heavenly lineage beyond the 1st coming of Christ we found ourselves confronted with what may have seemed at the time a most unlikely candidate to complete the second phase of our family tree, the 7 churches of Rev.

At that time we immediately shifted gears and proceeded on a specific quest to determine if in fact there was any existing Biblical basis for a theory many have called "duality of Scripture". The findings of our research provided conclusive proof that not only is "duality" a common and much used method of interpretation, but more than that it is a God inspired instrument exclusively created for the very same purpose in which we intended to exercise it.

It was primarily through this discovery that we pushed forward in our concrete comparisons of the 7 churches of Revelation and the widely known historical record of the past 2,000 years of church history, only to find them to yield the amazing synchronicity of a hand in glove identical fit.

It was at this juncture that we set our course on a purely logical theme of comparative analysis by testing the conclusive "fig tree" generation with that of the prophetic observations of the "end time", or "last days" generation, as given to us by the authority of Scripture. To no surprise we found a world revealing itself to be in a close alignment with the prophetic utterances of the prophets, declaring loudly that we are that 69th generation.

We additionally examined the possibility of determining the length of time that might constitute a plausible measurement for that generation that would usher in the second coming of Christ. Although vague and somewhat ambiguous we found ample proof that this time period could be rationally considered to be a representation of a 70 year time frame, and thereby leaving us to the intelligent assumption that not only are we participants of this most unique of all generations, but that we are for a certainty well in to that generation, even to the point of at the door of its conclusion.

Upon the completion of the second phase of our Daniel timeline there remained but one final rung of our ladder to climb, and that being the last and final generation of Daniel's 70th week. At which time we forged ahead with yet another comparison between that of the final generation of Dan. 9 and the treasure of Biblical prophecy that clearly defines the Millennial Kingdom, and once more only to arrive at a synonymous and perfectly constructed illustration of the two.

And lastly, and certainly equally as important, we considered ever so briefly what all of this should mean for each of us, saved and otherwise, backslidden, or staunchly cemented in the faith, what is our likely response to these stunning observations?

In conclusion, in studying Daniel's 70 weeks we discover a Genealogical Record of all of man's history, from Adam to the end of the Millennium.

Second, it likewise is the beginning and the end of all recorded time itself. Time starts and finishes with Daniels 70 weeks. Before Adam there was only eternity, and after the Millennium, all things shall return to eternal time. Therefore, Dan.9 is also God's record of "time" itself.

Third, it is the detailed ancestral lineage given by their generations, of every Christian and Jew. It is the detailed accounting of the "earthly and spiritual bloodline" of the Lord Jesus Himself. It is His Genealogical claim to the nation of Israel, and to His church.

Fourth, it foretells of the ministry of the Holy Spirit, and His arrival.

Fifth, because it is the architectural blueprint of all time, it likewise is the structural overseer of every cyclical pattern of all prophetic scripture, it is in fact the blueprint of "Biblical duality".

Sixth, it does more to prove the inerrancy and authenticity of the word of God, perhaps more than any other scriptural evidence that we have. In its understanding lies the tangible proof that God exists, while subtly and ingeniously announcing that our God is of a Triune nature.

Seventh, it is the trumpeting herald of every "visitation of God" to the earth down through the ages, both for judgment, as well as for blessing, anointing, restoration, and deliverance.

Eighth, it equally leaves no doubts whatsoever as to who the Messiah is. It is a royal proclamation of Jesus, and no other. Likewise, it exalts Him as God and Creator, proving beyond any shadow of doubt that He is who He said He was.

Ninth, it acts as a faith fertilizer on steroids. For the one that gains its understanding, it emphatically brings us to the reality of the authenticity of the Word of God and His Divine authorship.

Tenth, it loudly proclaims the Millennial Reign and the Kingdom of our God, and the glorious restoration of all things; and more than all the rest, it announces the coming of the Father to abide with His creation, setting all things in their creative order and God given design.

In short, it is the master key that unlocks the door to the deepest of all of God's hidden Biblical revelation, ever given by God to man (outside of course of His own actual Son in person, which could never be adequately paralleled), and all of this because it is the soul expression of the God man Jesus in all of His varying manifestations throughout all recorded time, and beyond.

Oh yeah, and I almost forgot, it does all of this, and so much more, with just a mere 4 verses of scripture (Dan.9:24-27).

It was for this cause, that when the disciples asked Jesus in **Matt.18:21-22 "Lord, how often shall my brother sin against me, and I forgive him?"**, that Jesus replied, **"I do not say to you, up to seven times, but up to seventy times seven."**
By this statement Jesus is using the passage of Daniel 9 to indicate that forgiveness has been firmly set in its place from Adam to the end of the Millennium, and thereby, as God forgives us over its full duration, so shall we forgive others over that same duration.

Then there's the 70 elders that receive of the anointing that was on Moses (Num.11:16-29) in the wilderness, again a picture of Christ delegating His anointing over Daniel's 70 generations.

And then there's the 70 that Jesus sends out Himself in Luke 10:1-20, which testifies of the same.

Not to mention the 49 days from the Feast of Passover to Pentecost, plus the 21 days from the Feast of Trumpets to the conclusion of the Feast of Tabernacles, and once again we have a total of 70 days, concluding with the last day of the feast, otherwise known as "the Great Day of the Lord". This patterns once again the genealogy of Dan.9, showing that God's own feast days (Lev.23), as they represent the "visitations" of God to the earth, are in close alignment with this very same prophecy.

It should also be noted as a side-bar, that the Hebrew word for "feasts" is "moed", which carries the definition of: "an appointment, a fixed time or season, appointed (sign, time)".

Add to all of this, that the 7 of Daniel can represent 7,000 years as stated in II Pet.3:8, and at the exact same time the 70 represents 70 generations (Dan.9) spread over those same 7,000 years, and what we see is that they are perfectly synonymous to one another. One entity of time spoken in two very different ways, while remaining identically as one. Just as God the Father, and God the Son remain as one God, while simultaneously representing the total expression of singularity and individualism.

Likewise, the common thread that binds the two is the Holy Spirit, who is one with them, and also distinct in His person, just as the 49, or 490 of Dan.9 exists separately within the timeline, while being inseparably one and the same timeline. A perfectly seamless amalgamation of the Triune God as found in Dan.9, and throughout every use of the numbers 7, 49, 70, 490, 1,260, and 2,520, throughout all of Scripture. Everything testifies to the King of Glory, His ancestry, and His various ministries, and the various times of His "visitations".

ARE YOU READY?

If you are among those who have followed along closely in this study, then I believe you have been blessed, and privileged to behold, and to understand the time-line of God. You have been given an extraordinary gift and it has not come to you accidentally. You have come to the knowledge of **I Chron.12:32 "And of the children of Issachar, which were men that had understanding of the times, to know what Israel ought to do..."**

Notice that the understanding was given to them for the benefit of all of Israel. It was God's instrumental method for guiding and directing His people. At the same time it served to give an advanced notice and warning so that the people could prepare for what would lie ahead.

And unless we forget, this also is the ministry of the Holy Spirit. Jesus Himself spoke these words in **John 16:13 "...when He, the Spirit of truth, is come, He will guide you into all truth; for He shall not speak of Himself; but whatever He shall hear, that shall He speak, and He will show you things to come."**

If you have been awakened through this study it is only because the Spirit of God has revealed it to you. Neither you nor I have the ability within ourselves to see these things, let alone the ability to understand them, or even to believe them for that matter, this is the work of the Spirit of truth.

And if you're wondering "why me?" Jesus Himself explains it best in **John 14:29 "And now I have told you before it come to pass, that, when it is come to pass, you might believe."**

This is a call to faith my dear friends, it cannot be mistaken for anything else.

I can look back at my own life and see clearly the various stages of faith and relationship that God has brought me through, and continues to do so. Early on I spent decades as a devout follower of drugs, alcohol, sex, violence and rage, cursing, lying, and stealing. I was loud, and arrogant, and cruel, unthankful, selfish, and unloving. There was no sin that I am aware of that I did not readily engage in, and I cared little about religion, let alone a person called God. This was the horror that my life had become over the many years of committed practice of every type of evil. I had become a street animal, sleeping anywhere, eating anything, and doing everything, while barely resembling a man. My mind was a sewer, a pit of disgust and torture, and there was no way out for me.

I was continually haunted in my alone time by my many failures and inadequacies, and the many people that I had hurt. I had turned my back on a dying father, I had totally abandoned an innocent young daughter, I had scammed and abused every relationship I had ever known, and I had injured many physically as well as those I had scarred emotionally.

I had never owned anything, never held on to any job, never married, never even had a driver's license; I was a throw away, and the worst part of it, was that I knew it. Year after year was passing, decades rolled painfully by, and as no surprise to me I was actually growing worse. Imprisonments and incarcerations, attempted murders, and those that attempted to murder me. Drug overdoses, some intentional, others were not, house fires, car crashes, gun shots nearly missing, home invasions and armed robberies, you name it, this was my life.

And one night I laid broken and shattered on a cold kitchen floor in the dark, crying shamelessly, and I said "God, I have heard about the people that you have changed their lives. If you can do this for them, why can't you do this for me? You know that I cannot change myself, if you don't change me I will die." That was it. No great theological prayer, no one there to hold my hand and lead me through the dos and don'ts of petitioning God properly. Just a crushed and hopeless heart giving up, tired and beaten down, crying out on a naked kitchen floor in the dark.

I didn't even know if He had heard me. There was no lightning or thunderbolts, no visions, no appearance of angels, no heavenly voice, no anything. I remember eventually getting up and wiping the tears from my face and moving on to whatever the next thing was. But I tell you this, from that next day and forward I did feel something, something new and strange, but unmistakably real. For the first time in my life I could feel within me an opposing presence to the evil that was my life. I didn't know what this thing was, but it was actively resisting me on every wicked front that I use to perform so freely before. There was a wrestling match going on so violently within me, it was impossible not to feel, or notice it. I knew nothing about a Holy Spirit, or the Word of God, but I now know this much, that night God did hear me, and I was saved by His mercy, and the road to change had begun for me.

I would like to say that from that moment on my life was completely changed, externally i mean, but that did not happen for me. It would be over many years still that this progression would take place, even at times as it would seem to be at a snail's pace. But for me, none of that matters now, as I have come through it to be the man that I am now, as I sit at this keyboard. Not perfect by any stretch of the imagination I can assure you, but unquestionably and undeniably forever changed.

For several years now I have been drug and alcohol free, no longer a slave to either. Additionally I have been sexually abstinent now since 2009 since I am still remaining unmarried. At the same time, I no longer fight, steal, lie, or curse, among many other things that were so common to me, but these are but the beginning of the change that God has done in me. The greater changes have occurred, and still occur within the hidden recesses of my heart and mind. Today I love God, and I am an addict to His Word. The knowledge of Him has stolen me away from this world, and it is the sweetest and most pleasant thing that I could have ever imagined. Consequently, I feel a deep abiding love and concern for others, and it is for this reason that I have written this book for you.

My heart bleeds for you to know Him, my soul pleads for you also to cry out to him, as I once did, and still do. I tell you as truthfully as I know how, He is loving, and merciful, and forgiving, and patient, and He is anxiously waiting for you. He will hear you, and He will answer mightily all the pain that is in your heart. You only have to ask. Yes time is short, so think of it this way, every second that you do not call upon Him is another second that you have to go without Him, and equally as important, He without you.

Perhaps you may already be saved, but over time and circumstances you have fallen victim to the many landslides of life, seemingly separating you ever farther from your Father. To you I would say this: He has not been moved away from you, neither has His opinion changed, or His heartfelt desire concerning you. Past guilt is behaving as your enemy, give that also to Him. Let us not ever forget that Jesus died to bear your shame and your guilt, in addition to your sin. Run back to your Father just as the "prodigal son" was so wise to do. He is forever looking over the barren landscapes of our lives hoping only to see us in the distance as we approach. With arms spread as wide as the beams that fastened wide the nail pierced hands of Christ, He welcomes you to come home to His certain embrace. I beg you not to walk, run my beloved, run hard and fast to your God and Father, and King. Run now!

And lastly, for those of you who have and do know Him well, all blessings and mercy, and peace and grace be to you. To you I say, reach farther, go deeper, seek more, grow, stretch, change, learn, and mature. Never become complacent, nor comfortable within this world. Yearn, thirst, and hunger, for His presence, to hear His voice, and to serve.

Ask yourself earnestly, what does this message mean for you? What is the appropriate response given all that we have learned? Where do you go from here? Do not do as the servant that hid his lord's "talent" in the ground as he awaited his lord's arrival, but rather be as the faithful servants that put their "talents" to use and did produce an "interest" to present to their lord at his return.

Take the message and make it your own. Study it, meditate on it, speak it and teach to others. Become that "watchman" that sits on the wall alerting the others to the seriousness of the times in which we live. Be bold and courageous, stand up and work for the good. Be fearless in your faith, and open wide your mouth and testify "in season and out of season". Be the "salt" and the "light" that you were created to be. The God of all creation has chosen you to live in this, the most crucial time in all of human history. You are stronger than you know you can be. Launch out in faith, and trust God to lead you and direct you in all of your paths. Jesus is coming, and God has preordained that you should be His welcoming committee. Blow the trumpet and sound the alarm, the King is coming!

So there it is, the cold hard facts staring you in the face. The future doesn't hold a new and better career for you simply because God desires to bless you. For that matter, you know that mystical debt cancellation you've been waiting on from God, or that new home, or that new husband or wife that God has been planning to get to you, none of this is as high on His priority list as it is on yours.

The truth is difficult times are ahead of us all. And until we face that, we are as far away from being prepared for it as we could possibly be. We are not here for God to bless us, were actually here to be a blessing. We're not here to take but to give. We were never meant to serve self, not while there's a great King to serve.

"SATISFIED IS WHAT I AM"

Satisfied is what I am.

Your voice comes to me most unexpectedly, what gentle calm embraces my soul.

Your words spoken softly and secretly, they do stir all of my being.

I am captivated once more in all of my entirety, is there anything sweeter in life, than to hear your still small voice?

I am fully enamored with you, while severely immersed in my pursuit of you.

Like a childish boy ensnared by first love, I am useless to every endeavor that would wish to distract me, even momentarily, from the yearning of my heart.

Sheltered in your Spirit, I am lost to this world, and altogether thankful for it, you have wet me with your mercy.

There are many songs in me, and they do sing, out of the sight of all those that would look in.

Your melodies and rhythms, they flow most elegantly within my soul, out of the reach of everything that surrounds me.

Oh, what precious cords they do pluck upon the ready strings of my heart. My spirit fly's into dance, and all the while I sit most unassumingly upon my bed.

All of this is simply too wonderful for me... satisfied is what I am.

Oh, what manner of a God you are, You who visits man, even him who is basest in his nature.

You humble yourself and bow down from your holiest of habitations that You might seek him out. What wonders so magnificent, as to think upon Your desire to abide with man.

How unsearchable are the riches of Your royal visitations, and yet done totally in the silence, separated from all fuss or fanfare, is your desire to make Yourself known.

What beauty must reside in your presence, and where you are, my person swirls when I set my mind upon these things.

What radiance you do give off each time, you so graciously provide the experience that is You.

I am saturated in your oils, Your fragrance lingers, and subtly demands that my senses find no rest.

Oh, how life has broken open, I am Your well and You do fill me up.

I have perished in my own eyes, and do perish from everything that does not choose to behold You, and this too is to my liking.

For I am Your constant creation, with all of its immensity, the divine nature of You, exploding and unrestrained in flesh and blood.

Forever moving forward, the when, and the where, is my sweetest propulsion. For again, and once more, You shall speak, and I will live in earnest expectation, as I listen for Your voice.

But until then... satisfied is what I am.

ABOUT THE AUTHOR

Steven Medley was born in 1961 in the inner city of Chicago. Born to a middle aged father and a young but alcoholic mother, it would be less than a year before his maternal mother would abandon them both. The next nine years would be spent being shipped around from various foster homes, and from one school to the next. At age 10 he would finally come home to stay with his quickly aging father. These would be the happiest years of his life.

At seventeen Steven would enlist in the U.S. Marines and four short years later he would receive an honorable discharge. Upon his return home his father would die of lung cancer only a short single year later. This would begin the darkest time of Stevens life. Alcoholism, drug addiction, and a wide array of criminal activities would eventually land him in the state penitentiary where he would serve a total of forty-two months behind bars. It would be there behind those same bars that he would give his life to Jesus in 1991.

This would begin years of cultivating a personal and intimate relationship with his newly discovered Savior. It would be during this period of his life that he would uncover the ever present gift of prophecy lying previously dormant and undetected within him.

Since then Steven Medley is a dedicated student and researcher of the Word of God, with more than over 40,000 hours of collective study in the field of biblical prophecy. Medley was born in Chicago Illinois, and currently resides there with his newly gained wife and teenage daughter. He is also the father of another daughter, and grandfather to three young grandchildren.

Printed in the United States
By Bookmasters